KOREANA

KOREAN CULTURAL HERITAGE

Volume II

Thought and Religion

Korea Foundation
한국국제교류재단

FOREWORD

The Korea Foundation is proud to present *Thought and Religion*, the second volume in its *Korean Cultural Heritage* series. The first volume, entitled *Fine Arts*, was published in 1994 in response to a growing demand for Korean Studies research materials. It has been well received by both scholars and general readers in Korea and abroad.

Thought and Religion examines traditional values, such as loyalty and filial piety, Korea's scholarly tradition, Buddhism, Confucianism, popular folk beliefs and contemporary religions. The articles in this new volume show how traditional philosophy and religion continue to influence Korean life and thought today.

The Korea Foundation hopes this volume will serve as a useful reference for Korean Studies scholars and as an informative resource for general readers who want to learn more about Korean culture. Subsequent volumes in this series will focus on other aspects of Korean culture and history.

We wish to offer our special thanks to those who have contributed to this volume.

Joungwon Kim, Ph. D., J. D.
President
The Korea Foundation

KOREANA

KOREAN CULTURAL HERITAGE

Volume II

Thought
&
Religion

Copyright ©1996 by
The Korea Foundation

This book is mainly a compilation of articles published in KOREANA from its inaugural edition in 1987 through 1995 and the second of a series on Korean culture. Some articles have been added or edited for style and space in some cases.

Publisher/Editor
Joungwon Kim

Art Director
Park Seung-u

Copy Editor
Julie Pickering

Layout & Design
Art Space Publications, Seoul

All photographs, except where otherwise indicated, are the property of Art Space Publications, Seoul

Printed in September 1996 by Samsung Moonhwa Printing Co, Seoul

Price: US$40.00 (₩30,000)

ISBN 89-860-9008-2

CONTENTS

VILLAGE RITES

SHAMANISM

RELIGION IN MODERN TIMES

APPENDICES

INTRODUCTION

We begin our investigation of Korean thought and religion considering the spiritual potential of the Korean people and the definition of the origins of Korean Religion. Professor Park Sung-bong focuses on the Korean spiritual make-up, first examining the influence of geographical and climatic conditions. He argues that Koreans' early spiritual potential was expressed in the acceptance and creative adaptation of imported thought systems, such as Buddhism and Confucianism, but in the modern era, their native creativity and cultural strength deteriorated with the decline of the Chosŏn Kingdom and the imposition of Japan's colonial culture. Professor Hwang Sun-myoung examines the development of religious beliefs from ancient tribal society to the modern era. After reevaluating the nature of Korean Shamanism and the relationship between religion and state in the Unified Silla, Koryŏ and Chosŏn periods, he concludes that religious practice in Korea is essentially supplicatory, but more developed and specific than primitive magical animism.

The Spiritual Potential of the Korean People

Park Sung-bong

The spiritual potential of the Korean people is a significant factor in any consideration of Korea's tradition and historical development. Looking back over Korean history, we find that the Korean people have always maintained and expanded their inner, qualitative culture, rather than concentrating on superficial force based on physical stature.

Koreans' spiritual and psychological potential is born of the agrarian culture they developed from early times. With its mild climate, the Korean peninsula was perfect for the development of agriculture, and, over the centuries, the Korean people developed a unique agrarian culture. Their peace-loving nature is clearly born of the geographical location of their country.

It was on the foundation of this geographic condition that the Korean people developed their national culture and world view. One could say the Korean pattern of historical development was culture-oriented. When economic and political systems were geared to cultural development, the nation flourished; when they were not, Koreans faced extended periods of decline.

Historically, Koreans held culture in high regard. As a result, education was revered, the fine arts flourished, and cultural assets were treasured. This love of and respect for culture grew from Koreans' acceptance and development of Confucianism, Buddhism and Taoism.

During the Koryŏ Kingdom, Taoism played an important role, combining elements from Korean and Chinese culture. However, unlike Buddhism and Confucianism, it did not have a productive or creative influence over a broad section of society. Buddhism, since ancient times, and Neo-Confucianism, since the early Chosŏn period, had a far greater influence on Korean history. Let us first consider how the Korean people's spiritual potential has manifested itself in the acceptance and creative adaptation of these thought systems.

Korea's encounter with Buddhist culture is significant in that it was an international cultural exchange, but more importantly, it represented the transcendence of the limitations of traditional society. Koreans struggled to create their own Buddhist tradition, and, over the course of two or three centuries, managed to adapt the religion to their own culture in ways the Chinese had not been able to do.

During the Silla period, foreign culture was adopted on a firm foundation of indigenous culture to create something new and different. After the unification of Paekche and Koguryŏ under Silla in the seventh century, a period of even richer creativity bloomed amid a new atmosphere of stability and prosperity. Silla embraced Buddhism somewhat later than Paekche and Koguryŏ, but it was the first to receive *sarira*, sacred relics of the historical Buddha and launch a thorough study of the complete Buddhist texts.

Buddhist thought was taken seriously in Silla. People from all walks of life studied Buddhism in earnest and, as a result, shared a firm belief in patriotism, native religion and Buddhism, which served to unite them as a nation. As Ch'oe Nam-sŏn, the renowned 20th century scholar-writer, once noted, if Indian Buddhism is basic and prefatory, and Chinese Buddhism is diversified and detailed, then Korean Buddhism is a conclusive unifying religion.

Several prominent Silla monks provided the spiritual force behind the unification of the Three Kingdoms and the successful defense of Unified Silla in their writings. Won'gwang (542-640) contributed to the development of the patriotic *hwarang* tradition, while the eminent Wonhyo (617-686) advanced the concept of harmonizing doctrinal disputes (*hwajaengnon*). Wonchŭk (631-696), one of Wonhyo's contemporaries renowned for his writings and translations while studying in Tang China, helped develop the unifying philosophy of the Yogacara Consciousness-only school of Buddhism (*yusikhakp'a*).

After unification, Silla combined the cultures of Paekche and Koguryŏ amid an atmosphere of political stability and economic prosperity. The spiritual energy of the two incorporated kingdoms was particularly evident in the arts. Unfortunately, most artworks made of wood have been lost in the wars, invasions and natural disasters that have plagued the Korean peninsula over the centuries. Many fine Buddhist statues, bells and roof tiles have survived, however, testimony to the spiritual brilliance of this period. Among these, Pulguksa Temple in Kyŏngju reveals the depth of Koreans' Buddhist thought during this period, combining elements originating in the *Saddharmapundarika-sutra*, the *Avatamsaka-sutra* and the Pure Land school.

Nearby Sŏkkuram Stone Grotto, built by Kim Tae-sŏng, creator of Pulguksa, reflects the artistic and scientific achievements of the Silla people who joined together from all levels of society to develop their country. The main Buddha and surrounding statues and wall carvings enhance each other's beauty and are, together with the Emille Bell of Pongdŏksa Temple, world-class cultural assets.

The spiritual strength of the Silla Kingdom was carried on in the Koryŏ Kingdom which followed. During the early years of the kingdom, the carving of the entire Buddhist canon, the Tripitaka, was undertaken in an effort to ward off foreign invasions and systemize the Korean understanding of Buddhist thought. The original set of 80,000 woodblocks was destroyed in the 13th-century Mongol invasions and replaced by a new collection, carved five years later. These woodblocks are now stored at Haeinsa Temple near Taegu.

The Koryŏ period saw the active development of arts and handicrafts thanks in large degree to the luxurious lifestyle and religious devotion of the aristocratic class. Ceramics were highly developed, especially the celadons, treasured today for their exquisite color and design.

The Chosŏn period which followed is notable for its reorganization of cultural pursuits, including scholarship and the arts, and the creation of *han'gŭl*, the Korean alphabet. The motivations of the alphabet's creators are still a matter of debate. Some scholars argue they were politically motivated while others see the alphabet as a reflection of an emerging ethnic consciousness. Whatever the motivations of King Sejong and the scholars at the "Hall of Worthies" (Chiphyŏnjŏn) who invented han'gŭl, the alphabet reflects an important historicity linking the ruler to the ruled. It also

opened the way for artistic growth among the common people.

The 16th century saw the blossoming of Koreans' spiritual potential once more in the spirit of the *sŏnbi*, learned gentlemen. The political and social climate of that era gave birth to a new breed of rural Neo-Confucian scholars who stood up for their beliefs despite repeated threats of political retribution and persecution. Many merit comparison with the great scholars of the Silla era for their creativity and wisdom.

They contributed not only to the advancement of metaphysics, but also to Korea's ethnic heritage by adapting Confucianism to Korea's unique cultural conditions in the form the *hyangyak* village code system.

Sixteenth-century Neo-Confucian scholars also advanced the study of Neo-Confucian theory, influencing Japanese Confucian thought in the process. During the Japanese and Chinese invasions of this period, Korea's Neo-Confucian scholars organized "righteous armies" (*ŭipyŏng*),

The Buddha at Sŏkkurram Stone Grotto (opposite) and the Tripitaka Koreana woodblocks stored at Haein Temple (above) testify to the Korean dedication to Buddhism. Both have been included in UNESCO's World Heritage List of unique and irreplaceable cultural assets.

mobilizing the populace in the defense of the nation. The spiritual fortitude of these gentlemen-scholars was responsible in part for the longevity of the Chosŏn regime.

In the early 17th century, the Practical Learning (Sirhak) school of reformist thought emerged, and in the 18th century, Catholicism became an important influence on the spiritual life of the Korean people. Practical Learning was motivated by an awareness of self, which went beyond simple personal reflection or phenomenal realization. Independent, practical thought born of a new self-awareness and the research and development of that thought had considerable significance for the emergent Practical Learning movement. It did not, however, manifest itself in government policies or elicit a positive response from a broad cross section of society.

The Practical Learning Movement influenced the development of the Enlightenment (kaehwa) Movement of the late 19th and early 20th centuries and had considerable historical significance, but was powerless, both militarily and culturally, in the face of the imperialist pressures of that period.

Well before this encroachment by foreign powers, Korean Catholicism had withstood serious persecution through its own self-preservation efforts. Lay people became priests and bishops, proving once again the latent spiritual potential of the Korean people. The Catholic Church was, to a large degree, responsible for the introduction and dissemination of modern culture and institutions, including the compilation of the first Korean dictionary and grammar text used in the publication of a Korean Bible and missionary efforts to abolish outmoded concepts and customs. Equality, regardless of sex or age, was actively promoted by the Catholic community.

Toward the end of the 19th century, Protestant denominations arrived in Korea, joining the Catholic Church in the promotion of the Enlightenment and other social movements. Christians also played an active role in the independence movement before and during the Japanese occupation of the Korean peninsula.

Despite these achievements, however, Christianity served as an avenue for economic and political imperialism. It also failed to open a channel of communication between the classes, unlike Buddhism and Confucianism which preceded it. For example, in the early years of the modern period, Catholicism was criticized for failing to identify with the masses participating in the Tonghak peasant movement and the righteous armies. The theological basis for active participation by Christians has yet to be established in our society today. Greater effort is required by all Christian denominations to clarify the role of christians in Korean society.

Ch'ŏndogyo, the "Religion of the Heavenly Way," such a powerful force in the Tonghak movement, played a decisive role in the March First independence movement during the Japanese occupation but has failed to excite much enthusiasm in more recent years. In fact, Tonghak has had a greater influence on other newly established religions such as Chŭngsangyo and Won Buddhism, which have attracted many believers in recent years. These religions still lack an advanced logical structure and any real popular appeal, however. Given the immense spiritual power of religion in traditional society, one cannot help but feel our modern religious institutions have a great task ahead of them.

Over the last century, as they began to accept Western science in the course of industrialization, the Korean people have suffered many hardships. The native creativity, cultural traditions and inner strength that might have served them in the modernization process were dulled toward the end of the Chosŏn period, and ultimately their nation fell victim to Japanese aggression. With Japanese rule, Koreans' traditional culture was suppressed and Japan's colonial commercial culture was mindlessly accepted. Since liberation in 1945, low-grade Western culture has been accepted in large doses, and only a very passive approach to the higher quality culture that gave birth to advanced Western science has been made.

The introduction of foreign culture with little attention to process or consequences is hardly the correct path to advanced culture. Rather, it gives rise to abuse and deception.

Today, 50 years since liberation from Japanese colonial rule, the absorption of Western civilization appears, on the surface, to be well underway, but any real transformation of our spiritual consciousness remains quite distant. The simple transplant of cultural elements may bring quantitative expansion, but without true absorption of those elements, a qualitative transformation and creation of a new culture is difficult. If we are to effectively absorb Western culture, all activities—political, economic and social—must be evaluated from a cultural perspective which takes their creative significance into account. To build a civilized society, we must establish, expand and realize in practice an advanced culture on the basis of this kind of cultural evaluation. ◆

The Origins of Korean Religious Beliefs

Hwang Sun-myung

The Yemaek tribe, distant ancestors of the modern Koreans, founded the Minusinsk bronze culture along the upper reaches of the Yenisey River in central Russia. When the tribe migrated to the Korean peninsula they brought Shamanism, a unique religious form still found in the Arctic region, with them. The path by which Shamanism came to Korea has been substantiated by numerous scholars, but any consideration of the close relationship between Korean culture and that of the Asian continent as well as climatic and geographical conditions reveals the obvious connection.

We must remember, however, that while Shamanism was Korea's ancient religion, that does not mean Koreans *believed* in Shamanism. This may sound like a play on words but I believe it is the first step toward a true understanding of the origins of Korean religion and the reality of religious life in ancient Korea. Early religious practitioners did not necessarily believe in Shamanism *per se*. Some scholars argue that early Koreans' worship of the sun and celestial gods, practices often found in nomadic tribes, prove they believed in Shamanism. Others assert that Chinese accounts of early Korean rites to the heavens prove they have believed in Shamanism since ancient times. Certainly, there is no denying Shamanism existed in ancient society, but we can only guess at its central transcendental concepts and the object of its belief.

In primitive or ancient societies, where the various branches of culture were not yet fully differentiated or developed, religious concepts played a centripetal role, influencing the entire social system. Transcendental concepts on which faith was based must have been the same for all members of society. While many different religious beliefs coexist in our modern society, in ancient tribal societies and more developed walled-town states, special objects of worship and religious rites honoring them enjoyed the unanimous support of the entire populace.

Many Korean historians assume totemism, found in Oceania and certain parts of North America, is unique for its system of marriage across tribal lines and for taboos that originate from this practice. They assume Korea's ancient religious traditions must derive from a totem culture because its foundation myth includes bear and tiger motifs and marriage between a heavenly father and a woman from a bear-totem tribe. I believe this assumption is overly simplistic. As evidenced from an account in the *Memorabilia of the Three Kingdoms* which suggests Silla's founder, King Namhae, who reigned from 4 B.C. to A.D. 24, was a shaman, Shamanism promoted unity and stability in tribal society. The question is: What was the belief system for individual members of that society? That is, was there a clear object of religious transcendence for people in tribal society? Did they distinguish the present world from the "other world"? Did they perceive their society in these terms? They clearly lived in a primitive state of magical animism, in which they could not distinguish their social system from nature. *Logos* had not yet emerged from *mythos*, so we can hardly expect them to have transcended the object of their belief. Generally speaking, it was not until centralized kingdoms emerged from the walled-town states that an absolute symbolic system embodying a more powerful mysticism was necessary.

Other Korean historians see Korea's ancient religion as animism. While this may be true in a certain sense, it does not adequately explain Korea's religious origins in the context of Korea's unique culture.

The magical animism mentioned above was not unique to ancient Korea; it can be found in any society where human beings have not yet differentiated themselves from nature. In Korea, animism had not developed to the extent that it could serve as the religious foundation for state building.

Even today, Shamanism remains at the bottom of the religious hierarchy. It is considered a backward folk belief because it never evolved to the level of a national religion. In fact, it is more a

A shaman making a food offering to spirits in a rite from the Kyŏnggi area

Villagers participating in the Ŭnsan pyŏlsin-gut parade to the village shrine with pieces of white paper in their mouths to prevent evil pollutants from entering.

system of customs than a religion. Overwhelmed by Chinese culture, Korean Shamanism was unable to develop into a more sophisticated religious form.

The bronze culture founded by the Yemaek people was soon overpowered by China's iron culture. In 109 B.C. Han China completed the Four Commanderies which marked the beginning of a powerful Chinese influence over Korean society and culture. The Chinese writing system was rapidly absorbed, and new concepts were introduced together with the language.

Confucianism arrived during the Unified Silla period but did not have a significant influence on the spiritual lives of the common people. A Chinese political structure was adopted and many renowned Korean Confucian scholars were produced. However, Confucianism's influence was generally limited to intellectuals familiar with Chinese culture.

In China, Confucianism took on religious significance when Former Han China's Emperor Wu systematized state rites. In Korea, it was not until the beginning of the Chosŏn Dynasty that Confucianism was embraced as the state religion and practiced by elite scholar-officials. During the Unified Silla period,

Confucianism was simply a ruling ideal; Buddhism and Taoism, introduced to Korea at a much earlier date, dominated the religious life of the common people. The atmosphere of *mythos*, protected from foreign influences by the walled-town states for so long, was suddenly absorbed by Buddhism and Taoism. The *Memorabilia of the Three Kingdoms* suggests belief in the Buddhist Pure Land was popular during the Three Kingdoms period, while a Taoist-influenced belief in Maitreya, the Future Buddha, was prevalent around the time of Silla's unification of the Korean peninsula. Maitreya faith was a prominent element

of religious life. The Silla people came to believe in reincarnation in a Taoist paradise where the Maitreya Buddha resided and sought to remake their world in the image of the future Buddha.

This period produced many revered Buddhist monks influenced by Pure Land thought and a belief in the future Buddha. The period is also notable for a boom in Buddhist construction and artistic activity. The many Buddhist statues, pagodas and temples produced during this period testify to the Silla people's devotion to Buddhism.

Political leaders emerging from aristocratic families toward the end of the Unified Silla period and during the early years of the Koryŏ Kingdom relied on the common people's religious fervor. Respected throughout society, Buddhism was embraced as the founding principle of the new kingdom. Koryŏ's rulers sought to enhance state power by resorting to a higher supernatural authority. Koryŏ's King Kwangjong introduced a Confucian civil service examination in 958, hoping to establish a rational bureaucratic political system, unlike the old system controlled by aristocrats, but he did not change the overall atmosphere of the country. He still entrusted the state's existence to a supernatural authority and the religious faith of the people. This is all too evident in the Koryŏ belief in prophesy and the protective powers of woodblocks of the Buddhist canons.

Belief in Tan'gun, the legendary founder of Korea, originated among the common people, despite their subordination to the Mongols. It offered them escape from the shackles of slavery. Thus I believe the Korean people's religious prototype is essentially supplicatory, more concrete and specific than primitive magical animism.

Conventional views about why the founders of the Chosŏn Dynasty revered Confucianism and suppressed Buddhism must be reconsidered. While the new elite, who took part in the establishment of a new regime by supporting Yi Sŏng-gye, demolished the old system in an effort to protect their own interests from widespread corruption in the Buddhist community, a disorderly system of land ownership and the emergence of large-scale landholdings, their independent consciousness is evident in their introduction of rites honoring Tan'gun and discussions about the construction of a replica of the Chinese people's ceremonial shrine where the God-Emperor was said to reside.

Still, Korea was transformed into a Confucian country for political and social reasons. The Confucian system was reinforced by the promotion of rites to be held in the home. With the development of Neo-Confucianism, scholars began to call for the abolition of Shamanistic rites. This could be interpreted as a direct challenge of the king's authority. From the founding of the kingdom, the kings and women of the court continued to participate in Shamanistic practices unofficially, despite Confucian scholars' persistent calls for propriety.

By linking Confucianism with national religious rites, the Chosŏn Dynasty emphasized the exclusive and absolute rights of Confucianism. The ruling elite and scholar-officials were expected to follow the system meticulously. Familial rites, including the most important ancestral rites, were systematized, and the social structure was

Spiritual traditions live on in rites held at Sajiktan, the altar established in 1394 by the founder of the Chosŏn Dynasty to honor the gods of land and grain (above), and in images of the Maitreya Buddha at Unjusa Temple in Chŏllanam-do province (right).

revamped accordingly. Under these metaphysical principles, practical morals, such as filial piety and loyalty to the country, were reinforced as norms in everyday life.

By strictly differentiating between the king, scholar-official elite and commoners, Confucian rites provided the fundamental principles behind the class system. The king and scholar-official elite enjoyed in the material world exclusive privileges in direct proportion to their obligations in the supernatural world. Commoners, or *ch'ŏnmin*, were not obliged to honor their ancestors, but by the same token enjoyed no privileges and were subject to numerous obligations in the practical world.

As a national religion, Confucianism linked the real world with the transcendental world. The social structure based on this view allowed the scholar-official elite class privileges. In order to guarantee that the system worked properly, the number of scholar-officials, or *yangban*, had to be limited and backed up by a large population of commoners and laborers dedicated to production. In order to firmly establish this system, the importance of familial rites had to be inculcated among the people. It was for this reason that the study of rituals (*yehak*) was promoted, and we see the emergence of renowned Confucian scholars such as Kim Chang-saeng and Song Si-yŏl.

For Confucian rituals to take hold, other religious faiths had to be streamlined. This is why Buddhism was suppressed in early Chosŏn. The persecution of Buddhism took the form of the seizure of temple property, the closing of temples and the conscription of monks into the service to the state, but this did not mean Buddhism, with its deep roots, could be eradicated overnight. Through the middle of the Chosŏn Dynasty, there were more than 5,600 temples serving a population of approximately 2 million.

Toward the end of the Chosŏn period, dramatic social and economic changes took place, undermining the class system itself. The existing class system deteriorated to the extent that commoners falsified their family records to obtain greater social privileges. As a result, ancestral rites were formalized and became increasingly complicated, promoting a trend toward conspicuous consumption.

Korean history clearly indicates that Shamanism is the means by which traditional culture has been transmitted to new generations since earliest times.

This period also saw the development of a family-oriented mindset manifested in the formation of villages composed of people from one clan. This family-orientation is thought to have been the reason Confucianism never developed into a proper religious institution despite its early status as a state religion. The emphasis on bloodlines made it impossible for individuals or factions unrelated by blood to unite or cooperate despite a shared national affiliation.

This exclusivity prevented Koreans from sharing a universal value system. When Catholicism was introduced, Practical Learning (*Sirhak*) scholars of the Southern (*Namin*) faction and missionaries attempted to realize a certain philosophical universality by focusing on the similarities between the Confucian concept of heaven (*ch'ŏn*) and the Christian concept of God (*Hanŭnim*). In the end, however, they were unable to overcome the concept of ancestral worship based on familial ties of blood which stretched back for so many generations. Catholic missionary work in the 19th century failed because it was unable to transform the value system that ruled the general public at that time.

While it is impossible to characterize Korean religious life in a few sentences, when we look back over archeological, linguistic and folkloric data, it is clear that Shamanism, handed down from ancient times, constitutes Korea's fundamental religious system, albeit an insufficient one. It is not a religious belief *per se.* Rather the world view and symbolism found in Korean Shamanism can be seen as a religious foundation for belief. The study of Shamanism has thus far focused on certain specialized elements such as ecstasy and possession, but many more important questions remain to be asked. For example, What specific religious symbols do we find in Shamanism? What are the Shamanistic concepts of deities and the transcendental world? How did these develop and how were they reflected in the Korean people's consciousness over the long term?

Korea's modern religious life can be likened to a religious museum where all types of gods and religions are on display, but I believe that the orgins of religious practice in Korea are based on animistic and supplicatory belief dominated by a magical faith in a transcendental authority. The concept of ancestral worship was emphasized in the Chosŏn period as part of the regime's efforts to establish Confucianism as the national ideology. While ancestral worship is to a certain extent universal, the Korean people's extended devotion to it stems from their unique social and historical circumstances. ◆

FUNDAMENTAL PRINCIPLES

Several principles and concepts run throughout Korean thought and religion. In this section, Professor Suh Kyoung-yo considers two of the most significant: loyalty and filial piety, moral standards of Confucian society which remain important in modern Korea. The *sŏnbi* gentleman-scholar embodied these values; in fact, he was the personification of Confucian ideals.

During the Chosŏn period, he was responsible for putting Confucian morals, such as loyalty and filial piety, into practice, whether serving as a government official or residing as a gentleman-scholar in the countryside. Professor Keum Jang-tae describes the life and values of the rural sŏnbi in his discussion of mountains and their inextricable link to the Korean psyche. While the images and significance of the mountain differ in Confucianism, Buddhism and Taoism, it is revered throughout Korean literature, art and daily life.

Loyalty, Filial Piety and the Sŏnbi Spirit

Suh Kyoung-yo

I n Korea, part of the Confucian cultural sphere of East Asia, thc concepts of loyalty, filial piety and the *sŏnbi* spirit, a learned devotion to country, have long served as a spiritual backbone, reinforcing social unity and the national consciousness.

Loyalty and Filial Piety

Loyalty and filial piety are not simply moral standards emphasizing what one *must* do. Modern Koreans generally think of the Three Bonds and Five Moral Disciplines when they think of Confucianism, and often find its "learned men," or sŏnbi, conservative and old-fashioned. However, Confucianism is actually dedicated to harmonizing the principles of the changeable and the unchangeable, hardly a reactionary enterprise.

In the 20th century, as Western civilization and democratic thought patterns which valued freedom, equality, and justice flowed into Korean society, many Koreans dismissed tradi-tional ethical standards as "pre-modern" and "feudalistic." The concepts of loyalty and filial piety, virtues governing the relationships of father to son and sovereign to subject, were considered obstacles to the democratic spirit, and traditional social values were rejected.

While hardly the intent of Confucian scholars, there have been some negative effects when the concepts of loyalty and filial piety are put into practice. Filial piety can result in blind subordina-tion to a patriarch, and loyalty sometimes means unconditional devotion to a sovereign. Confucianism is also criticized for treating human beings as members of a group rather than indi-viduals, for robbing them of their independence.

Historically, the concepts of loyalty and filial piety have been misunderstood and misused on numerous occasions. Modern Western philoso-phers and sociologists, especially Hegel and Weber, lacked a full understanding of Eastern

For many people like the elderly gentlemen pictured here Confucianism and the sŏnbi sprit are still a way of life, even down to their choice of clothes and hats.

A respect for learning and a dedication to state and family are essential elements of Korea's Confucian culture. While the 20th century has seen the introduction of Western culture, loyalty, filial piety and scholarly dedication remain ideal moral standards for many Koreans.

societies. They viewed the East in terms of absolute monarchies and pointed to the limitations of loyalty and filial piety in human relationships, labeling the concepts political and biased, and concluded that filial piety meant complete subordination which led in turn to unquestioning loyalty to the sovereign.

This perception resulted in a prejudiced view of traditional East Asian culture. On the whole, these Western scholars saw traditional Oriental society as authoritarian and criticized the concepts of loyalty and filial piety for rationalizing the authoritarian structure.

However, the fundamental spirit of these concepts emphasizes the idea of admonishment (*jianzheng* in Chinese or *kanjaeng* in Korean). Loyalty and filial piety should not be viewed narrowly as the subordination of children to their father or subjects to their king. Children and subjects were encouraged to remonstrate, to

Confucian rites, honoring one's own ancestors, the king or Confucius himself, are solemn affairs, rich in symbolism. Adhering to the strict ritual procedures is a gesture of respect to the deceased and a lesson in etiquette to the younger generation. Below, a young man and woman undergo a coming-of-age ceremony, a major Confucian ceremony.

make sure kings and fathers acted justly, thus preventing unjust acts by their superiors.

Loyalty and filial piety are not unilateral moral standards. They are based on a love of humanity derived from an ideal of "father's love, children's filiality" (*puja chahyo*), and a sense of duty springing from the concept of "king's righteousness, subjects' loyalty" (*kunŭi sinch'ung*). A father's love for his son and a son's sense of duty to his father are the utmost expressions of humanity and love. Without them, human life would be hollow.

A loving, respectful and sincere mind is the fundamental basis for moral human relationships. We can hardly expect moral behavior when the parent-child relationship lacks love and respect or when human relationships lack sincerity. This is true of all societies, feudalistic or democratic. Insofar as the family and the nation are communities, unity and a sense of

camaraderie are essential to the solution of difficult tasks. This is true of personal ethics as a family member and as a citizen.

Filial piety, brotherly love and loyalty were first mentioned in the *Analects* of Confucius. According to Confucius, one must be dutiful in the home and respectful outside, and one must always try one's best to be loyal and sincere.

Filial piety and brotherly love are the roots of love and respect. To children they constitute affection, to parents filial piety, and together they are the expression of benevolence. There is a saying that a child does not leave its parents' bosom until the age of three. And indeed, children are nurtured in the affection and strict teachings of their parents. Before they are ever instructed in their duties or correct behavior, they experience paternal love. Parents' love for their children and children's filial piety are the most natural expressions of humanity and the healthiest experience of love. Lacking these, humans fall into a void, become emotionally unstable, and may easily lose sight of life's meaning. Therefore, starting with the fundamental spirit of respect for one's parents and love for one's children, we move outward, into society and act with true and heartfelt patriotism through which we love our people and nation.

In the Sino-Korean expression for loyalty—ch'ungsin—ch'ung denotes the sincerity with which one acts according to one's own heart and will. In other words, it means being sincere to oneself. In the context of human relationships, this manifests itself as truthfulness or fidelity (sinŭi). Without a sense of personal sincerity or public trust, everything is reduced to false impressions. Loyalty is the foundation of sincerity and credibility, the fundamental principle of independence for the individual and of civic spirit for a member of a community.

Ethics are not unrelated to human universality or historical circumstances. They must be observed in the context of time and space. In practice, the concepts of loyalty and filial piety are significant in a number of ways.

First, they help us recognize our home and nation, repel invasion, resist oppression by outsiders, and guard our national sovereignty.

Second, they promote the veneration for ancestors, fraternal love, and love of family and the human race, thus promoting a humanitarian outlook. Filial piety within the parent-child relationship is vertical, while brotherly love is horizontal. The reverence of ancestors transcends time in that it extends to a love of one's fellow countrymen. It not only means respecting one's parents while they are alive; it also means appreciating and honoring them with memorial

ceremonies after their death. It is in these ceremonies that filial piety maintains the continuity of life.

The *Sŏnbi* Spirit

The Korean word *sŏnbi* refers to a person of knowledge and good bearing. More specifically it denotes a man of character or class who embodies the precepts of Confucianism. A sŏnbi is a gentleman, kindhearted and knowledgeable, an intellectual who acts upon principles. The Chinese ideograph *sa*, often used to refer to such gentlemen, means "scholar," and connotes a certain knowledge and skill in service of the government.

When discussing academic achievements, the gentleman is sometimes called *susa*—a person of scholastic excellence and virtuous conduct—or *chinsa*—a successful candidate for the second level of the civil service. More than anything else, however, Confucius emphasized the following as the true features of a gentleman. First, the gentleman devotes himself to the *to*, or "right way," and is never ashamed of dressing humbly and eating simple food. Second, he is armed with a sense of right and wrong in his own actions, and exhibits frugality, a moral sense transcending his governmental and social position, and a moral nature in his personal bearing. Third, he is a leader in society and an

Men of character and knowledge, the sŏnbi *have long been a model of loyalty and manhood for the Korean people. From early times, they were responsible for putting Confucian ideology into practice, whether as government officials serving in the capital or as scholars in the countryside.*

The sŏnbi study (opposite) reflects the traditional scholar-official's humble devotion to learning and the "right" way. The furniture in the study was fastidiously selected for it was visible evidence of the scholar's financial situation and intellectual sophistication. A reading table, a table for calligraphy, a table for smoking accessories, a stationery chest and book chest were standard equipment, and anything gaudy or overly decorative was strictly banned.

educator both to the general public, by carrying his beliefs into action, and to the ruler, by rectifying customs and administering government affairs in a just manner.

When a pupil asked him what made a true gentleman, Confucius replied, "A man who has a sense of shame in the way he conducts himself and does not disgrace his lord when serving as an envoy abroad can be called a gentleman." For Confucius, gentlemen were always true to their convictions and never risked transgressing virtue. Rather, they worked to realize virtue, even at risk to their lives. Zhuang-zi, on the other hand, emphasized righteousness. When a gentleman encounters danger, he thinks of benefiting others, even if he must sacrifice his life to do so. Mencius said the gentleman maintains a steadfast mind even if he lacks a fixed occupation. For him, integrity and a commitment to principles were essential to the gentleman.

In terms of social position, the sŏnbi and the class immediately above them, the *taebu*—an honorific term for scholar-official—were *sadaebu*, or "illustrious officials." As mentioned above, the ideograph sa means "scholar"; taebu is an honorific term for scholar-official. The combination of terms refers to the possibility of movement between the two classes. On the other hand, when speaking of personal bearing, the sŏnbi are called *sagunja*—sa meaning "scholar" and *kunja* meaning "man of virtue" in the sense of an ideal man who embodies Confucian principles.

Through scholarship, the sŏnbi was also a social leader. In this sense, he stood at the top of society's four classes—scholars, farmers, artisans and merchants—complementing the role of those engaged in farming, manufacturing and commerce. Some sŏnbi were more akin to the common people and could be called *sasŏin*, gentlemen who are also commoners. This distinction shows that while the sŏnbi could rise to the ruling class, they were also subjects. Through these titles, we see that the concept of sŏnbi almost always revolved around personal bearing and a moral sense of etiquette, right and wrong.

Korean history is full of examples of model sŏnbi. Ŭlp'aso, a Koguryŏ man who rose from a hermit's life in the countryside to the post of prime minister, aptly described the ideal sŏnbi at the time of his appointment: "When times are not right for the sŏnbi, he lives in seclusion, and when times are right, he emerges to take government office. That is the rightful action of the sŏnbi."

When the father of Kangsu, a Silla writer

with Confucian convictions and a profound knowledge of Chinese letters, scolded his son for taking a wife from a lowly class, Kangsu replied, "It is not shameful to be poor and humble; what is truly shameful is having knowledge of duty but not practicing it."

Sŏlch'ong, son of the renowned Silla monk Wonhyo and a Confucian scholar who developed the *ku'gyŏl* system of explicating Chinese texts, presented a letter of admonishment to King Sinmun, in which he warned the monarch against carnal pleasures and asked him to strictly observe moral standards. Sŏlch'ong has long been considered a model of sŏnbi behavior.

In Koryŏ times, the sŏnbi's official activities expanded noticeably, as did their training in educational institutes. By the end of the Koryŏ period, Neo-Confucianism had been imported from Yuan China, Taoism was being reinterpreted according to Confucian principles, the sŏnbi had a deeper awareness of their role, and their sense of social reform had matured. Chŏng Mong-ju, Yi Saek, and Kil Chae, three Koryŏ scholar-officials who refused to serve the first Chosŏn king because they believed he had violated Confucian principles in his seizure of power, are model sŏnbi for their scholastic achievements and moral strength.

In early Chosŏn times, Confucian ideology was embraced as the ruling principle of government. The sŏnbi were responsible for putting that ideology into practice, whether serving in a governmental post or living a hermit's life in the countryside. Wherever they were the sŏnbi illuminated the proper path of Confucianism and made an effort to realize it. Therefore, the sŏnbi were respected and honored by the common people and exerted a great influence on policy.

Sŏnbi were not born. A man became one through training and study. In this sense, the sŏnbi had to be a scholar. The aim of his learning was finding the correct approach to problems encountered in daily life.

The sŏnbi had to cultivate their personal morality, and at the same time, act upon it. They accomplished this by harmonizing their intellectual work, which consisted of studying principles, with their actions, whether in service to the government or as scholars.

In government they served their superiors and the king, and cared for the general public. As subjects they did not, however, obey the king blindly. The king and the subject were related by their moral sense, and the subject was obliged to correct the king's wrongdoing through admonishment. If correction was impossible, however, the sŏnbi resigned his position. Government service was not a life-long profession. The official had to maintain a moral sense of his own origins and his ascension to and retirement from the government. He had to recognize the difficulty of rising in the government and the ease of losing his post, realize he should not concern himself with wealth and fame, maintain a critical attitude and reject injustice. It is for this reason that the hermit sŏnbi who did not ascend to a government position was even more respected.

Ordinary people act in accordance with their desires. The sŏnbi strived to realize humanity's moral sense. When called upon by the king, Pak Che-sang, a fifth-century Silla official and model of sŏnbi behavior, said, "If I calculate the difficulty of the task before acting, that can not be called loyalty. If I calculate my chances of surviving in battle, that can not be called bravery." In Pak's words we detect strength based on loyalty and bravery. The sŏnbi was a patriot who worshiped moral values. He never acted from selfish greed. He always maintained a spirit of self-sacrifice and moral duty.

Cho Kwang-jo, a reformist scholar-official (1482-1519), described the sŏnbi attitude: "In general he cares not for himself but seeks to benefit the country; he does not calculate the difficulty of a task but acts bravely in the face of danger." The spirit of the sŏnbi meant transcending selfishness and maintaining a stately fair-mindedness. The sŏnbi was unbending, firm and free of suspicion.

Pak Chi-wŏn, the *Sirhak* philosopher and writer (1737-1805), once said the sŏnbi's opinions, or *saron*, should be based on public opinion, that the sŏnbi's influence, or *saryu*, should benefit society, that the sonbi's morals, or *sagi*, should manifest the righteous opinions of all people, that the killing of sŏnbi, or *sahwa*, is the murder of innocent men of virtue; and that *sarim*, lectures on learning and duty, are the collective responsibility of all sŏnbi scholars. In this, Pak prescribed the sŏnbi's social functions. In traditional society, the sŏnbi were the social conscience, the social intellect and a vigorous driving force.

Throughout Korea's history, the sŏnbi have taken a leadership role. In modern times the struggle for independence demanded virtuous and patriotic leaders. The sŏnbi played that role. They set the moral standard, for the individual and the community. The sŏnbi were not simply a class; they were intellectuals who put their values into practice, who were unbending in their pursuit of those values. Their spirit continues to serve us well today. ◆

Mountains in Korean Thought

Keum Jang-tae

Mountains are a fact of life in Korea. They are all around us. Throughout history sunny mountain slopes have provided a home to communities large and small. We have dug wild greens on these mountains. We have collected firewood there. In the era before cities developed, we were born in the mountains, we lived there, and we eventually were buried there. This was the pattern of our lives; house and tomb were tied to the moun-tains. They were everyone's home, everyone's final resting place. The idea of returning to the mountains was deeply root-ed in the minds of our ancestors and remains part of the Korean psyche.

During the Chosŏn period, when Confucian thought domi-nated, literati choose between two roads: the road to officialdom or the road back to a simpler life in the mountains. The road to officialdom meant going to Seoul, preferment, success, and the glitter of the capital. It also meant having to endure the noise and dust of the mundane world. The road to the mountains, on the other hand, meant a return home to a life buried in sleepy wooded valleys, where one might pursue a leisurely life of aca-demic interests, cultivating clear thoughts and transparent wis-dom.

Fame and honor accompanied the road to officialdom: a man could unburden his heart and might even be given a chance to

save the world. Every man embarking on an official career meditated on the writings of the great Chinese statesman Chu-ko Liang (181-234): his reflections on war brimmed with the spirit of loyalty and legitimate aspiration. But the road to officialdom was beset by the twin snares of dishonor and intrigue. A man sometimes lost his heart; sometimes he lost his life.

In contrast, the road to the mountains, while hardly exciting, provided peaceful repose and a sense of well-being. One discovered there a life admirably suited to fattening body and heart and cultivating deep clear thought. Those who returned to the mountains invariably echoed the Chinese official-turned-poet Tao Yuan-ming's "Return to My Mountain Home," in which he recounts the joys of life in the mountains after retiring from his magisterial post in the Eastern Chin kingdom. Academic pursuits in the mountains as a young man, an official career in middle age, and a final return to the mountains in one's declining years—this was the pattern of literati life. In "Return to My Mountain Home" Tao characterizes his official career as "heart becoming the slave of the body." Presumably a return to the mountains means "body becoming the slave of the heart." The heart should be master; it is wrong for the heart to be enslaved by the body.

The Chosŏn Confucian philosopher Yi Hwang (T'oegye, 1501-1570) was fifty before he finally built the mountain study of his dreams, Hansŏam. The day he moved there he wrote a poem rhyming with Tao Yuan-ming's "Moving House" from which the following comes:

This is a remote place: visitors seldom come.
The mountains are deep, the sun sets easily.
Life here I know is poor,
but it is better than having body rule heart.

Among the Chosŏn literati there were some who worked hard to be admitted to officialdom and some who worked hard to get out. In the 16th century, Cho Kwang-jo and Yi I (Yulgok) are examples of the former, while Yi Hwang and Cho Sik (Nammyŏng) are examples of the latter. It is difficult to say which side is right. Yi Hwang was likened to a mountain bird because he always wanted to leave office and return to his mountain home, whereas Cho Sik was typical of the lofty-minded hermit who from the outset turned his back on public office and buried himself in the remote countryside.

The trend among literati to retire from public office seems to have been venerated in Chosŏn society. Retiring to the country meant laying aside ambition, something thought difficult for ordinary mortals. A more important reason for the admiration given a return to the mountains is that it meant an opportunity to cultivate one's mind.

Mencius says: "If a man does not gain preferment, he should make himself virtuous; if he achieves distinction, he should make heaven and earth virtuous." Thus Mencius points the way both for those who attain high office and for those who live in poverty in the countryside. Obviously making oneself virtuous is easier than making all heaven and earth virtuous. At the same time, the point is being made that the personal cultivation process forms the root of an attitude toward government administration calculated to make heaven and earth virtuous. Personal cultivation is thus given greater priority. Retreating to the remote countryside and cultivating the inner man through learning is therefore regarded more highly than rushing after preferment in the bureaucracy.

Life with city people leads to inner confusion, making progress in learning difficult. Living in the quiet of a gentle mountain valley, reading and thinking, facilitates the pursuit of pure learning. In fact, the fostering of learning that occurred in these country retreats during the Chosŏn Dynasty helped to give real body to the thought of the period.

Studying personal cultivation in the mountains and studying in the city are quite different. In the city, the tendency is to pursue practical skills and develop knowledge of practical problems, while in the mountains, interest centers on personal cultivation, ranging from philosophical considerations of the origin of the universe to ethical considerations of human conduct. It follows that in traditional society, mountains were not only places where people lived but also a cradle for learning and thought.

When it comes to personal cultivation, the kind of mountain deemed suitable for intellectual exercise varies according to objective and methodology. Confucian literati preferred mountains with gentle slopes, watered by quiet streams flowing through quiet valleys. They avoided mountains that were too rugged or high. They also avoided water that was too deep or swift. They preferred a middle ground, something in between flat plains and towering peaks. It was this temperate terrain that served as the incubator of Confucian thought.

In contrast, Buddhist monks and Taoists sought rugged mountains with deep pools for their ascetic practice. High, rough, remote mountain areas are ideal if one's ascetic objective is, by transcending the world, chewing pine leaves and practicing personal cultivation, to become the Buddha or an Immortal.

Rugged mountains are best for practicing the truth of the void and the ideal of eternal youth. Some ascetic monks wander the mountains and countryside like "clouds and water," seeking spots of exceptional natural beauty and never staying in one place for long.

Korea's mountain terrain is singularly suited to the objectives of the ascetic monk. Buddhist and Taoist monks often cut their ties with the human world and retire deep into the mountains where they seek a truth that transcends life and death. The literati, in contrast, while leisurely cultivating the heart in the mountains, looked outward as they searched for a truth that might serve the human world. The literati on their mountain slopes lived apart from the world, but in another sense they remained very much a part of it, distinct and yet never separate, just like the *i-ki* (*li-chi* in Chinese) concept in Neo-Confucianism.

Why are the mountains so suitable for ascetic practice? Above all they are quiet, removed from the world's complexities, places where one can concentrate, where the spirit can spread its wings in the wind and green. In fact, young Chosŏn literati intent on study often left their homes in the foothills in search of the quiet of a hermitage higher up the mountain. Many religious groups and followers of folk religions still use the mountains for prayer and devotional exercises. In the mountains, faith deepens and learning is more refined.

Mountains and water are like *yin* and *yang*, harmonizing with each other so the whole may retain its balance. Mountains and water are not in conflict. Their relationship is one of mutual support: one serves the interests of the other. The contrast between the loftiness of the mountains and the depth of water

sets off the mountains' height; the quiet immobility of the mountains highlights the unceasing movement of water. Human life, art, learning and religion have always thrived where mountains and waters meet in harmony.

Confucius says: "The wise man delights in water, the good man delights in mountains. The wise man is active; the good man stays still." Using mountains and water as images of wisdom and goodness, Confucius contrasts the two basic divisions of human virtue, intellectual wisdom and moral character. Knowledge is like water in that it implies an unbroken flow of reasoning ability. Goodness is like the mountains in that it is fixed and unchanging in its devotion to justice. Mountains and water provide a noteworthy environment for cultivating wisdom and goodness: while enjoying the mountains, a man can increase his goodness. While enjoying water he can increase his wisdom. A combination of wisdom and goodness is the ideal.

This old *hansi* (a poem composed in Chinese characters by a Korean poet) figuratively links mountains and water with classical literature and classical music.

Blue mountains are wordless
but they are a book for all ages;
Flowing waters are stringless
but they are the kŏmungo of a thousand years.

Blue mountains of old are as eternally unchanging as the truths contained in the classics. In contrast, the sound of flowing water is as varied as the melody of the kŏmungo, a six-string Korean zither, over a thousand years. Indeed, when the literati left government service and returned to their homes in the mountains, the classics and the kŏmungo were the most prized possessions they took with them.

One day after the summer rain cleared, Yi Hwang climbed Chaha Peak and sang of the fresh, tingling pleasure he experienced there:

The fields are broad, the skies are high,
the summer rain has cleared.
Blue mountains surround me;
I hear the tinkle of jade waters.
Now I know the boundless excitement
of mountains and waters;
I do not wish for embroilment
in the hollow sins of the world.

When the literatus retires from the complexity of the world, mountains and water serve as a space within which he can give himself to the pleasures of learning and personal cultivation. Mountains and water are not desolate, dreary places. They overflow with the excitement of nature and the joy of truth garnered deep in the heart.

In Confucian society, a self-sufficient life among mountains and water represented "home," an ideal life for retired scholars and officials. Some of the characteristics of this ideal life can be found in *sijo* vernacular verse.

First of all, man and nature find harmony in mountains and water. A sijo written by Yi Hwang's friend, the scholar Kim In-hu, is very close to the Korean heart. It deals with the greening of human life amidst mountains and water.

Blue mountains go their way;
green waters go their way.
Mountains their way, waters their way,
and me my way among them.
I have grown my way among them;
among them my way I will grow old.

Secondly, mountains and water represent a transcendent world. Yi Yu, a scholar-official of the late 17th century, followed Yi Hwang's example and wrote of the joys of life in harmony with nature.

I build a three-room hut
on the banks of the blue stream in Tosan Valley.
Fish jump up on the bank,
white gulls alight in the field in front of my house.
I fear the world may discover
these two pleasures.

The heart, so thrilled by life in communion with nature that it fears its pleasures may be discovered by the world at large, reflects a sense of self-sufficiency associated with the Taoist Peach Blossom Paradise and the World of the Immortals. It testifies to the grace of the lives of literati in pastoral retirement.

Thirdly, mountains and water are a place of learning and personal cultivation. Life amidst the mountains and streams did not simply mean whiling away pleasant hours in a transcendent natural environment. It meant living a life that reflected the acquisition and practice of Confucian moral standards as revealed in this sijo by Yi Yu.

I close my mountain door
and sit at leisure.
I live with ten thousand books, my joy endless.
Should my love
come to see me, tell her I am not here.

Yi Yu emphasizes reading and the cultivation of learning as the supreme joys of a literatus buried in nature. He seems determined to cut himself off from the temptations of the outside world. Kim Su-jang, a poet and minor official in the military ministry around the same period, wrote a sijo in which he uses objects commonly found in the countryside to compare the natural order with the order of man:

I cut a tree on Great Learning Hill
and make a Bright Virtue Boat.
I row across Citizen's River and tie up at Supreme
    Goodness Point.
Ah!
I will fish for the Three Principles and Eight Articles.

The literati who returned to the mountains took great care in choosing the place where they intended to pursue learning and cultivate moral character. They often constructed lovely little gardens for themselves and took regular strolls, appreciating the exceptional natural beauty, giving names to the mountains, rocks and bends in the rivers, creating in the process a living environment of enhanced meaning. The "eight scenes" and "nine songs" motif, so common in Korean poetry, is the most obvious example of this practice.

The nine songs (or "bends" as the Chinese character *kok* translates as both "song" and "bend") theme is particularly noteworthy. The nine songs refer to nine beautiful spots found in the area about which so many of these poems were composed. The original is the Chinese Neo-Confucian philosopher Zhu Xi's "Nine Songs of Wuishan" (in Korean, Mui Mountain). Zhu also wrote a ten-poem Wuishan boat song series which Chosŏn literati subsequently used as a model for their own nine-poem series. The nine songs of Wuishan are described from one through nine and correspond to the progress achieved through learning, to stages of the Taoist Way, or simply to the natural beauty of each valley. Chosŏn literati often composed poems in response to Zhu Xi's boat song or discussed the character of the nine-poem boat series. Sometimes they even designated nine "bends" or beautiful spots in their own areas and composed nine-poem series celebrating that beauty.

After reading a book by the Song Chinese scholar Liu Kui recounting anecdotes associated with Wuishan, Yi Hwang wrote a nine-poem series rhyming with Zhu Xi's boat song. While studying in Haeju, Yi I designated nine local beautiful spots and wrote his "Nine Songs of Kosan." Kim Su-jang developed the area around Hwaŭmdong, on the northern slopes of Mt. Hwaak in Hwach'ŏn, into a scenic area featuring nine beautiful spots which he then commissioned the artist Cho Sae-gŏl

to paint.

In the mid-19th century, Yi Won-jo built a pavilion for his retirement on Mt. Kaya, creating his own nine-songs (bends) area which he celebrated with a nine-poem series, rhyming with Zhu Xi's Wuishan boat song series. Yi is recognized for collecting and editing materials related to Wuishan from China and Korea.

The literati did not simply build houses on mountain slopes and river banks. They went deeper and climbed higher to devote themselves to learning and personal cultivation, freeing the inner spirit. What Mencius refers to as "reviving one's spirit" is easier to achieve on a mountain ridge where the vista of a broader world spreads before one's eyes. At the top of a mountain, opening the heart and shouting with all one's might brings a refreshing release to the crumpled inner man. According to traditional Korean beliefs, the mountain has a spirit, and those who live beneath or climb the mountain receive that spirit and experience a deepening of their humanity.

Chosŏn literati left many accounts of "leisurely days in the mountains." While climbing Mt. Kaya, the scholar-official Chŏng Ku (1543-1620) stressed "washing the eyes and opening the heart on the mountaintop." Looking out on a landscape of clear blue water flowing down a mountain valley, he sang of his heart being "cleansed." Washing the eyes and cleansing the heart imply inner purification. In order to study effectively, one must cool the fires of desire that burn in the heart and free oneself from thoughts and feelings born of daily life's conventions. Thus climbing the mountain does not merely involve broadening one's vision; it also means striving to broaden one's heart.

Those pursuing classical learning are encouraged to take frequent walks in the yard in order to free the spirit, to close the book and take time to reflect, so that learning and thought may be parallel, to engage by day in exercise that consumes energy and to nurture at night *ki*, the energy that fosters life. Both static and dynamic elements, yin and yang, are essential for personal cultivation and the acquisition of learning. A session of reading the classics is static and crimped; climbing the mountain afterwards opens the mind and heart.

Chŏng Ku realized "the good man reflects on himself when he sees the mountain." The dictum "Approach good as if it means climbing up, approach evil as if it means falling down" assumes that good is perfected in the effort to go upward, while evil is realized in the luxury of going down. The refreshing vista that opens before one's eyes on the mountaintop symbolizes the blinding moment of truth one will inevitably experience if one continues to strive for a perfect knowledge of natural law as envisioned by Zhu Xi. The refreshing vista from the mountaintop expresses the ultimate state of transcendence which follows learning accumulated over a long time.

In an account of leisurely days on Mt. Sobaek, Yi Hwang tells us, "What at first was blocked, now is free," confirming in the course of mountain-climbing the process by which learning is acquired and enlightenment is attained. The Buddhist master Ch'ŏn-in (1205-1248) understood leisurely days in the mountains in terms of personal cultivation: "We view towering mountains and listen to tinkling waters not simply to gladden the heart, but to enable ourselves to follow the Way by reviving the inner man through the pursuit of the goodness and wisdom that comes from a union with nature."

Climbing mountains brings a wider world into view, a broadening of one's vision. Confucius said that when he climbed Dongshan (East Mountain), he considered his native kingdom of Lu small, but when he climbed Taishan (the great eastern mountain of China), all heaven and earth seemed small. When we accompany Confucius to the top of the mountain, we take in the world at a glance and become awakened to the Way. Kim Chong-jik, a 15th-century Confucianist, says the reason he admired Confucius for climbing Taishan and seeing heaven and earth and the reason he admired the Tang poet and essayist Han Yu (768-824) for climbing Hengshan was not because he wanted to climb himself but because he wanted to experience their breadth of vision.

When *Sirhak* (Practical Learning) scholar Pak Chi-won (1737-1805) crossed Mach'on Pass on his way to China and saw the vast Liaodong Plain below him, he sighed: "It is a fine place to cry. I think I will give it a try." As the baby cries when it leaves the narrow dark womb and goes into the world, so he wanted to cry upon seeing the broad expanse of China after living in the choking confinement of the Korean peninsula. He also felt like crying when he stood on top of Piro Peak in the Diamond Mountains and looked down on the East Sea and when he saw the hazy skyline as he walked the golden sands of Changyon beach. Pak Chi-won's superior consciousness is clearly evident in the cry of rebirth and release he emits upon viewing a new world after agonizing in the dark, choking, contradictory confines of his society.

In the mid-15th century, the Sallim Faction, founded in the spirit of Chong Mong-ju and Kil Chae, scholars of the late Koryo period who remained faithful to the Koryo monarch after the founding of the Choson Dynasty, came into conflict with the Hun'gu Faction, literally the "Faction of the Meritorious and Conservative," all-powerful in the court of King Sejo. At the heart of the Sallim Faction's ideology was a reverence for loyalty: Chong Mong-ju died because he refused to serve two kingdoms; Kil Chae refused an official post in the new kingdom and retreated to the mountains. When Sejo usurped the throne from his nephew Tanjong in 1455, powerful Hun'gu Faction officials like Chong In-ji and Sin Suk-chu made sure the Sallim Faction remained buried in the country. A new generation of young bureaucrats emerged in the footsteps of Cho Kwang-jo, the young Neo-Confucian reformer, but repeated purges forced them to retire deeper into the countryside.

Throughout the period, the Sallim Faction was confined to the mountains and forests, while the Hun'gu Faction firmly established itself in Seoul. The Sallim Faction continued to cultivate learning and revere loyalty, thus arming themselves with a critical sense of justice in the face of official greed and corruption, a sense of justice which became the literati mind-set of Choson. Literati who believed in righteousness were always prepared to leave their official posts without regret and return to the countryside. They were even prepared to devote themselves, from the outset, to learning in the beauty of the countryside and never assume a post at all.

Kim Sang-hon (1570-1652) and Song Si-yol (1607-1689) were representative of the anti-Qing ideology that emerged during the Manchu Invasion of 1636. Kim Sang-hon established himself in a cave on the banks of the Han River, and many of his followers went deep into the mountains along the upper reaches of the Northern Han. They lived in the secluded harmony of the mountains and waters, and their strong, incisive opinions served to transmit the values of the age. These were the Sallim scholars of the later Choson Dynasty, men armed with a strong sense of justice.

While studying in Hwayang-dong near Ch'ongju after his retirement, Song Si-yol carved the "Nine Songs of Hwayang" and some writings by the Koryo king Uijong and the Choson King Sonjo in large letters on the face of a cliff. These writings expressed in condensed form the spirit of righteousness. The writings by Uijong recommended that one never violate etiquette, and the Sonjo piece proclaimed that the Yellow River always flows east, symbolizing the steadfast nature of loyalty.

In the late 19th century, as the Japanese encroached on Korea and Western pressure to open ports mounted, scholars supporting the "reject heterodoxy" ideology emerged around the country. Yi Hang-no (1792-1868), a pioneer among them, founded his own school in the mountains near Pyokkye, nurturing a group of leaders pivotal in the propagation of "reject heterodoxy" thinking. They renounced the reform program being pushed by the Western powers and devoted themselves to a radical expurgation of Western and Japanese influence.

When Queen Min was murdered by the Japanese in 1895 and Japanese influence became dominant, Yu In-sok organized a "righteous army" known as the Chech'on Volunteers. Yu proposed three possible courses of action for literati to respond conscientiously to the national calamity: raise an army of volunteers and sweep out the enemy; leave for the mountains and follow the old ways; or demonstrate their fidelity by dying for the cause. Most chose the "leave and follow the old ways" dictum. Some left the country as exiles, and others retreated deeper into the mountains. Most major scholars chose to retreat into the mountains.

The life of the literatus who retired into the mountains and gave himself to study and the appreciation of the wind and the moon reflected the traditional spirit of resistance: ties of worldly temptation were cut, worldly desires were bridled. By retreating deeper into the mountains, sticking resolutely to Confucian principles, rejecting Japanese aggression, and refusing all contact and compromise with Korea's invaders, the scholars at the end of the 19th century preserved a solid spirit of resistance in the face of aggression.

For them, the mountains were a snug nursery that fostered and protected Korean thought and the literati mind-set. This was hardly an active response to life's challenges, however. Intrinsically negative, it tended to weaken in its exclusionist stability. Nevertheless, the learning cultivated in the mountains did have positive aspects. In fact, much of the Sirhak, or Practical Learning program, that emerged in the 17th century was developed in the mountains by men like Yu Hyong-won and Chong Yag-yong. ◆

(Poems translated by Kevin O'Rourke)

BUDDHISM

In the 1,600 years since it was introduced to the Korean peninsula, Buddhism has provided Korean rulers with an effective tool for unifying the country under a central government and the common people with a rich source of spiritual strength. It has also nourished a magnificent blossoming in the arts and literature. In fact, it would be difficult to find an element of Korean life that has not been influenced by Buddhism directly or indirectly.

In this section, our contributors consider the influence of Buddhism on Korea's history, philosophy, art, music, dance and literature. What distinguishes Korean Buddhism from that of other cultures? What are the goals and practice of Korean Buddhists, and what is Buddhism's role in modern society?

Korean Buddhism: Harmonizing the Contradictory

Chung Byong-jo

The teachings of the Buddha penetrated China around the first century A.D. The towering Himalayas were a formidable barrier separating China from the Indian continent, but a thread-like trade route, the Silk Road, found its way through the treacherous mountains and the deserts and forests. It was over the Silk Road that India and China came to know one another. They were, however, very different in temperament, ethnicity and culture. The Indians were religious and transcendental, while the Chinese were practical and interested in the concrete. Indeed, in many ways, the relationship between these two cultures was like that of the East and West today—forever running parallel like two railroad tracks racing toward the horizon.

It is no wonder that Buddhism, a product of Indian soil, ran counter to the Chinese disposition. The Indo-Aryan culture was extremely logical and rational, while the Chinese relied on intuition over reason. The Chinese people chose to accommodate Buddhism on their own terms in the form of Chan (better known in the West by the Japanese transliteration, Zen) and Hwa-yen (or Avatamsaka) Buddhism. Chinese Buddhism tended to emphasize intuition over logic and reflected a distinct Sino-centrism.

It was in this modified form that Buddhism came to Korea. Although some scholars still assert Buddhism came to Korea directly from India, existing data do not support this view. Few are persuaded by "evidence" such as Indian-style place names in the Kimhae area or mention in the 13th-century *Memorabilia of the Three Kingdoms* of a statue of the Buddha sent to Korea by King Asoka of Maurya in the third century B.C.

Buddhism was introduced to Koguryŏ in A.D. 372, to Paekche in 384 and to Silla in 527, a natural order given the Three Kingdoms' geographical locations. The arrival of Buddhism seems to have caused little friction in Koguryŏ or Paekche. Koguryŏ's King Sosurim instructed his people to "seek happiness by respecting the Buddhist dharma (teaching)" in 373, one year after its introduction to his land. It was also around this time that nine temples, including Ibullan Temple, were built in P'yŏngyang, Koguryŏ's capital. When the Paekche Kingdom decided to embrace Buddhism as the state religion in 384, the king welcomed monks from China with the utmost courtesy, traveling several miles from his palace to greet them.

These incidents show that both Koguryŏ and Paekche adopted Buddhism in a top-down fashion. At the time, the Early Chin was the strongest of a number of warring states on the Chinese mainland, and for Koguryŏ, which shared a border with the Former Chin, armed conflict was hardly desirable. Thus when the king of the Former Chin sent statues of the Buddha and Buddhist scriptures to Koguryŏ, they were welcomed as symbols of amicable relations between the two countries. Paekche embraced Buddhism on similar terms. Silla, on the other hand, did not accord official recognition to Buddhism for another 150 years.

Why was this? Prior to the reign of King Pŏphŭng in the sixth century, Silla had been a federation of six founding clans. There was no centralized royal authority and, as a result, Buddhism could not spread from the court down to the commoners. Rather, it flowed in the opposite direction, and there was undoubtedly friction between the new religion and existing popular beliefs.

Another factor slowing official recognition of the religion may have been the Silla rulers' concern with internal cohesion, rather than foreign affairs. For Koguryŏ and Paekche, the acceptance of Buddhism meant not only friendly relations with China but also the accommodation of an advanced culture. Silla, on the other hand, was not yet mature enough to take this step.

Ironically, Buddhism ultimately flourished in Silla, to the extent that Silla Buddhism is taken as the prototype for Buddhism during the Three Kingdoms period. Silla Buddhism represented an evolution in the eastward diffusion of Buddhism from India.

We cannot be certain as to the nature of the beliefs and practices of the earliest Korean followers of Buddhism. Nevertheless, it is safe to say that until the Koryŏ period, Korean Buddhism's central tenet was the cultivation and practice of the spirit of the Bodhisattva, absolute selflessness on the path to enlightenment, one of the defining characteristics of Mahayana Buddhism. Countless truth seekers pursued Mahayana Buddhism, the greater vehicle for universal salvation. For them, Buddhism was a prescription for the sufferings of the masses and developed to become the backbone for many traditional Korean philosophies.

As with most religions, Korean Buddhism is really two religions in one: first, the ideology of the ruling class, and second, a popular religion of the masses. History has been shaped to a large degree by the ideology of the ruling elite, and over the centuries Buddhism has taken different forms depending on the attitudes of those in power. Having said this, however, we must remember that the masses' faith in the religion was constant. Of course, popular faith was not always lofty or refined; at times it bordered on superstition. Nevertheless, we must remember that this grass-roots faith reflected the spirit of the times.

The great Chinese military strategist of the sixth century B.C., Sun Wu, once said winning over the hearts of the masses was essential to victory in war. Without popular support, brave troops and brilliant tactics were no guarantee of battlefield success. Sun Wu's advice can be applied to Buddhism as well: it will never prosper without the support of the masses. This does not mean, however, that the religion should cater to the people's every whim. Rather, Buddhism must always enlighten the spiritual life of the people, taking them to a higher place.

What do ordinary people want from Buddhism? Their demands tend to be definite and immediate. They expect their belief to bring prosperity to their families and success for their children in important examinations, for example. Their immediate concerns are not with abstract ideas such as the four noble truths or the six perfections. They want cures for their illnesses, answers to their prayers.

Often their desires can be satisfied with simple magic, but an over-reliance on magic is bound to reduce Buddhism to a kind of sorcery. Hence, true Buddhists must elevate the immediate and materialistic desires of the laity to a purer belief.

How is Korean Buddhism different from the Buddhism found in other cultures? From

earliest times, the Silla people had a tradition of worshiping mountains. This tradition, exemplified by notions such as the "five holy peaks" or "three divine mountains," was expressed in slightly different forms over time, but the essence remained intact.

Stemming from a Shamanistic sense of awe in the face of natural forces, this primitive worship of nature took on a Buddhist tone over time. Buddhism provided the theoretical underpinnings for primitive thought. This syncretism facilitated the acceptance of Buddhism. By smoothly integrating primitive belief and Buddhist thought, Silla became the ideal "Buddha Land." Ultimately, Buddhism was viewed as an indigenous religion, rather than an import from abroad. So began the indigenization of Buddhism in the Silla Kingdom.

This process of indigenization and the concept of Silla as the "Buddha Land" are to a great extent the fruit of the efforts of a few prominent monks, including Master Chajang (608-686), National Preceptor in seventh-century Silla. Chajang initiated the worship of Mt. Odae in Kangwon Province. This worship was later popularized by Poch'ŏn and Hyomyŏng who are believed to have been Silla princes. Determined to leave the secular world, the two princes built hermitages on Mt. Odae and spent their lives studying there. Historical records suggest they worshiped the five peaks of Mt. Odae daily and finally witnessed the 50,000 "Bodies of Truth" and their transformation into different forms.

The five peaks of Mt. Odae, one for each of the four directions and the center, were believed to have been inhabited by five different bodhisattvas. Worshipers of the mountains paid their respects in two shifts that stretched throughout the day, chanting and reading texts specific to each peak. Given the obvious connections with the Taoist concept of directions, this practice demonstrates Silla's syncretism of Taoism and Buddhism.

The unique historical consciousness of the early Silla people as revealed in the worship of Mt. Odae is best characterized by the tendency to accept the various bodhisattvas as a whole rather than to prefer a particular bodhisattva. The Silla people tended to pursue unity amidst diversity rather than uniformity. The glorification of Mt. Odae was a means of returning to the spirit of Ekayana (literally "one vehicle"), the ultimate reality leading to supreme enlightenment; it was not a simple dogma. The Silla people's worship of Mt. Odae embodied both the pursuit of Ekayana and the notion of ideological diversity.

This distinctive tendency exerted a great influence on the Silla people's conception of art and left its mark on virtually every artistic creation of this period, including sculpture, painting and architecture. Indeed, through Silla's artistic legacies, we confirm the nature of Buddhism during that period.

The unification of the Three Kingdoms under Silla can be analyzed from a number of angles. For example, it is often seen in terms of

Silla's military prowess and successful exploitation of diplomatic ties with Tang China. Sometimes it is explained with reference to Silla's social solidarity built around the youthful *hwarang* ("flower of youth") elite force. However, a major factor enabling Silla to achieve unification was the spiritual power flowing from the state's sound accommodation of Buddhism. The ruling elite had a clear understanding of the religion, and the masses were willing to follow them. Buddhism thus enhanced solidarity within Silla society.

During the early years of Silla Buddhism, the spiritual ties between the rulers and the ruled owed much to a belief in Maitreya, the Future Buddha. This utopian doctrine satisfied the popular longing for a land of happiness, free of suffering. At the same time, it encouraged the ordinary people to identify their own monarch with a Buddhist deity.

From the reign of King Chinhŭng in the mid-sixth century, Silla became involved in a series of wars through which it greatly expanded its territory. While rapid progress was made throughout society, the continued war sharpened the sense of crisis among the people and created a gulf between the rulers and the ruled. It was in this context that Buddhism was actively embraced. Of the Three Kingdoms, Silla was the only state in which Buddhism served as a centripetal spiritual force, a catalyst transforming a clan-based society into a cohesive one committed to unification.

In fact, unification of the Korean peninsula under Silla can be seen as an example of Buddhism realizing its historical mission—transforming a clan society embedded in a primitive belief system into a unified and future-oriented consciousness. Buddhism helped the Silla rulers alleviate the anxiety of those they had defeated by presenting them with a religion that offered a new way of life. By showing the path to the "other world," Buddhism encouraged them to pursue their lives in the new environment with renewed enthusiasm. In short, Buddhism served to bring the dispersed people of the former Three Kingdoms together.

Silla was also far ahead of the other two kingdoms in terms of Buddhist doctrine. The theoretical depth and maturity of Silla Buddhism was especially indebted to Mahayana Buddhist texts such as the *Avatamsaka-sutra*, the *Saddharmapundarika-sutra* and the *Samadhi-nirmocana-sutra*. These texts guided Silla Buddhism toward the pursuit of "oneness."

The *Saddharmapundarika-sutra* teaches the

merging of three states of being into one, the Ekayana (One Vehicle). The *Avatamsaka-sutra* emphasizes the doctrine of all-encompassing harmony. For the Silla people, these teachings suggested an ideology on which territorial unification could be based as well as the means by which it could be achieved. The visible world seems to consist of conflicts and confrontations, but when approached from the standpoint of the Ekayana, it reveals its true image: a seamless web of delicate harmonies.

According to Ŭisang (620-702), a prominent Silla monk, the world is a totality which cannot exist without individual units, but when the individuality of the units is emphasized, that totality disappears. The relationship between a group and its individual members is inevitably the same. An efficient group is one that respects the unique abilities of its members, while at the same time promoting the good of the whole.

However, if something is to be called "a whole," its individual units must share a certain quality. Ŭisang called this quality "identity" (*tongsang*). The unique characteristics of the composite parts must be able to mold into a unified identity. The whole, in turn, must strive to achieve a perfect harmony among its individual units, a goal that cannot be achieved without self-sacrifice on the part of the individual components.

When seen from this dialectic perspective, the relationship between the state and individual citizens is much like the relationship between the one and the multitude as defined in the Doctrine of the Six Phenomena: the one (the state) contains the multitude (individuals) and yet the multitude is as one. This doctrine defines the attitude that the state and individual citizens should take toward one another. The code of action it provides can be applied to the king, his court officials and the people at large. This dialectic regulating the relationship between the state and the people is the essence of the historical consciousness that fueled the Silla Kingdom's unification of the Korean peninsula.

While Buddhism during the Koryŏ period was not without unwholesome elements in terms of doctrine and practice, it made significant contributions to the development of national culture. For example, the Tripitaka Koreana (the Korean compilation of Buddhist texts) was produced with what were at the time the world's most advanced woodblock printing techniques.

The carving of the Tripitaka that exists today began in 1236 amidst an all-out struggle against the invading Mongols. The original woodblocks, completed in 1087, were destroyed during these invasions, and the ruling king, Kojong, ordered a new edition carved after he and his court moved from Kaesŏng, the capital, to Kanghwa Island in 1232.

From the historical sources available to us today it is impossible to tell exactly how the Tripitaka was produced. The woodblocks are believed to have been carved from white birch trees from islands off the southern coast. The wood was soaked in brine for a long period of time, then dried in the shade before carving. The main office overseeing the production of the woodblocks was established on Kanghwa Island in 1236. Later branch offices were set up in Namhae and Chinju for the actual carving.

Most of the woodblocks were carved from 1237 to 1244. In 1248, a list of the woodblocks, a kind of table of contents, was also carved. It was not until three years later that the entire Tripitaka, totaling 81,340 blocks, was completed.

What is the significance of the Tripitaka? First of all, it symbolizes the Koryŏ people's commitment to the defense of their country. Internal unity in Koryŏ society was essential in the face of the Mongol invasions, and the Tripitaka project provided a focus for that unity. Confronted with the "barbaric" Mongols, the military regime of the Ch'oe family, the power behind the throne, no doubt wanted to inspire a sense of cultural pride and mission among the Koryŏ people.

Second, the Tripitaka underscores the solid spiritual and cultural foundation of Koryŏ Buddhism. While Koryŏ Buddhism tended to incorporate some elements of Shamanism, it also achieved significant progress as the official religion of the ruling regime. The inauguration and subsequent evolution of the Chogye Order greatly popularized Buddhism and provided the basis on which the colossal Tripitaka project could be successfully completed.

Third, the Tripitaka is the world's oldest extant set of Buddhist Mahayana texts and, at the same time, the most precise. It is also one of the main sources of information on the original Mahayana texts, many of which have been lost or destroyed. In short, the Koryŏ Tripitaka was the crystallization of a national culture of which Buddhism was an essential component.

When Japan invaded the Korea in 1592,

Buddhist believers perform t'aptori,
a ritual in which they circle a pagoda,
praying and chanting sutras.

Yŏnggyu, a disciple of the Master Sŏsan (1520-1604), mobilized a group of monks to fight the invaders. The guerrilla force attacked the Japanese troops occupying Ch'ŏngju Castle in Ch'ungch'ŏngbuk-do Province, driving the them from the castle. This was the first victory for the Korean side since King Sŏnjo fled the capital of Seoul for Ŭiju in the north. Yŏnggyu then joined forces with Cho Hŏn, another guerrilla leader, to wage a major battle against the Japanese at Kŭmsan, Ch'ungch'ŏngnam-do province. Unfortunately, the combined force lost the battle and Yŏnggyu and Cho Hŏn were killed.

It was around this time that the king ordered Master Sŏsan, who was staying at Mt. Myohyang, to organize an army of monks. Sŏsan took the role of commander and appealed to monks around the country to come to the nation's defense. His disciples also organized many guerrilla units around the country.

The patriotic activities of these monks stood in stark contrast to the passive stance of the Chosŏn ruling elite and Confucian literati. The monks had been subjected to harsh repression since the beginning of the Chosŏn period and yet they were the ones who rose up to rescue it. What motivated them? First, it was their commitment to protect the dharma (the teachings of the Buddha). This spirit of mission, calling for the destruction of evil so that good may survive, was deeply ingrained in Korean Buddhism by this time.

A second source of motivation was the monks' patriotism and dedication to "benefit the people." This reflects Buddhism's close relationship to the masses. Also the practical goal of revitalizing Buddhism must have played a role. Buddhism's image was tainted during this period, and demonstrating the unity of the Buddhist community and promoting a proper understanding of Buddhism helped to overcome this negative image.

As a result, Chosŏn Buddhism was rejuvenated by the Japanese invasion. Sŏsan left behind a number of theoretical works on Zen Buddhism as well as a collection of Zen poetry, all of which served to pave the way for the revitalization of Buddhism, at least on a doctrinal level, if not on a practical level. Sŏsan is also known for his cultivation of a number of distinguished disciples, including Samyŏng (1544-1610), Ŏngi (1581-1644) and T'aenŭng (1562-1649) who together established the mainstream of Chosŏn Buddhism. Ch'oe Nap (1717-1790), a Buddhist scholar well versed in the classical literature of both China and Korea, blazed new

paths for the doctrinal (Kyo) school and the Zen meditation school of Buddhism.

Buddhism did not prosper during the Chosŏn period, however. This was only natural considering the Chosŏn regime's pro-Confucian/anti-Buddhist policy. During this period Buddhism was characterized by Shamanistic practices, pessimism and a sense of frustration. It managed to survive in this hostile environment thanks to the Buddhist community's efforts to provide religious consolation to the suffering and to protect the masses when the nation was in peril. In my view, it was no coincidence that the great independence leader and poet Han Yong-un who fought against Japanese colonial oppression in the first half of the 20th century was a Buddhist. Han is just one more example of the vitality and tenacity of Korean Buddhism.

What has been the spiritual mainstay of Korean Buddhism over the past 1,600 years? As I have noted above, there were three important elements. The first was the pursuit of Ekayana, or "one vehicle." Korean Buddhism has constantly explored ways through which conflicting views and contradictory ideas can converge. The pursuit of Ekayana extends to the dimension of bringing the masses and the Buddha into unity.

Next is the protection of the dharma, the Buddha's teachings. When the protection of the dharma was linked to national interests, Buddhism made an active effort to defend the nation. However, this crusade for national defense was only meaningful in Buddhist terms when it was motivated by the desire to protect the dharma.

The third element is the spirit dedicated to rendering benefit to everything in the universe. Korean Buddhism has always tried to respect and offer benevolence to all living things.

These three elements run throughout the history of Korean Buddhism, although they have manifested themselves in varying degrees at different times. As in all religions and philosophies, the historical flow of Korean Buddhism has not been constant; it has ebbed and flowed with time.

Today, the most important task for Buddhists is attaining the wisdom to recognize the degeneration of Buddhist ideals, while at the same time endeavoring to establish these ideals as important forces in our society. By doing so, Buddhists can contribute to the formulation of proper relationships between humanity and society and humanity and nature, thus achieving what could be called the "functional virtue" of religion. ◆

Buddhist Legends:
Light the Path to Enlightenment

Choi Rai-ok

Buddhist legends handed down by word of mouth or recorded in historical chronicles are rich in universal truths and have helped many along the road to enlightenment. A survey of these legends not only provides us with a better understanding of the fundamental principles of Buddhism but also offers us a unique opportunity to reexamine our own values and priorities.

Buddhist legends or stories can be divided into two general categories: ancient myths from India selected for inclusion in the Buddhist texts taught here in Korea and tales born of incidents specific to Korean Buddhism. One could say the roots of these legends are found in both India and Korea.

The legends originating in Korea since Buddhism was introduced 1,600 years ago fall into five categories: stories about the Buddhist texts, stories about temples, pagodas and other Buddhist edifices, anecdotes about monks, stories combining or contrasting elements of indigenous Kŏrean beliefs (that is, Shamanism) and Buddhism, and allegorical fables aimed at promoting a better understanding of Buddhism among the common people.

Though legends include both lengthy epics and short, simple stories, they nearly all share an edifying and moralistic outlook on the world.

The renunciation of greed is an important theme found in Buddhist legends. "The Tale of the Magic Hollow" is just one example.

Long ago there was a young monk who secluded himself in a stone cave behind a temple to meditate and practice asceticism.

One day his teacher, a senior monk from the temple, came to him. "You will find a hollow in the stone here," he said. "Every morning one serving of rice pours from it, but if you poke into the hollow with a stick, the rice will come no more." With these words the older monk left the cave.

At first, the young monk followed his teacher's instructions carefully, but his curiosity grew with each passing day until finally he could restrain himself no longer. He found a stick and poked into the hollow. Can you imagine what happened? First, water poured out. The young monk poked into the hollow once more. This time blood poured out, and just as his teacher had warned, the hollow produced no more rice. The young monk soon had to give up his practice and leave the cave, only to be severely scolded by his teacher.

There are dozens of versions of "The Tale of the Magic Hollow." But what do they mean? Greed and suspicion are considered evil in Buddhism. A person pursuing an ascetic life must not lust for material objects coveted by the rest of society. They must be thankful for the small portions of food they receive and dedicate themselves to their studies and self-cultivation. The young monk was not satisfied with his lot and so desired greater abundance. He was punished as a result.

Another tale demonstrating the evils of greed and the virtue of renunciation is "The Story of the Two Cups."

Long ago a Confucian scholar, active in politics, went to see a famous monk at a Buddhist temple.

"Teach me everything you know about Buddhism," he demanded arrogantly. "I've come to learn."

"Oh, there is nothing for you to learn here," replied the monk.

"What? Am I really that perfect?" asked the scholar.

"No, it's not that. If you want to learn from me, there must be space for my teachings, but your mind is already full. A cup that is full cannot be filled with something else. Just as we must empty a cup before we fill it anew, so too must you empty your mind before you can accept a new truth. Your mind is already filled with arrogance, greed and contempt for others. Return when you have emptied it."

The Confucian scholar's face flushed with embarrassment and he rushed from the temple.

This tale is one of many depicting the conflict between Buddhism and Confucianism in the Chosŏn period. Buddhism was oppressed and many Buddhists persecuted following the founding of the Chosŏn Dynasty in 1392. In fact, Buddhist monks were not even allowed to enter the capital of Seoul. Nevertheless, Buddhism continued to develop during this period, and many Buddhist monks fought bravely in the defense of their country when it was threatened by a Japanese invasion in the late 16th century. As a result of the monks' contributions, oppression of the religion was relaxed for a time.

Nevertheless, the Chosŏn period gave birth to many interesting tales of the conflict between Buddhist and Confucian scholars. "The Story of the Two Cups" is just one example which also reveals the importance of the Buddhist doctrine of "emptying one's mind."

Overcoming religious oppression is another important theme of Korea's Buddhist legends, most graphically revealed in the many tales of temples riddled with bedbugs.

As everyone knows, the bedbug makes its living sucking blood. Bedbugs are rare in modern society, but in the olden days they were found in every household. The pesky insects also made their homes in Buddhist temples, so harassing the monks they could hardly sleep. In some places, there were so many bedbugs the monks had to abandon the temples, and the bedbugs died for lack of food. Turn over a stone in one of those abandoned temples today and you will find the remains of thousands of bedbugs!

It was not until I heard the story of a temple near Chŏnju in Chŏllanam-do province that I finally understood the significance of these bedbug tales. According to this story, a group of monks were driven from their temple by bedbugs, but as they left the temple and headed down the mountain, they all stopped to kick the tombstone of a devout Confucianist that stood by the side of the path. The monks should have been angry at the bedbugs so why were they kicking the tombstone of a local luminary who happened to believe in Confucianism? They did it because the bedbugs symbolized the oppression of Buddhism by the Confucian powers running the Chosŏn Dynasty . The monks were leaving their temple because they could no longer endure the hardships imposed on them by the local Confucianists.

Of course, the bedbug tales do not always symbolize religious oppression and the destruction of temples during the Chosŏn period, but they are, for the most part, an accurate reflection of circumstances under the Chosŏn regime.

Some Buddhist legends involve a fundamental principle of Buddhism: causality or retribution. Buddhism deals with life in three worlds: the world in which we are living now (*isŭng, kŭmsaeng*), the world in which we lived prior to birth in the present world (*chŏnsaeng, chŏnse*), and "the other world" (*chŏsŭng*) or "the world to come" (*naese*) where we will go after our death in the present world.

The life we live in the present world is the result of our actions in the previous world. Our previous lives are the cause and our present life is the effect. By the same token, when we look into the future, our present lives are the cause and our lives in "the other world" are the effect. Thus, we must be circumspect in all actions. The happiness I enjoy in the present is all thanks to virtuous actions in my previous life, and if I wish to enjoy a happy life in "the other world," I must be virtuous in my present life. In this respect, Buddhism constitutes a moral conception of time, a conception found in many old legends such as the story with the unusual title, "Better the Wife of a Salted Shrimp Peddler than the Wife of a Prime Minister."

Once upon a time there was a respected prime minister who returned home from court one day to find his wife gone. His wife was a happy woman by any standard: she had a beautiful house, a fine husband and many successful children. However, the neighbors said she had run away with the salted shrimp peddler, a ugly little man of low social status, who had come to the neighborhood to sell his salted shrimp. The moment the prime minister's wife saw him, she called out, "My darling!" and disappeared down the street with him.

The prime minister could hardly believe his ears. How could any woman prefer a lowly peddler to a famous prime minister? He and his wife had spent such a happy life together, full of love and good fortune—how could she possibly leave him for another man?

After puzzling over the problem for days, the prime minister

went to the king to resign from his post. He left the capital and spent nearly ten years scouring the country for his wife. He finally found her working in a restaurant near the seashore.

The husband sat down at one of the tables and placed his order. His wife responded in a happy voice. Indeed, she seemed much happier than when she was living with him in their fine house in Seoul. The prime minister could not understand it. How could she be so happy working in this wretched restaurant?

"Don't you recognize me, woman?" he asked.

"Oh, it's you, my beloved husband," the woman replied.

"Yes, it's me. Give up this life and return to Seoul with me. I'll forgive everything. I've been searching for you for ten years."

The woman shook her head sadly.

"I'm sorry. I can't go with you. I'm happy here."

"Happy? How can you be happy as the wife of a salted shrimp peddler? Do you mean to say you'd rather be the wife of a salted shrimp peddler than the wife of a great prime minister?"

"Oh yes," she replied without the slightest hesitation.

And so the prime minister's ten-year search ended—in a baffling riddle with no wife.

He became a monk and prayed to the Buddha for an answer. For years he studied the relationship·between love and hate, meeting and separation, longing and forgetting, husbands and wives, nobility and humbleness. Then one day, after ten years at the temple, he looked into the sky and saw the morning star. Suddenly he realized what had happened. He had achieved enlightenment and everything from his previous life appeared before him like a movie on a screen.

In his previous life he had been a monk studying in a large temple. This monk had a serious problem. A louse had attached itself to his body but he could not kill it because of the Buddha's precept against killing living things. The louse grew larger and larger, sapping the monk of his strength. What should he do? He tried to get the louse to let go but to no avail. An ordinary person would have simply crushed the louse between his fingers, but how could a monk do such a thing?

One day as the monk headed down to the village below the temple to beg for alms, he saw a large ox.

"Louse, please make your home with that ox. I can't take this anymore!"

And so the louse attached itself to the ox.

The former prime minister suddenly realized the importance of causality. He was the monk, his wife the louse, and the ox the salted shrimp peddler. In his previous life, the monk had served the louse, offering it love and sustenance, and in return the louse had felt gratitude toward the monk. As a result, the two had become husband and wife in the present world.

According to Buddhist thought, there is a reason why certain people marry. A woman marries a man because of the gratitude she feels for him from a previous life. We generally think of marriage as an expression of love and respect but this story reveals that gratitude and service to others is the real foundation of a marriage. The woman in the story repays her debt of gratitude to both the prime minister (the monk in her previous life) and the peddler (the former ox).

Many Buddhist tales deal with the concept of emptiness or nonexistence. Everyone has desires. In East Asia as a whole, and in Korea in particular, people long for riches, hope, long life, good health, success, marriage, fertility and a peaceful death after a long, healthy life. They struggle to fulfill these desires; indeed, these desires serve as the motive force behind many people's lives. However, a preoccupation with the fulfillment of these desires can lead to greed that harms others, to deteriorating mental and physical health, even premature death. A person cannot live a humane existence if preoccupied with such material desires. That is why religions instruct us to restrain our desires. They ask us to search for spiritual and religious happiness rather than material or physical pleasure. Wealth, status and glory do not last long. In fact, life is no more than a fantasy, a dream as transient as the morning dew, as clouds, as fog, as lightning, as a fragile bubble.

The Buddhist admonition against a preoccupation with rank, prosperity and material gratification does not mean we should embrace pessimism or nihilism. Rather, we should awaken to the realities of life and live fulfilling lives.

The Buddhist concepts of "nothingness" and "emptiness" are extremely difficult to explain to the average person. That must be why the following stories about relationships between the sexes were created.

There was once a young woman who could not understand the Buddhist concept of "emptiness." Why were people always saying life is empty?

One day the young woman went to the well for water. As she poured scoop after scoop into her pail, she thought about the word "emptiness." All of a sudden, a handsome young monk walked up and asked her for alms.

"Monk, monk. I will give you all the alms you want if you will explain what 'emptiness' means," the young woman pleaded.

The monk smiled and grabbed her arm.

"Come with me," he said, and the young woman followed him, leaving her pail at the well.

"Let us marry and live a prosperous life with many sons. I will give you everything you've ever wanted," the monk said.

"Oh, thank you, my darling husband," replied the young woman, and so they began their life together. The monk let his hair grow long and became a farmer. The woman gave birth to three healthy sons who grew up to be strong, intelligent young men. All three boys went to Seoul to take the state examinations, and, remarkably enough, all three passed the rigorous exams. What more could a mother want?

Not long after that, the eldest son returned home to visit, but as soon as he stepped in the courtyard, he keeled over and died. His mother ran to him but there was no reviving him.

The second son walked through the gate, but what do you think happened? He fell down and died too. Then the third son walked in, but he too died as soon as he set foot in the courtyard.

Why had all their sons died? The woman and her husband buried them in a sunny spot in the mountains and collapsed in tears at their grave side.

"Oh, I feel so empty. In a single moment, all my beautiful

hopes have turned to despair. Life is empty." cried the woman.

All of a sudden the woman felt someone tapping on her shoulder.

"Why are you lying here crying when you should be filling the pail with water?"

The young woman looked up in amazement to see her husband's uncle standing over her. It was all a dream. She had been dreaming from the moment she had asked the monk begging for alms what "emptiness" meant. The uncle told her to go look for the three graves in the mountains, but there were no graves, only pots of treasure representing the Three Treasures of Buddhism: the Buddha himself, Buddhist teachings, and the community of Buddhists. These treasures represent the truth.

Through her dream, the young woman had learned that one's earthly desires are merely a dream, as fragile as a bubble. She went on to become a devout Buddhist and led a truthful life. Learning is enlightenment; enlightenment is truth.

The legend related above has been passed down through the ages by storytellers. "The Tale of Chosin," recounted below, is included in the *Memorabilia of the Three Kingdoms* and was the basis for the 20th-century novel *Dream* by Yi Kwang-su and a number of modern-day films.

Once there was a young monk named Chosin who fell in love with the daughter of the local magistrate. Chosin prayed to the Buddha, asking him to make the girl love him, but his prayers went unanswered, and the lovely daughter was married off to another man. The young monk cursed the Buddha for his heartlessness.

Then one day the magistrate's daughter came to Chosin's door and confessed her love for him. She said her parents had forced her to marry another but she had escaped and wanted to become his wife.

Imagine how Chosin must have felt! He left his temple with the beautiful girl and returned to his home village where they loved each other deeply, had five children and lived happily for 40 years. But alas misfortune overtook them. They could no longer feed their many children and had to take up the life of beggars. Their eldest son died of starvation and was buried along the side of a road. One of their daughters was killed by a dog when she was out begging. The rest of the family was on the brink of starvation when the wife finally suggested they divide the remaining children between them and try to make their way begging separately.

"Oh, is this what love brings? It's so miserable," Chosin sighed, and then he opened his eyes to see his lamp flickering dimly in the dawn light. It had all been a dream—from the moment the magistrate's daughter had appeared at his door.

That morning Chosin went to the spot in the road where he had buried their eldest son in his dream, and there was a stone image of the Maitreya Buddha. Chosin decided to take the Buddha back to the temple and worship it. All thoughts of women and worldly desires melted away like ice in a fire. "Life is a dream, I must not spend it wrapped in desires," he thought as he walked to the well to wash. When he leaned over the basin of water and saw his reflection, he realized his hair and beard had turned white as snow, evidence of the fifty years he had spent in his dream.

The *Memorabilia of the Three Kingdoms* also relates "The Tale of the Two Monks, Puduk and Pangpak."

Puduk and Pangpak were two young Silla men who left their village and went to the mountains where they each built houses, far removed from each other, and pursued the life of ascetic monks. One night an indescribably beautiful young woman appeared on Pangpak's door and asked him to take her in for the night for she had lost her way.

"I am a monk," Pangpak proclaimed. "I have forsaken all distractions in search of the proper way. You must not try to tempt me with your youthful body. Leave me alone. That is the only way I can live my life."

The young woman left his house in tears and crossed the mountains to Puduk's house.

"A man studying the ways of the Buddha should not get involved with women," Puduk said. "But the mountains are dangerous at night and I cannot refuse you. Please come in."

Did Puduk's resolve waver as he sat in that tiny room with the young woman? No, he simply remembered the Buddha. But then, toward dawn, the young woman suddenly doubled over in pain. Puduk had no choice but to draw closer and ask what was wrong.

"I'm going to have a baby. Please help me."

He assisted her and she gave birth to a baby. Even after this experience, her body was very beautiful.

"Monk, I need to take a bath. Please heat some water," she said.

Puduk filled a tub with hot water and the young woman undressed. She was so beautiful!

"Please come and scrub my back," she asked. "Why don't you get in? I'll bathe you."

Puduk had no choice but to bathe with her. He was careful not to let his resolve waver, but suddenly a wonderful fragrance filled the air.

"Who are you?" he asked.

"I am Avalokitesvara, the Bodhisattva of Compassion. I appeared to you as a beautiful young woman to help you achieve enlightenment. This bath water is really golden water which will help you become a great monk, brilliant as gold."

The following day Pangpak, fearing Puduk might have fallen under the spell of the beautiful young woman, came looking for his friend, only to find him bathing in a tub of golden water.

"My dear friend, may I take a bath in your golden water?"

"Of course," Puduk answered. "There's plenty of water left."

And so Pangpak became a brilliant monk as well, although his sparkle was not so bright as his friend Puduk.

This tale sings the praises of Mahayana Buddhism, which emphasizes self-sacrifice for the good of others.

Perhaps the most dramatic legend in the *Memorabilia of the Three Kingdoms* is the tale of the great monk Wonhyo's journey to Tang China.

The story takes place 1,400 years ago when two Silla monks, Wonhyo and Ŭisang, set out to study in Tang China, known

for its advanced development of Buddhism. Night fell as they traveled toward China, so the two monks scurried into a cave to sleep. During the night, Wonhyo woke with a great thirst and found a bowl of water beside him. He drank the water, which had the most marvelous taste, and slept soundly through the rest of the night.

The following morning Wonhyo woke to find the cave was filled with dead bodies and the bowl from which he had drunk was actually a human skull filled with rain water! Wonhyo vomited in disgust, but then realized something.

"The water was so sweet and my sleep so restful when I didn't know where I was. Ignorance can be medicinal and

knowledge can be harmful. Everything depends on one's mind. Water from a skull can be sweet and fresh water can be bitter. A skeleton can be beautiful and a beautiful woman as hideous as a skeleton. It is all in the mind. I can understand the world if I study the mind, so why do I need to go all the way to China?"

And so Wonhyo returned to Korea. Later he became one of Silla's greatest monks, as did Ŭisang after he returned from his studies in Tang China. The experiences of these two great monks help us realize there is more than one way to come to the truth and show us the power of legend in the Korean Buddhist's search for enlightenment. ◆

Sŏn

Choi Hyun-gak

The meditative sect of Korean Buddhism, Sŏnjong, formed under the influence of the Chinese Chan meditative sect (better known by the Japanese term Zen), but as time passed, it established its own unique character. This process began in the late Unified Silla period and was not completed until the early Koryŏ period when Buddhism played an important role as "state protector."

Sŏn showed remarkable development during the Koryŏ period. However, in the Chosŏn period, Buddhism was severely oppressed. The religion survived by retreating to the mountains where monks practiced in isolation. Fortunately, there were many monks dedicated to meditative practice, and the Sŏn tradition lives on today.

Sŏn constitutes the mainstream of Korean Buddhism. In many ways, the Sŏn spirit pervades all Korean Buddhism, and the Sŏn tradition, including eating customs, clothing, and lifestyle, is still maintained at every temple.

How is Sŏn practiced in everyday life? In this article, I will focus on Sŏn's status within Korean Buddhism and how Sŏn principles are being passed on to future generations.

Sŏn is generally understood as a kind of meditation. However, in the Buddhist tradition, Sŏn is distinguished from other meditative techniques and referred to as *chodo,* "the teachings of the masters." The esteem that Sŏn enjoys is, in part, the result of the achievements of the great Sŏn masters. It is also distinguished from preexisting Buddhist thought by certain unique features.

The practices performed in temples can be divided into three traditions: *Kyo* ("the study of the Buddha's teachings") which focuses on the Buddhist texts, *Yul* ("the discipline") which studies the rules of monastic life, and Sŏn meditation. All aim toward the attainment of enlightenment but Sŏn practice is considered the most important.

Kyo involves research into the teachings of the Buddha, or the *dharma.* This study takes place in a school inside the temple, known as

kangwon. Buddhist masters are invited to teach young monks and nuns on a professional basis. The master hands down the tradition to able disciples, and thus a family tradition is formed. This tradition is known as the Kyo lineage.

Yul involves the study of the discipline or rules of temple life. These rules are to be kept by all monks, but certain monks, known as *yulsa*, dedicate themselves to the research and perpetuation of these rules, thus establishing what is known as the Yul lineage. The Yul lineage is only established when proper behavior as well as intense study is achieved. Hence, from a religious point of view emphasizing practice over study, the Yul lineage is more important than the Kyo lineage. This may in part derive from the fact that the Yul lineage has been handed down from Sakyamuni Buddha (the historical Buddha born in northeastern India in the fifth century B.C.), whereas the roots of the Kyo lineage are unclear. In any event, the preference for the Yul lineage indicates the importance of Buddhist practice.

The Sŏn lineage attempts to achieve the Buddha-mind (enlightenment), transcending letters or words. This tradition contains a profound message which can only be conveyed from mind to mind. It is thus seen as a higher practical tradition than the Kyo or Yul lineages. Like the Yul lineage, the Sŏn lineage has succeeded directly from the Buddha and maintains the orthodoxy of Buddhist practice.

Korean Sŏn sustained its unique characteristics through the Koryŏ period, but under the persecution of the early and middle Chosŏn period, the distinctive features of each sect were lost as they were amalgamated. The sects were mixed as a result, and Buddhism became a kind of "pan-Buddhism."

The concept of a dharma (literally "the teachings") lineage has been handed down from the time of Sakyamuni Buddha. It is more important in the Sŏn tradition than in the Kyo or Yul lineages. The system of "standing the flag of dharma" when a person inherits the dharma from his or her teacher is much like a rite of passage, initiating the new monk into the orthodox lineage of Sŏn Buddhism. Therefore, the system is governed by strict procedures and forms. The teacher is the dharma teacher and the newly ordained monk or nun is the dharma disciple. A *bhikkhu* (monk) or *bhikkhuni* (nun) can take on his or her own disciples ten years after being ordained. However, from the point of view of the dharma lineage, any monk or nun who has achieved enlightenment, even a *sami* (male novice) or *samini* (female novice), can have disciples.

The dharma lineage is the most important aspect in the Sŏn tradition. Anyone who succeeds the dharma of his or her teacher must impart the dharma to his or her own disciples.

"Succeeding the Buddha-Dharma" is another expression for nirvana or enlightenment, the

The spirit of Sŏn *pervades all Korean Buddhism, from lectures at temple schools to the individual monk's quest for enlightenment.*

64

AHN JANG-HUN

final goal of Buddhism. The dharma lineage has traditionally been considered the most orthodox because it has been carried down from the Buddha. Unlike a familial lineage in which hierarchy is established by age, in the dharma lineage, the degree or stage of enlightenment, not simply age, is the criterion by which the hierarchy is set. Thus, a novice, or even a lay person, can be a member of a dharma family.

The dharma lineage was introduced to Korea from India through China. Korean dharma lineages originated from Chinese Sŏn masters through the late Koryŏ period but they were cut off and obscured in the early Chosŏn period when Buddhism was politically and socially persecuted. It was only during the 16th century that Master Sŏsan (1520-1604) revived the system and restored the dharma lineage of Korean Sŏn. As a result, all monks and nuns of Sŏn Buddhism belong to Sŏsan's dharma lineage. After the restoration of Sŏn and Kyo by Sŏsan, Korean Buddhism moved in the direction of a pan-Buddhist Sŏn Buddhism.

Sŏn monks live together in *sŏnbang*, meditation centers separated from other monks. In Korea, there are very few *yulwon*, discipline halls, although kangwon study facilities and sŏnbang are quite common. Temples located in towns are usually meant to propagate Buddhism, so they do not maintain special sections, such as yulwon, kangwon, or sŏnbang.

Traditionally, Sŏn temples are found deep in the mountains. Many of Korea's most famous temples are known as sites for Sŏn meditation. There are also many small Sŏn hermitages scattered throughout the mountains around the peninsula. According to a 1992 survey, 1,415 monks and nuns are practicing in 54 Sŏn centers around Korea.

Practicing Sŏn monks and nuns account for approximately 14 percent of the Chogye Order's membership. These monks and nuns devote themselves to the practice of Sŏn exclusively. While a relatively small percentage of the entire order, they are regarded as its elite and have a strong voice in the order's affairs.

Sŏn monks and nuns practice a special tradition known as *chosasŏn*, the way of Sŏn handed down from the great masters. Chosasŏn is divided into two branches: *kanhwasŏn*, which involves the study of great masters and meditation and *mukchosŏn*, the practice of silent meditation. Korean Buddhism is fundamentally based on the kanhwasŏn school.

While Chosasŏn transcends Kyo (study), Korean Sŏn does not neglect the importance of study. As I have already mentioned, contem-

Meditation restores life by bringing it into the present, overcoming conceptions of the past and imagination about the future. Through meditation the monk becomes aware of the "three poisons" of greed, anger and ignorance.

porary Korean Sŏn is a pan-Buddhist Sŏn. Chanting and the study of Buddhist texts, part of Yul and Kyo practice, all coalesce in Sŏn. The amalgamation of these practices has given birth to a synthetic view of the practice of Sŏn. Hence, Sŏn is considered the best of all Korean Buddhist practices, and Sŏn monks and nuns are respected.

The actual practice of Sŏn is quite technical. There is a standard meditation position. First, one must sit up straight. The spine is held erect and firm, and the head is balanced, facing forward. The legs are crossed and the knees touch the floor.

Controlled breathing and concentration are essential. The meditator must look straight ahead and breath deeply and quietly. Consciousness is focused on the belly, just below the navel. This meditative technique restores life by focusing on the present and reality, overcoming conceptions of the past or imagination about the future. Through meditation we become aware of our consciousness and behavior—the three poisons—greed, anger and ignorance. By obtaining a proper understanding of our mind and body, we finally attain enlightenment filled with freedom and happiness.

Such practice is essential to Chosasŏn, established in China during the middle of the Tang period. In Chosasŏn, concentration is focused on *hwadu*, enigmatic problems more commonly referred to by the Japanese term, *koan*, established by Sŏn masters, upon which thought is concentrated as a means of attaining inner unity and illumination. Three things are essential when trying to solve the problem posed in a hwadu: one must be filled with a sense of doubt and questioning and eager to understand the hwadu fully; one must firmly believe in the potential for final enlightenment embodied in the solution of the hwadu; and one must question the master's selection of the hwadu. The solution cannot be obtained through words but rather from mind to mind and finally from one subconscious mind to another.

In Sŏn, enlightenment can only be transmitted from one mind to another. It is here that we find the fundamental difference between Sŏn and Kyo, which conveys ideas by words or letters. Kyo is limited to the boundaries of consciousness, while Sŏn transcends consciousness. The Kyo tradition emphasizes the study of Buddhist texts, that is the teachings of the Buddha, whereas Sŏn cuts through all ordinary thinking and mental discrimination.

Sŏn, Kyo and Yul are often described as the mind, the teachings and the behavior of the

Meditation can be accomplished anywhere, in the rugged mountains, a temple meditation hall, wherever life takes the believer.

Buddha, respectively. All originated in the Buddha and differ in appearance only. This phenomenon is best understood through a metaphor. When someone looks at a mountain covered with red and yellow autumn foliage and explains how beautiful it is, that conception of beauty is a most complicated thing. In order to understand how that person feels, we must understand not only their emotional state but also the external conditions influencing the situation and that person's relationship with others. Everyone feels something unique when they see that mountain. A poet experiences nature in that scene, a painter sees the profundity of the colors, a musician hears the harmony of nature, and a religious person sees the message embodied in nature. The possibilities are limitless. In order to best understand the inner conditions of the mind of the person, we must communicate intuitively between his or her mind to our own, rather than try to logically understand the meaning of the words they used to express their conception of beauty.

This is the way of Sŏn. It transcends the boundaries of ordinary logical ideas and, in that sense, is only achieved through a high level of mutual mental exchange.

However, this is not easy. The practice of Sŏn requires passage through a number of set stages. First, Kyo must be practiced; that is, words or letters must be learned in order to attain the wisdom to overcome the knowledge of those words or letters. Kyo is the gateway to Sŏn, and when Kyo is completed, the practice of Sŏn begins. To use another metaphor, Kyo is the boat which is essential for crossing the river but which becomes unnecessary when we reach the other side. Stepping out onto the bank on the opposite side of the river is analogous to entering Sŏn after leaving Kyo behind.

Korean Sŏn Buddhism and Sŏn masters believe it is best to move ahead after completing Kyo. That is, the core of Sŏn begins with words to ultimately achieve a stage where no words are needed.

Most Buddhist lineages in Korea have been sustained by the Sŏn lineage. Buddhism is known as the "religion of enlightenment or awakening," and the transmission of enlightenment from mind to mind forms its core. Buddhism is, after all, a religion or philosophy of self-realization based on the manifestation of universal truth. The vigor with which Korea's Sŏn monks and nuns pursue their practice is living evidence that the dharma lives on in the Korean Buddhist community. ◆

Buddhism and
Early Korean Literature

Lee Jong-chan

When people speak of the origins of Korean literature, they generally start with stories from the Three Kingdoms period when the Korean peninsula was divided into the Koguryŏ, Paekche and Silla kingdoms, or the Unified Silla period when the three kingdoms were united under Silla's rule. The source of most of these stories is the *Memorabilia of the Three Kingdoms*, a chronicle compiled by the Buddhist monk Iryŏn in 1285, well after the founding of the Koryŏ Kingdom.

Much of the *Memorabilia of the Three Kingdoms* deals with Buddhism, a natural consequence of its compiler's interests and the intellectual trends of that era. Nearly all the *hyangga*, literally "native songs," or Old Korean Poems, recorded in the history are based on Buddhist themes. The hyangga were originally performed as songs but have survived as poems, remarkable for their rhetorical style and expression.

What made the hyangga so exceptional? Clearly it was the literary skills of their authors, a handful of learned Buddhist monks, including the masters Wonch'ŭk (613-696) and Wonhyo (617-686). In the preface to his commentary on the *Prajnaparamita-sutra* (*Pulsŏlpan'gomilta-simgyŏngch'an*), Wonch'ŭk laid out what could be seen as his literary philosophy:

A great work is one in which principle runs deep and profound, breaking the limits of existence and nothingness so that the reality of the universe transcends all that may be expressed in words.

What did Wonch'ŭk mean by "breaking the limits of existence and nothingness" and "transcending all that is expressed in words"? Literary theorists today might call this a kind of transcendentalism, much along the lines of what, in the field of modern literature, is known as surrealism.

Similarly, Wonhyo used the metaphor of a man awakening in a room lined with mirrors, dreaming a dream within a dream, to dramatize the state of meaningless fantasy that the average unenlightened person experiences in everyday life. Considering the emphasis placed on the dream analysis in literary theory today, I cannot help but feel proud that a Korean scholar came up with this concept 1,300 years ago.

When I am drowsy
Sleep envelops my mind
And in my foolishness
I am plunged into a vast body of water.
Unaware that it is all a dream
I am swept downward

And a great fear is born in me.
Before I wake from that dream
Another begins
And I think
'Ah, this is just a dream!'
Unaware that I am still in my bed,
I thrash about
Struggling to awake,
And when I do,
I grope through my dream
To find that everything that was,
The deep water, my floating body,
Is not,
And all I see is my bed
Lying in silence.
Even my longest dreams are thus.
Confusion envelops my mind.
I am foolish,
Swept up in the six ways of the world
Flowing in the eight hardships of life.

Wonhyo's surrealistic perspective shows both Buddhism and literature are dedicated to the discovery of the true nature of human existence and thus belong together.

Buddhists of the meditative sect of Korean Buddhism (Sŏnjong) do not appreciate the written word because enlightenment cannot be expressed through language, which by its very nature is limited. Nevertheless, there is no avoiding the use of language as a tool for conveying information. The danger is that, through the use of language, we may make the truth, reality, more complicated than it actually is, thus confusing the issues at hand. This is why the language we use to express life's truths must be simple and concise. Whether expressed in spoken language or the written word, the object is the substance of existence, that is, truth itself, the origin of the true form of the universe. This is best expressed directly and simply. To use an old Korean expression, there is no need to stir up a storm on a quiet plain. When words are unavoidable, they must be simple.

Thus the language expressing truth is decidedly ordinary. However, if that ordinary language is an authentic representation of truth itself, that language is nothing more than a tool, and it is the truth that is ordinary. According to the Zen rules of language, the ordinary is, in fact, not ordinary. From this we can

This youthful Maitreya in
meditation is one of the finest gilt-bronze
Buddhist sculptures in East Asia.

induce that this ordinary and yet extraordinary language is the language of literature. It is the link between Buddhism and what we know as literature.

Many of the collections of writings left behind by Korea's great Zen masters are simply called "analects," literally "collections of sayings." This is, of course, partly a reflection of the modesty one would expect from a Zen monk, but also it reveals their belief that ordinary language is truth. The content of these "analects" is extremely simple, and yet therein lies their profound truth.

The teaching delivered one New Year's Day by the National Preceptor Chin'gak (1178-1234) is one example of the expressive power of ordinary language.

Today I would like to discuss the meaning of time. At the New Year, children are always eager to grow a year older but old people wish they could grow younger with the passage of time. In fact, neither wish can come true. There can be no more or no less.

In Korea, everyone becomes a year older on New Year's Day. Individual birthdays are celebrated, but age is calculated from the first day of the year in which one is born. In that instant between the old and the new years, everyone ages 365 days, and consequently that instant takes on great meaning, bringing joy to the young and sorrow to the aged. Imagine an old man's feelings as he sits across the breakfast table from his young grandson on New Year's Day. The grandfather can feel the wrinkles forming on his brow while the young boy is filled with joy at his approaching manhood. Really, there is no difference between that morning and the previous morning. It is all a matter of perception. If one were not conscious of the connection between the passage of time and the advancement of age, there would be nothing to worry about. The existence of time is simple; the problem is our consciousness of that time. Only by breaking free of this consciousness can we achieve Buddhist enlightenment or emptiness.

This state of emptiness is achieved when we accept the ordinariness of truth. Wishing we were a year older or a year younger means we have not accepted the passage of time in its true form. We embellish time with our own useless emotions. The bipolarity of emotions manifested by the grandfather and grandson on New Year's morning occurs when we attach ourselves to one side of a conflicting relationship. Buddhism warns against this in the principle of moderation.

Chin'gak's New Year talk includes the following instruction:

Who says there are no superhuman ascetics in the human world? We must believe that each bottle contains unique space.

What is the significance of this paradox? Logically humanity does not possess divine powers, and yet Chin'gak says it is possible. A person who can accept the reality of existence as reality is divine. A simple glass bottle meant to hold water can also hold

Stone stupas near the entrance to Paek'yangsa Temple

The mystical atmosphere of the temple is heightened by the gentle tinkling of the p'unggyŏng, wind bells hanging from the temple eaves (above). To reach the temple proper, one must pass through several gates like Pul'imun at Paek'yangsa Temple (opposite).

as the truth itself. I believe it is because of this simplicity, this truth, that Buddhist writings constitute true literature. When writing is forced, when a writer tries to embellish his or her work, there is danger of glossing over the truth, of burying it in "words." Indeed, literature has much to learn from the simplicity of Buddhist language.

When you think about it, the birth of a human being is a mysterious thing. By "mysterious" I mean the action or event itself does not intend to be anything and therefore inspires a sense of "mystery" within the observer.

Such mystery was a natural part of life for primitive man and thus the source of primitive belief. The songs and dance of primitive society, what we call primitive art, are born of primitive man's fascination with the mysterious. Over time, these songs and dances have taken on the form of ceremonies or rites to become part of folk religion or shamanism.

Buddhism, as it spread around the world, embraced such native religions, harmonizing with local belief. Buddhism's tolerant nature, based on the expansive concept of emptiness which allows it to attach and grow anywhere, made this possible. As a result, the mysteries found in indigenous religions have been incorporated into Buddhism over the centuries.

During the Silla era, Buddhism firmly rooted itself in Korean life and was accepted as the national religion. A perusal of the hyang-ga vernacular poetry surviving from this period reveals literature rich in mystery. While Iryŏn, the monk who compiled the *Memorabilia of the Three Kingdoms* in which most of the hyang-ga are recorded, may have had a vested interest in recording works with a Buddhist theme, there is no ignoring the profound literary content and inspirational power of these religious songs.

Just one example is the "Hymn to the Thousand-Eyed Bodhisattva," the song of Hŭimyŏng, a country woman from eighth century Silla. When Hŭimyŏng's child was blinded at the age of five, the woman took him to a temple where she sang the following song to a portrait of the Thousand-eyed Bodhisattva, Avalokitesvara, painted on the northern wall of one of the buildings.

> *I fall on my knees and implore you.*
> *Thousand-eyed Bodhisattva.*
> *Your compassion is so great*
> *And you have so many eyes.*
> *Can you not spare two for my child?*

And with that, her child's sight was restored. The roots of this song lie in the *Saddharmapundarika-sutra* in which the compassion of the Buddha and bodhisattvas is revealed. Hŭimyŏng expresses her heartfelt wish with such simplicity the song inspires sympathy in all who come in contact with it.

The songs of Silla monks are equally compelling. Master Wolmyŏng, or "Bright Moon," earned his name for his brilliant flute playing. According to legend, the moon stopped in its path when it heard the sound of Wolmyŏng's flute.

In the ninetteenth year of Silla king Kyŏngdŏk's reign, the sun split in two and hung in the sky for ten days straight. This was truly a strange incident, especially in a society where the sun was a metaphor for the king himself. Clearly, the double sun was a sign someone coveted Kyŏngdŏk's throne. Naturally,

divine space. Everything we observe as simple truth becomes its own unique world born of that simple truth. The conception of truth as a simple thing is expressed in a number of Buddhist sayings, such as "Mt. Sumeru (the mountain at the center of the Indian cosmology) is hidden within a tiny grass seed" or "All the universe can reside on the tip of a single strand of hair."

Enlightenment is a simple thing, and if we must express its meaning in words, those words must be as simple and ordinary

Kyŏngdŏk responded by summoning the mysterious powers of religion. He called in the official in charge of astronomical phenomena who suggested they enlist the aid of a Buddhist monk with whom the king had an affinity. The monk Wolmyŏng appeared at that very instant. They asked him to perform a Buddhist ceremony but Wolmyŏng replied that he knew only hyangga and nothing of the "Brahmans' ceremonies," a reference to pŏmp'ae, ceremonial Buddhist chants. The king had no choice but to accept. Wolmyŏng sang his "Requiem" (Dosolga) and the two suns melted back into one.

Did Wolmyŏng have mysterious powers or were the words he wrote the source of that power? Literature embodies the inspirational power of the writer. This is what makes the works of the great monks of Silla so powerful.

This tradition was carried on by the Great Master Kyun-yŏ (923-973) of the Koryŏ period. Kyun-yŏ was extraordinary from birth. Born prematurely to a 60 year-old mother, Kyun-yŏ's life was the source of many inspirational stories. According to one story, Taemokhwanghu, the queen ruling during Kyun-yŏ's lifetime, had a large growth on her genitalia. Of course, she could not show the growth to a doctor so she summoned Ŭisun'gong, one of the great monks, and asked him to treat her with Buddhist techniques. Ŭisun'gong prayed that the queen's malady would be transferred to his own body, and soon the queen was cured. Ŭisun'gong was incapacitated as a result, however, and

Kyun-yŏ prayed that the growth detach itself from Ŭisun'gong and grow on a tree standing to the east of the main temple building. It did and the tree soon sickened and died. Kyun-yŏ was so deeply impressed by this mystery that he wrote eleven devotional poems known as Pohyŏnsiwŏn-ga. In his introduction to this collection, he explained the motivation behind them.

Songs are usually sung for enjoyment but they are also the core of human effort to become a bodhisattva. Just as one must pass through the shallows to reach the depths, just as one must begin nearby to reach afar, one cannot find a simple path without understanding the ways of the real world, nor can one communicate the deep meaning of causality without relying on the language of the real world.

Kyun-yŏ suggests that the spiritual bridge between humanity and the gods must be found in common language. The words of the songs are like a bodhisattva's prayers; herein lies their inspirational power. Each of his poems embodies a devout attempt to achieve enlightenment. They were so popular that people often wrote them on walls and used them as objects of worship. These religious songs, and so much of the early literature influenced by Buddhism, testify to the inspirational energy created when the spiritual power of human language is combined with profound aspirations. ◆

Buddhist Thought as Revealed in Temple Architecture

The Ven. Popchong

Taeungjŏn—The Main Hall

The central building of a Buddhist temple is the Main Hall, or Taeungjŏn, which enshrines the image of the Buddha himself.

Taeung refers to the Buddha, literally the great man who is enlightened and spreads the truth around the world. Originally only Sakyamuni, the historical Buddha, was enshrined in this hall, but later the bodhisattvas Kashyapa and Ananda were established to the left and right of the Buddha. Kashyapa was the Buddha's loyal disciple who actively promoted the religion following the Buddha's passage to the Western Paradise. Another disciple who faithfully attended the Buddha for 25 years, Ananda was known for his remarkable memory and specialized in the recitation of Buddha's teachings which he, of course, had heard directly. Thus the meditative branch of Buddhism started with Kashyapa, and the teaching branch was launched by Ananda.

In the center of the Main Hall, a statue of the Buddha is enshrined atop a pedestal. While hardly an efficient use of space, the Buddha is placed at the center so believers may circle the statue, a custom handed down from ancient India where people honored a revered figure by circling him three times in a clockwise direction. References to this practice can be found in many Buddhist texts. Only by placing the statue in the center of the hall can it be circled. For this reason, the doors of most Buddhist structures, not only the Main Hall, are placed in front and to the left and right. It is customary for the head monk and elder monks to enter through the front door, while younger monks and believers enter through the side doors.

The Main Hall at T'ongdosa Temple in Kyŏngsangnam-do province (above) and Songgwangsa Temple nestled in the mountains of Chŏllanam-do province (right) typify the beauty and symbolism of Korea's temple architecture.

Taechŏkkwangjŏn—The Hall of Vairocana

The "three bodies" of Buddhism are *pŏpsin* or Vairocana, the body of Sakyamuni, *posin*, a body created as a result of the search for truth through retribution, and *hwasin*, the physical body that exists in the present world, an incarnation.

According to the *Avatamsaka-sutra*, Vairocana, the first of the five transcendental Buddhas, teaches the truth in a world of eternal peace and brightness (*sangchŏkkwangt'o*). Thus the main Buddha in the Taechŏkkwangjŏn, or Hall of Vairocana, is not the historical Sakyamuni, but Vairocana who is often called the Brilliant One. In some temples, a posin Buddha and a reincarnated Sakyamuni Buddha (hwasin) sit to the left and the right of the Vairocana Buddha. In other cases, two bodhisattvas, one symbolizing knowledge and the other virtue, are found in this building. The bodhisattvas signify the existence of wisdom and virtue in the pure form of Vairocana.

And where is this world of eternal peace and brightness? Within the human heart, the pure Buddha nature. The moral nature of humanity embodies both knowledge and virtue, and thus living a humane life means living with an awareness of our human moral nature.

The Vairocana Buddha symbolizes the spreading light everywhere; that is, our original pure moral nature shines as tranquility and light around the universe. The Vairocana Buddha enshrined in a temple hall is simply a statue, but it serves to remind us of the body of Buddha which lives within all of us.

The Hall of Vairocana at Haeinsa Temple in Hapch'ŏn

Sŏlbŏpchŏn or Musŏlchŏn

In the past, temples following established custom had a separate hall for lectures and ceremonies called the Sŏlbŏpchŏn, but in recent years, as temples have been reconstructed, this building has been left out.

Songgwangsa Temple in Chŏllanam-do province still has a Sŏlbŏpchŏn, and a Musŏlchŏn, literally a "no talking hall" was included in the reconstruction of Pulguksa Temple in Kyŏngju. Paradoxically, *musol* or "no talking" is synonymous with *sŏlbŏp*, or teaching, for if a teacher is overly attached to his words or to the listening audience, he can neither teach nor accept learning. The teachings of the Buddha live and move only when we teach without preaching and listen to silence.

Kŭngnakchŏn or Muryangsujŏn—The Nirvana Hall

The Amitabha Buddha, who presides over the Western Paradise, is found in the Kŭngnakchŏn or Nirvana Hall. Derived from the Sanskrit Amitayus meaning "infinite life," Amitabha is translated into Korean as *muryangsu* (infinite life) or *muryanggwang* (infinite light). The Buddhist chant *Namas Amita Buddha* is an oath to embrace the Buddha of infinite life and wisdom. "Namas" means to return and depend on.

While this oath seems to signify the embracing of the Amitabha Buddha who exists in a faraway Western Paradise, in fact, it is a promise to return to our original selves which were formed through knowledge (muryanggwang, infinite light) and compassion (muryangsu, infinite life). In his final talk, the

79

Sakyamuni Buddha urged believers to depend on themselves, the truth and nothing else.

The Pure Land of Paradise is located in the West because the people of ancient India believed the West was the ideal world. The Amitabha Buddha of Pusŏksa Temple's Muryangsujŏn is enshrined on the western side of the hall for this very reason.

Kwanŭmjŏn—The Hall of the Bodhisattva of Compassion

The Avalokitesvara Bodhisattva (Kwanseŭm posal) is the incarnation of compassion, said to have been born from a ray of light emanating from the head of the Amitabha Buddha. This bodhisattva is generally considered the receiver of the world's pain, a rescuer who exists everywhere in the world as an instrument of knowledge.

Belief in the Avalokitesvara Bodhisattva has become a sort of folk religion in Korea. When in trouble, Buddhists often chant the bodhisattva's name over and over. The belief in the bodhisattva's miraculous powers remains strong today. In fact, many believers favor temples known for the powers of their Avalokitesvara Bodhisattvas, such as Naksansa Temple's Hongyŏn Hermitage in Kangwon-do province, Pomunsa Temple on Kanghwa Island and Poje Hermitage in Namhae on the southern coast.

The Avalokitesvara Bodhisattva has an infinite member of "bodies" and 1,000 hands and eyes to rescue those in distress. Bodhisattvas are usually sexless, but the Avalokitesvara Bodhisattva is often portrayed as a woman for compassion is generally considered a distinctly feminine, even maternal, concept.

Nearly every Korean temple has a Kwanŭmjŏn, reflecting the

importance of the Avalokitesvara Bodhisattva in the Korean consciousness.

Nahanjŏn or Ŭngjinjŏn—The Hall of Disciples

The Nahanjŏn houses images of *nahan*, the Buddha's disciples, each with his own distinct personality and appearance. The Korean nahan derives from *arhat*, the Sanskrit word for "worthy one," or "one who accepts the truth and helps others to enlightenment." The Sakyamuni Buddha once referred to himself as an arhat. This expression of respect is used not only in Buddhism, but also in reference to saints or holy men in other Indian religions.

In Korea, the Sakyamuni Buddha is enshrined in the Nahanjŏn, and the 16 nahan sit on either side of him.

P'alsangjŏn

The P'alsangjŏn houses an eight-panel painting depicting the life of the Sakyamuni Buddha. The best known examples are found at Pŏpchusa Temple in Ch'ungch'ŏngbuk-do province, Ssanggyesa Temple in Kyŏngsangnam-do province and T'ongdosa Temple near Pusan.

The Kwanŭmjŏn at Songgwangsa Temple in Chŏllanam-do province (left) and the P'alsangjŏn at Pŏpchusa Temple in Ch'ungch'ŏngbuk-do province (above)

Chijangjŏn, Myŏngbujŏn and Siwangjŏn

These three structures, all variations on a common theme, enshrine the Ksitigarbha Bodhisattva (Chijang posal). This bodhisattva is enshrined like any other except he is dressed like a Buddhist monk. The Ksitigarbha Bodhisattva vowed to save all those suffering in hell. In his left hand is a metal cane with which he beats on the doors of hell. In his right hand is a shining orb which lights the land of darkness. This merciful bodhisattva defends the reborn who stand in judgment before the King of Hell. He once swore never to leave hell until all the reborn held captive there were free.

The Myŏngbujŏn and Siwangjŏn earned their names as the homes of the ten kings (*myŏngbu siwang*) who stood as judges in hell, a concept clearly influenced by Chinese Taoism for it is not found in Indian Buddhism.

81

Mirŭkchŏn or Yŏnghwachŏn—The Hall of the Maitreya Buddha

The Maitreya Buddha (Mirŭk) is the Buddha of the future. Belief in this Buddha sprouted in the earliest years of Buddhism. According to this belief, the Maitreya Buddha will appear in the distant future when the world becomes a paradise, and all people live to be 80,000 years old. The Maitreya Buddha will redeem all those that the Sakyamuni Buddha failed to save.

The religious significance of the Maitreya Buddha is great, both for its popular prophetic tendency and messianic theme. Humanity has always relied on hope for the future to overcome its problems. The belief in the Maitreya Buddha most certainly was born of this human tendency.

The Sanskrit *Maitreya* means the "Loving One." Thus the Buddha of the Future is a Buddha capable of saving humanity through benevolent love.

The origins of the belief in the Maitreya Buddha in Korea are unclear, but Chinese influences were undoubtedly great. The many statues of this Buddha dating to fourth century Koguryŏ and Paekche indicate that the belief already flourished in that period. Artifacts and documents from early Japanese Buddhism, cultivated by monks from both these Korean kingdoms, also suggest the popularity of the Maitreya Buddha belief. The *Memorabilia of the Three Kingdoms* also contains many references to this belief.

The towering statues of the Maitreya Buddha erected at Kŭmsansa Temple in Chŏllabuk-do province and Pŏpchusa Temple as well as the ruins of Mirŭksa Temple (literally "Temple of the Maitreya Buddha") are vivid proof of the extent of this belief.

Chosajŏn—The Founder's Hall

Chosa refers to the founder of a sect of Buddhism, respected and revered by all future generations of followers. The Chosajŏn generally houses portraits of the temple's founder and

The Founder's Hall at Pusŏksa Temple in Kyŏngsangbuk-do province

The Ŭngjinjŏn, or Hall of Disciples, at Pusŏksa Temple

monks who have been instrumental in teaching the ways of the temple. Memorial services are held every spring and autumn.

In temples with no Chosajŏn, a separate pavilion is dedicated to portraits of these important figures.

Yŏmhwasil and Misosil

The Buddha once climbed to his seat at a lecture and stared silently into the audience, holding a single flower in his hand. The audience waited quietly, not knowing what to make of his behavior. Only the disciple Kashyapa smiled broadly, understanding the Buddha's true meaning. The Buddha then explained that true Nirvana had passed from him to Kashyapa without the use of words, a lesson in the power of immediate communication or telepathy between two spirits.

The room occupied by the head monk is called Yŏmhwasil (Telepathy Room) or Misosil (Smile Room), emphasizing the importance of communication from heart to heart.

Ŭnghyanggak and Hyangnogak

Whether a temple has many visitors or just a few, its main purpose is as a training ground for young monks. Each monk is assigned a task, from the head monk down to the cook. Monks responsible for the maintenance of the Buddhist sanctum live in structures called Ŭnghyanggak or Hyangnogak. *Hyang* is the Chinese ideograph for incense. Its inclusion in the names of these two structures refers to the monks' duty to light incense honoring the Buddha three times a day.

Ilchumun

Ilchumun is the first gate as one enters the temple. The term *ilchumun* literally means a gate standing on one column but it can also be interpreted as "one heart" or "one spirit." Thus ilchumun urges those who enter to study and search for the truth while carrying with them a common spirit uniting them with their fellow man and the Buddha.

Ilchumun, or "First Gate," at T'ongdosa Temple

Ch'ŏnwangmun and Haet'almun

After passing through the Ilchumun, the visitor generally encounters Ch'ŏnwangmun (Gate of the Four Heavenly Guardians) or Haet'almun (Gate of Deliverance).

Ch'ŏnwangmun houses the four Heavenly Guardians, supernatural kings who control the four heavens and guide the reborn to the right path.

Ch'ŏnwangmun Gate at Pusŏksa Temple 83

The concept of the Heavenly Guardians is referred to in ancient Indian texts and clearly predates Buddhism. In Buddhist thought, the guardians embraced the Buddha's truth and stand guard over the religion.

Each guardian represents a direction: the eastern figure holds a knife; the northern figure a lute; the guardian of the west a pagoda; and the southern guardian a dragon. The Haet'almun is erected to deliver or save (haet'al) from the cares of the mundane world all who pass through it.

Pŏmjonggak—The Bell Pavilion

Pŏmjong means "pure bell," the bell with a clear sound found in Buddhist temples. The "four instruments" (samul)—a bell, a drum, the unp'an, a flat cloud-shaped iron gong, and the mokt'ak, a hollow wooden clapper—are housed in the bell pavilion and used in the morning and evening chanting sessions.

Sammuktang

The Sammuktang refers to the temple's dining area, bathing

facilities and toilet. *Sammuk* means the "three silences" and refers to the prohibition against speaking in these three places.

Pŏptang—The Lecture Hall

The basic precepts of Buddhism are taught in the lecture hall. Novice monks study the Buddhist commandments and protocol as well as a set course in the teachings of the Sakyamuni Buddha. In addition, they acquire general knowledge about history and comparative religion.

The Four Heavenly Guardians protecting Pusŏksa Temple (above); the Bell Pavilions at T'ongdosa Temple and Pusŏksa Temple (far left and middle below), and the large drum housed in the Bell Pavilion at Pusŏksa Temple (right below)

Sŏnwon—The Meditation Hall

After completing the basic course of Buddhist study, monks train themselves through regular meditation. They learn Buddha's teachings in the Lecture Hall, and in the Meditation Hall, they attempt to experience the Buddha directly.

There is no statue of the Buddha in the meditation hall. The monks only bow to each other, even when honoring the Buddha himself. This is a means of realizing the Buddha's actions and experiencing the Buddha without depending on anything else. The monks sit empty-handed on a cushion, concentrating. When it is time to sleep, they lie on the hard wooden floor with only the cushion to cover them. Thus the meditation hall is also called *sŏnbulchang* or "a place to choose the Buddha."

In fact, the study of the Buddha's way is the study of oneself, the path to forgetting oneself. Only by forgetting ourselves can we become one with the experiential world and be delivered from our worldly bonds. ◆

Issues Confronting
Korean Buddhism Today

Lee Eun-yun

While Buddhism was introduced from abroad, it has long been one of Korea's "national religions." Over its 1,600-year history, Korean Buddhism has contributed significantly to the development of local culture and has penetrated the Korean mind to become a dominant element in thought and behavior. Buddhism flourished during the Three Kingdoms period and the Koryŏ Kingdom and remained strong during the Chosŏn period despite that regime's "Revere Confucianism and Suppress Buddhism" policy. Today, however, there is a great deal of concern and criticism over the role of contemporary Korean Buddhism.

In our rapidly changing industrial society, people lose touch with a Buddhism that cannot keep up with modern times. Implicit in this feeling is a sense of remorse about the decline of the Buddhist tradition which was once such a dynamic force in our history, culture, morality and ethics.

The history of Korean Buddhism is rich with references to monks respected for their intellect, moral influence, ethics and character. These monks were spiritual mainstays in times of national crisis so it is no wonder that today's Buddhism seems dwarfed in comparison.

Recently a Buddhist friend complained about never seeing any high-ranking government officials at the Buddhist functions he attends. He meant that temples no longer attract the elite of our society. This is, of course, an exaggeration. Many Buddhist believers are college professors or business and social leaders. However, they do seem reluctant to attend large religious gatherings, and they rarely visit monks or temples. Many do not even like to admit they are Buddhists. They study on their own and keep their religious revelations to themselves. It is not Buddhist doctrine that they are ashamed of but the musty attitudes of monks and temples.

This problem stems from several factors: the poor quality of ordained Buddhists today, shamanistic elements emphasizing the fulfillment of worldly desires, trivial factional disputes among sects, and careless secularization. I can hardly criticize believers who are ashamed of their religion without first discussing the problems plaguing the Buddhist community today.

In modern society, spiritual "poverty" grows in proportion with material abundance. Today many Koreans feel the need for a reexamination of their values and the reasons for human existence. As the limitations of Western culture become increasingly evident, they begin to search for new answers in their own culture.

The spiritual values for which the human race now yearns are embodied in the immutable truth that Buddhism has always embraced as its central principle. Buddhism clearly provides the spiritual values our modern times demand. However, in order to fulfill its mission and flourish, Korean Buddhism must discard atavistic habits and respond to the many problems facing it today.

Eminent Western scholars, warning of the collapse of modern Western civilization, have long considered Eastern thought an alternative to existing theories. Buddhism and Taoism are two philosophies that have attracted attention in the West. Western scholars' examination and reinterpretation of ancient Buddhist scriptures in light of contemporary circumstances have already confirmed that the doctrine taught by the Buddha 2,500 years ago had unparalleled religious significance.

What does it mean to be a human being? What is the essence of humanity? These age-old questions are urgent issues in modern industrialized society. Buddhist doctrine—teaching spiritual discipline and psychological control—is undeniably a vital source of philosophical insight.

Buddhist philosophical doctrine, through the practice of religion, has played an important role in purifying the human experience—transcending scholarly, contemplative and logical boundaries. However, contemporary Korean Buddhism has not only failed to serve as a cleansing force in our society but has also failed to promote human maturity, morality and ethics. Indeed, it seems to have degenerated into a secular occupation. If we are to reverse this deterioration and reestablish the religion as a dynamic social force providing the energy needed to help human beings live like human beings in accordance with Buddhist doctrine, we must reevaluate, in terms of our present circumstances, the principles embodied in the Buddhist texts.

Unfortunately, there have been few notable developments in the reinterpretation of doctrine by religious sects or Buddhist academia. Most religious orders seem to think the translation of Buddhist texts, which some consider their main task, is the goal of research. In fact, the translation of these texts involves little more than adding Korean endings to the Chinese or, at best, a literal interpretation in Korean. This can be a first step, of course, but it is a far cry from the colloquial translation needed to promote a broader understanding of the religion in contemporary society. Furthermore, there have been no attempts to translate directly from the Pali or Sanskrit, making it impossible to tell when or if Korean scholars will ever break away from their dependence on Chinese texts or Japanese publications.

One of the elements that have deterred the modernization and spread of Buddhism is the pedantic attitude of high-ranking monks who have, over the centuries, insisted on quoting difficult Chinese texts. There has been no modern reinterpretation of these ancient traditions nor has there been any attempt to preserve the original style of the old Zen poems and texts chanted

during Buddhist ceremonies. As a result, ignorance reigns.

We must reinterpret Buddhist texts in terms of contemporary sociology, economics, politics and ethics. The truth is immutable, of course, but the objects to which the truth is applied have been changing throughout history. While television sets and cars did not exist in the Buddha's time, they are necessities today. Korean Buddhism has not responded to these changes. Just one example of this obsolescence is found in precepts forbidding the use of makeup or listening to secular music by Buddhist monks or nuns. How can a monk avoid hearing popular songs while waiting for a bus or train? And every temple owns a television set nowadays. This is a trivial example, yet it reveals how Buddhism has been thrust into the modern world. Old rules must be reinterpreted in order to broaden modes of behavior. Unfortunately many Korean Buddhists still cling to antiquated rules they cannot faithfully uphold.

For modern Koreans, secular problems—human rights, a just distribution of wealth, and social welfare—cannot be separated from religion. The Mahayana branch of Buddhism has always asserted "worldly passions are the teachings of the Buddha" and "the secular world is Nirvana." In other words, Buddhism rejects the division of the world into the holy and the secular. It actively promotes religious practices that stimulate change, trying to transform the present world into Nirvana. The will to change reality and to become involved in the secular world has always been an important element in the tradition of Maitreya thought and Zen Buddhism.

In order to overcome weaknesses stemming from a speculative noninvolvement in the world, priority must be given to the reinterpretation of Buddhist texts. There are numerous interpretations for each verse of the Bible, and as a result, various branches of Christian theology have arisen, including the Liberation Theology now sweeping certain regions of the modern world. In Korean Buddhism, textual interpretation began with the great Silla monk Wonhyo's *Supplement to the Treatise on the Awakening of Faith of the Greater Vehicle* (*Taesŭng Kisinnonso*).

The reinterpretation of Buddhist doctrine within the context of contemporary politics, economy, society and culture is the most fundamental and neglected order of business facing the Buddhist community and academia today. The demands of contemporary society must be met through advances in fields such as Buddhist sociology, ethics, and economics so as to provide solutions to the problems of modern industrial society. If this does not occur, Buddhism will have a hard time finding a meaningful role for itself in today's world and will never be more than a primitive religion.

One of the most pressing problems facing Korean Buddhism today is the deteriorating quality of its ordained members. Few monks graduate from four-year colleges or universities, and the behavior of some is despicable by any standard.

The separation of politics and religion in modern society has resulted in a deterioration in the quality of the ordained members in all religions. Traditional religious values have deteriorated with the spread of materialism, and religious leaders can no longer depend on the younger generation's sense of "calling" to recruit the best and the brightest.

Thus, it is no wonder that today's ordained members do not
measure up to the religious elite that once shared, with the aris-

tocracy, a leading role in traditional government when politics and religion were linked. The numerical decline in prospective clergy is a worldwide phenomenon, and those people who do respond to the calling are often far from the cream of the crop.

When Buddhism was Korea's national religion, it was not uncommon for princes and preeminent intellectuals, the most intelligent and virtuous of their day, to join the Buddhist orders. Even during the Chosŏn Dynasty when Confucianism was the ruling ideology, many outstanding intellectuals dedicated their lives to Buddhism, playing important roles in the perpetuation of the religion. Recently, however, the quality of monks has declined. Except for a few special cases where a young person experiences a true sense of inspiration, the brightest high school graduates, students with the highest scores on the nationwide college entrance aptitude test rarely choose to go to theology schools or Buddhist colleges.

This is not, however, the only problem related to the general quality of ordained Buddhists. Temple school education is usually limited to reading Chinese or translated texts. English, one of the most important subjects in any formal education, is generally neglected. Some people may ask why a Buddhist monk would need English, but if monks are to participate in international society and read Western research on Buddhism, they must know English.

The education of ordained Buddhists also lacks in comprehensive interdisciplinary study. In some religions, prospective clergy go on for advanced degrees in other disciplines, such as sociology, economics, politics, literature and philosophy, then return to teach at theological seminaries. Interdisciplinary study rarely occurs in Buddhist academic circles, however. This lack of interdisciplinary expertise is an urgent problem, because, as I mentioned before, a reinterpretation of Buddhist teachings is essential in our modern times.

The deterioration in the quality of Korean monks also stems from sectarian discord which rocked the Buddhist community in the 1950s. This discord arose when President Syngman Rhee issued an order calling for the expulsion of married monks from temples nationwide. Celibate monks, vastly outnumbered by the married monks, welcomed this move but were unable to enforce it because of their small numbers. To build up their strength, they began recruiting indiscriminately. Many of these new recruits were former hoodlums who were dressed in monks' robes and sent out to expel married monks from temples by force.

The recruits were a thoroughly secular lot, hardly suited for the monkhood, and the sects intended to let them go after the cleansing movement. However, when a new government, established after the military coup of 1961, implemented a policy aimed at mopping up the criminal population, the gangsters-turned-monks found life safer in the temples. By and by they acquainted themselves with the customs of temples and became proper monks, partly of their own volition and partly as a consequence of the times.

Buddhists celebrate Buddha's birthday with many events at the temples. They hang paper lanterns bearing prayers for family members inside and outside the temple.

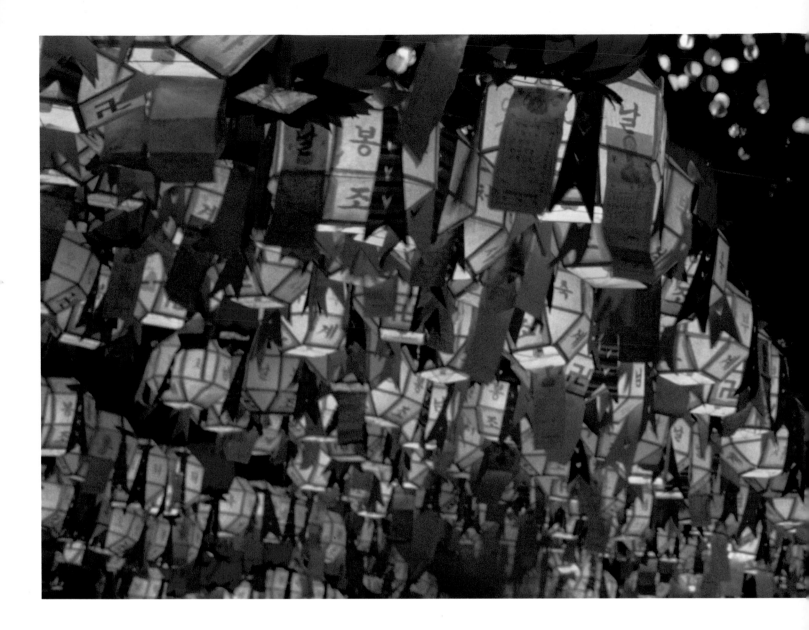

The cleansing of married monks was both a boon and a burden for Korean Buddhism, but ultimately it sowed the seeds of violence and corruption within Buddhist sects. The violence intensified when former hoodlums began inviting their old cohorts into the monkhood.

The admission of hoodlums tapered off after the 1970s, but the second-rate monks who entered around the time of the cleansing movement now occupy the middle rungs of the Buddhist hierarchy, and their behavior tends to muddy the entire community.

Another reason for the deteriorating quality of the Buddhist clergy is the tradition of ordaining lowly unfortunates, a legacy of primitive Indian Buddhism and the Buddhist suppression policy of the Chosŏn Dynasty. During the Chosŏn period, most prospective monks were orphans, the poor or illegitimate children. This trend persists today, albeit to a lesser extent, and some people still join the clergy to escape broken homes or misfortune.

Korean Buddhism is often seen as a nihilistic, secular religion, an image first acquired during the Chosŏn Dynasty. Many people accuse Buddhism of being a paradise for escapist pessimists. Indeed, the Buddhist tradition of personal discipline and transcendence of worldly affairs is more an object of criticism than praise.

In fact, Buddhist doctrine rejects selfish individualism. Mahayana Buddhism is based on compassion for humanity as a whole, as summarized in the phrase "My own disease cannot be healed as long as humanity remains afflicted." It also states, "One must work to enlighten humanity first, even if it means postponing one's own enlightenment."

Korean Buddhism belongs to the tradition of Mahayana Buddhism, which places a priority on helping others. Modern Korean Buddhists are wrong to insist on their own enlightenment. While self-cultivation must precede all else, it is not the end to which Mahayana Buddhism aspires.

Another problem is the tendency to concentrate on the fulfillment of worldly desires. Each year as university entrance examinations approach, mothers flock to Buddhist temples to pray for their children's success. Monks encourage this trend in order to collect more donations, but it bodes ill for the present and future of Korean Buddhism.

The most urgent problem from the point of view of the propagation of Buddhism is the lack of young male believers. Buddhism is often referred to as a "women's religion," and in fact, most active Buddhist believers are women or elderly people.

The main factor behind the lack of interest among young people and men could be Korean Buddhism's emphasis on personal good fortune and self-interest. The frequent use of difficult expressions derived from Chinese and lectures that have little to

The climax of Buddha's birthday is the lighting of lanterns illuminating the way for those seeking Nirvana.

do with the realities of everyday life also tend to alienate young people.

Of course, one could say all religions embody a certain supplicatory element, and the passive emphasis on self-enlightenment has always been a part of Buddhism. However, today's religions are moving toward an embracing of the secular world and a more mature concern for the human community.

The practice of faith and the management of temples are also important issues. The ultimate virtue in the practice of Buddhism is compassion or "active sympathy" (*chabihaeng*). This sense of compassion (*karuna* in Sanskrit) connotes a feeling of sympathy for all unfortunate beings and a sharing of pain. Korean Buddhists chant about compassion, but their actions reveal a desire for the Buddha's protection and sympathy for themselves.

From the time it was a national religion, Korean Buddhism has been a passive Buddhism. However, today's world demands the opposite: Korean Buddhism must take an active, giving role.

The management of temples is a case in point. Monks sit in flowing robes, as they accept bows and donations from believers. They use the money to decorate their temples, erect pagodas, commission statues, and take care of their daily needs. The custom of going on alms rounds, alive and well in Thailand, Burma and Sri Lanka, has disappeared from Korean Buddhism.

Another serious problem is the failure to actively seek out believers. No one seems to be playing the traditional role of the bodhisattva who shares the heartache and happiness of the lay believer. Rarely does a monk go to a believer's house to chant or help prepare a body for a funeral. Originally, the practice of Buddhism meant sacrifice and the performance of tasks avoided by others.

In short, Korean Buddhism seems to have lost sight of its original doctrine and teachings. It suffers not only from the low quality of monks, contemporary religious practices, and the failure to reinterpret teachings, but also from problems related to propagation, the observation of rules and reform. Recently revived practices, such as rules related to eating and behavior, suggest Buddhists are less interested in plumbing the depths of religious profundity than in indulging in superficial and eccentric behavior. Such behavior and ignorance of the true spirit of Zen Buddhism can hardly help believers live healthy, meaningful lives.

The human spirit, worn out by modern civilization, may long for the insight offered by Korean Zen. While Korean Buddhism is saddled with many pressing problems and weaknesses, it remains rich in the power and tradition needed to help modern humanity overcome the spiritual poverty it faces today. ◆

Pŏmp'ae:
The Sounds of Buddhism

Hahn Man-young

A ceremonial Buddhist chant, *pŏmp'ae*, resembles the sounds of a temple at dawn. In the early morning darkness, as the rest of the world sleeps, the gentle beat of the *mokt'ak*, a hollow wooden clapper, rings through the quiet starlit garden in front of the Main Hall. The crisper tones of the *unp'an*, a flat cloud-shaped iron gong, follows, and soon a clear-voiced monk makes the rounds of the temple, chanting "The bell rings over the world," a signal for the other monks to rise.

After the monk passes, a few moments of expectant silence settle over the grounds before the large temple bell sends its first sonorous sound into the quiet mountain valley. At the first toll, the rocks deep in the ravines shake from their sleep. At the second toll, the trees quiver awake, and at the third toll, the birds soar from their nests in a chorus of praises for the coming of a new day.

The sounds of the temple bell are like waves on the sea, surging forward, then rolling back to lap against the shore. And like the waves, they wash away the 108 passions Buddhists say humans are subject to in this world.

Pŏmp'ae is a combination of all these elements: the mokt'ak, the gong, the drum, the chants and a cymbal dance in praise of the Buddha. In China, it is known as *fanbai*, in Japan, as *bombai*. In Korea, it constitutes one of the three great vocal musical genres, together with *kagok*, classical songs, and *p'ansori*, dramatic narrative mono-opera.

A monody without rhythmic cycle, pattern or harmony, pŏmp'ae is only sung at Buddhist temples during certain established ceremonies.

These ceremonies include ordinary rituals for the dead, larger rites dedicated to the ten kings who are believed to reign over the underworld, rites for drowning victims, rites for persons expected to die soon, and large rites for villages or specific areas. Interestingly, these rituals all have counterparts in Korea's shamanistic rituals.

Stylistically, pŏmp'ae is divided into two groups: *anch'aebi* and *kŏtch'aebi*. Anch'aebi, commonly called *yŏmbul*, literally "praying to the Buddha," is an invocation or recitation of Buddhist sutras accompanied by small hand bells. Kŏtch'aebi is sung by monks specially trained in pŏmp'ae. They are invited to perform in ceremonies at their own temples as well as other temples.

In a narrow sense, the term pŏmp'ae refers to kŏtch'aebi, which comprises solo vocal music, or *hossori*, and the chorus-like *chissori*. The chant used at the five ceremonies mentioned above usually consists of anch'aebi and hossori. These Chinese-ideogram verses set to the chant praise the Buddha.

Chissori, which is always sung in unison, is a more elaborate form of pŏmp'ae. It takes between 30 and 40 minutes to perform, while the simplest hossori requires only four or five minutes. Because of its length, chissori has fallen into decline with the simplification of Buddhist rites in modern times. As a result, the chissori repertoire, which once comprised 72 pieces, has shrunk to only 13 which are sung by a mere handful of pŏmp'ae monks. Chissori's melismatic passages and dynamic range makes its performance extremely difficult.

Only monks can become pŏmp'ae singers. They do not begin training in chissori until they are thoroughly familiar with the more regular hossori chants. Since chissori is sung in chorus, a leader is needed to conduct with his hands or exaggerated movements of his lips. Chissori's elaborate melodies are delivered in long, drawn-out vocalization, and its dynamic range is remarkably broad, stretching from the barely audible to the extremely loud. Chissori has some solo parts, called *hŏjŏlp'uri*, usually taking the form of a prelude or interlude.

As in all religions, Buddhism often uses

Chants and dances such as the drum dance (right), performed by a single dancer beating on a large temple drum, enhance the subdued beauty of Korea's Buddhist ceremonies.

music to propagate its ideas. Sometimes the texts of simplified sutra were set to folk song melodies. *Hwach'ŏng* and *Hoesimgok*, popular Buddhist songs recorded in Korean, are two such examples.

Hwach'ŏng is sung by pŏmp'ae monks at the end of temple rituals. Similar to yŏmbul, it is a simple chant marked by long recitatory passages and performed in the *ŏnmori* rhythmic cycle, a fast, irregular 10:8 pattern.

Buddhist rites are often accompanied by three time-honored dances of purely Buddhist origin: the butterfly dance (*nabich'um*), the cymbal dance (*parach'um*), and the drum dance (*pŏpkoch'um*). The butterfly dance is performed by two or four nuns, holding peonies in one hand and wearing a monk's hat and robe. There are 15 varieties of this dance, each performed in a different rite.

The cymbal dance is performed by two or four monks wearing the same attire, except without the hats. This dance requires considerable strength and agility as the dancers must swing large cymbals in rhythmic motions up and behind the head. There are six versions of this dance.

The drum dance, of which there are two varieties, is performed by a single dancer who beats on a large temple drum. Again, the dancer wears the regular monk's robes.

All three dances are accompanied by the conical oboe (*t'aep'yŏngso*), the gong (*ching*), a drum (*puk*), and the mokt'ak wooden clapper.

Pŏmp'ae is generally believed to have been introduced to Korea by Master Chin'gam (774-850), a revered monk of the Unified Silla Kingdom. According to an epitaph on a monument at Ssanggyesa Temple in Hadong, Kyŏngsangnam-do Province, Chin'gam became familiar with the pŏmp'ae chant in 804 while he was serving as Silla's official emissary to Tang China. Upon returning to Korea in 830, he taught the music to his disciples at Ssanggyesa.

However, an entry in the *Memorabilia of the Three Kingdoms* suggests pŏmp'ae was already in Korea at the time of Master Chin'gam. According to the *Memorabilia*, in 760 the sun split in half, the two parts taking turns lighting the earth 24 hours a day. The royal meteorologist advised an agitated King Kyŏngdŏk to invite a pŏmp'ae monk to sing at court, asking the Buddha for a solution to this mysterious phenomenon. The king set up an altar and waited for the monk's arrival. Soon a monk named Wolmyŏng appeared. The king asked him to chant but Wolmyŏng refused,

The butterfly dance (nabich'um) *is performed at Buddhist rites by nuns dressed in flowing white robes.*

94

saying he knew only Korean folk songs, or *hyangga*. The story not only shows that pŏmp'ae existed at this time, but also that certain monks specialized in the chants.

In his *Record of a Pilgrimage to Tang China in Search of the Buddha's Law*, the Japanese monk Ennin, a contemporary of Master Chin'gam, describes a ritualistic lecture on sutra held at a Silla temple on China's Shandong Peninsula. According to the account, three types of pŏmp'ae were performed: pŏmp'ae of the Tang style, pŏmp'ae of the native Silla style, and an older genre similar to that which had been transmitted to Japan through Korea from China before the Tang Dynasty. Master Chin'gam's pŏmp'ae obviously was of the Tang style.

Hossori, as it is known today, is similar to the folk songs of the Kyŏngsang and Kangwon regions, the old territory of the Silla Kingdom. This suggests that Silla's pŏmp'ae was similar to today's hossori. "Old style" pŏmp'ae, quite different from either the Tang or Silla styles, is believed to have come to Korea through Central Asia and Mongolia and is similar to today's chissori. It also resembles Mongolian and Tibetan Buddhist chants.

Over the centuries, Tang fanbai is believed to have been Koreanized and assimilated into the existing hossori. This assumption seems justified since Chinese *ci* music, irregular verse with an instrumental accompaniment introduced during the Koryŏ period, much later than pŏmp'ae, was also Koreanized over a prolonged period of time.

One may assume that pŏmp'ae flourished in Koryŏ, which embraced Buddhism as a national religion, but there is no specific documentation to verify this. Koryŏ was in close contact with the northern Chinese dynasties of Liao (907-1125), Jin (1115-1234) and Yuan (1206-1368) both militarily and culturally. Koryŏ pŏmp'ae is believed to have been exposed to considerable influences from these three states, and through them, to have been influenced by Tibetan Buddhist chants as well.

The text setting of Korean pŏmp'ae is noted for its nominal vocables interspersed between text syllables. It shares this characteristic with Tibetan chants. These vocables are not found in Chinese fanbai or Japanese bombai. The logarithmic structure of the hossori and chissori is also reminiscent of a Tibetan chant called *gad*.

Some pŏmp'ae scores from the Chosŏn period are still available in the traditional notation, but much of the music underwent a drastic decline after 1911 when the Japanese colonial government enacted a law governing Korean

The cymbal dance (parach'um) is performed by several monks, deftly swinging the shining cymbals through the air.

Buddhist temples and banned the performance of hwach'ŏng music and Buddhist dances in temples. The chants were saved from complete extinction because Buddhist believers insisted on holding rites including pŏmp'ae and traditional dances.

With the current trend toward simplification, Buddhist rites that once took days now take less than an hour. Simple yŏmbul chants are popularly employed for ordinary rites, while hossori and chissori have all but been abandoned. They are barely perpetuated under the protection of the government which designated pŏmp'ae an Intangible Cultural Asset in 1969. At present, four monks, Pak Song-am, Chang T'ae-nam, Chŏng Chi-kwang and Yi Il-gŭng are recognized as government-designated "Intangible Cultural Assets" for their expertise in performing pŏmp'ae.

Aesthetically speaking, pŏmp'ae, a religious

Pŏmp'ae chants and their performers, accompanied by large temple drums and other percussion instruments, have been designated "Intangible Cultural Assets" by the Korean government.

chant, is not descriptive nor does it have a narrative text. It is like the sounds of a temple bell reverberating through a sequestered mountain valley. Its long sustained sounds, followed by multiple melodic ornamentations, are profoundly pure and clear and never secular.

Pŏmp'ae has exerted considerable influence on secular music. *Yŏngsan hoesang*, an important example of *chŏng-ak*, the "proper music" of the Chosŏn ruling class, suggests Buddhist influences in its title, which means the "Buddha's Teachings at Yŏngsan." *Kagok*, long lyrical chŏng-ak songs, also evince pŏmp'ae influences in their long melodic lines and sustained sound followed by multiple melodic ornamentation, the very essence of pŏmp'ae.

While Chosŏn's conservative Confucianism influenced court music and boisterous shaman music worked its way into folk music, the artistic concept of Buddhism, "subdued but not sorrowful, joyous but not carnal," left its own lasting mark on chŏng-ak. ◆

The Poetry of Han Yong-un

Translations and Introduction by Ko Chang-soo

Widely recognized as one of the greatest poets Korea has ever produced, Han Yong-un (1879-1944) was also a Buddhist monk and a patriot who played an important role in the independence movement against Japanese colonial rule. Han's collected poems, *Love's Silence*, are a landmark in Korea's literary history. Many of these poems deal with philosophical and religious questions concerning the relationship between the phenomenal world and ultimate reality. In his poems about love, inextinguishable religious aspirations underlie expressions of physical love. Nevertheless, Han's poetic diction remains plain and conversational, even when his subject matter is metaphysical and religious. The poet frequently employs, with great mastery, the language of paradox and irony in the manner of a enigmatic Zen question (*hwadu*).

Han's poetry often echoes the Buddhist dictum against "looking at the finger that points to the moon." The subtly incantatory quality of his narrative draws its dynamism from the Buddhist philosophy that permeates his poetry as a whole.

Han Yong-un's poems contain many layers of reference and meaning subsuming those of Buddhist thought, patriotic sentiments and human love. The beauty of his poetry derives in part from his free-ranging imagination and exceptional poetic sensibility. In his poems, Han weaves sound and sense into captivating works of art.

Nowhere is this more true than in "Love's Silence." Ostensibly, this poem is about the meeting and parting of two lovers, but it also addresses man's relations with an ultimate being. The "silence" of the lover suggests the silence of Truth as opposed to man's "dubious" verbal pronouncements. This poem is often referred to as a patriotic poem, the lover being the poet's country. Thus, the lover represents many things: a human lover, Han's motherland and a transcendental being.

"I Do Not Know" is perhaps the most cosmological of Han's poems. Individual details drawn from nature are mere symbols which seem to point to an ultimate being. Sensuous images evoke the mystery of existence and help the reader visualize an ultimate being.

"Come" is an excellent example of the use of paradox in poetry. The poet masterfully uses the logic and imagery of the ineffable. The speaker addresses his or her lover but the relationship does not seem entirely human. It resembles the relationship between man and a transcendental being which may be better explained through the language of paradox.

At first glance, "Boat on the River" seems a charming vignette. However, the person waving from the riverside tavern adds a new dimension to the scene. Whether it is because of the poet's longing for attachment to or detachment from a human love, or because of some transcendental perspective on the riverside scene, the person waving adds a pathetic beauty to the situation.

Love's Silence

Love has gone. Ah, my love has gone.
You have left, shaking me off and breaking
the green mountain light along the small path
toward the maple grove. The old promise that
was firm and bright as golden flowers has been
carried away like cold dust by a breath of breeze.
The memory of that keen first kiss has receded
changing my fate's course. Your sweet voice has
deafened me and your fair face has blinded me.

Love, after all, is a human affair; so I feared
our parting when we first met. But this parting
has been too sudden; my surprised heart is
bursting with new sorrow. To make parting
a source of idle tears will only mar love itself.
So I have poured my hopeless sorrow into a keg
of new hope. As we dread parting when we meet,
so we believe in reunion when we part.

Ah, my love has gone, but I have not let you go.
A love-song that cannot bear its own music
hovers over love's silence.

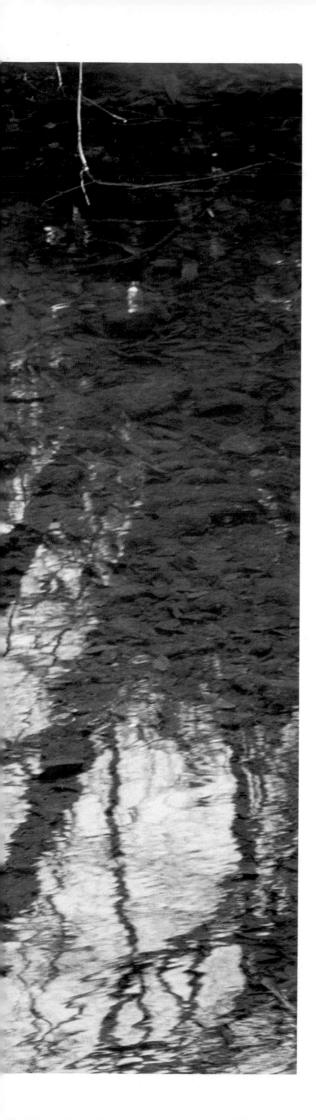

I Do Not Know

Whose footprint is that paulownia leaf
that drops softly, rousing ripples in the windless air?
Whose face is that blue sky
glimpsed between the dark, threatening clouds
blown by the west wind following a long rain?

Whose breath is that fragrance in the sky
over the flowerless tree, over the dilapidated tower?
Whose song is that bickering stream
that quietly flows, starting from nowhere
and making the stones moan?
Whose poem is that evening glow
that adorns the waning day,
its lotus feet on the boundless sea,
its jade hands patting the sky?

Burnt ash becomes fuel again.
My endlessly burning heart!
Whose night does this
Flickering lamp illumine?

Come

Come. It's time you came. Hurry up.
Do you know when it's time for you to come?
My waiting will signal your time to come.

Come to my flower bed.
Flowers are in full blossom in my flower bed.
If someone pursues you, go and hide in a flower.
I'll become a butterfly and sit on the flower
where you hide.
Then your pursuer won't find you.
Come, it's time you came. Hurry up.

Please come into my arms; I have a soft bosom.
My bosom is soft as water
when you caress me.
But it can turn into a golden knife
and a steel shield
if it's to protect you from dangers.
My bosom can become a withered flower
trodden under the hoofs of a horse.
But your head cannot fall from my bosom.
And your pursuer cannot lay his hands on you.
Come, it's time you came. Hurry up.

Come into my death.
Death is ready for you any time.
If anyone pursues you,
you just come and stay behind my death.
Nothingness and omnipotence are equal before death.
Death's love is infinite and eternal.
Warships and artillery become dust before death.
The strong and the weak are friends before death.
Then your pursuer cannot capture you.
Come, it's time you came. Hurry up.

Boat on the River

The small boat moves up the river,
loaded heavily with twilight.
The river's lucid wind fills its sails.
The plaintive boating song fades
in the spring skies.
Someone waves from a riverside tavern.

CONFUCIANISM

Scholars are not certain when Confucianism first came to Korea but it has been a way of life and system of political thought since ancient times. Confucianism is most clearly manifested in the Three Bonds and Five Moral Disciplines of human relations, concepts familiar to all Koreans, even today. Ritual filial piety, demonstrated in regular ancestral memorial rites, has long been a prescription for personal behavior and a mode of politics, which has influenced individual actions and the relationship between the individual and the state.

Our contributors discuss Confucianism's influence on Korean culture, focusing on education and political theory, and offer a vivid glimpse at Confucian rites, preserved more accurately in Korea than in any other country.

Confucian Thought and Korean Culture

Yun Sa-soon

The exact date of Confucianism's introduction to Korea is unclear, but it is generally traced back 2,200 years. To the extent that Confucianism has played a role in Korean history over these many years, its influence on Korean culture has also been immense. In this essay I consider the influence of Confucianism on Korean culture, how it contributed to the formation of our history and culture. I will also consider the relationship of national identity and independence in the context of Confucian influences.

The goals of Confucianism are self-cultivation and harmony or peace among people. In fact, Confucianism is often called the pursuit of *naesŏng woewang*—literally, achieving the inner dignity of a sage and the capacity to rule the external world as king.

The Great Learning (Da Xue), one of the main Confucian texts, established eight ways to practice Confucius' teachings. These methods are explained in terms of the relationship between sequence, cause and effect, and the importance of matter. Students begin with the pursuit of knowledge and self-cultivation and finish by governing efficiently for the peace of the nation. Possessing the prerequisite of self-cultivation, one proceeds to put one's family in order, then moves on to the ultimate task of wise and benevolent government. It is an ethical process centered around the concept of filial piety and a political method centered around the concept of loyalty. The mainstream of Confucianism in traditional Korean culture dwells in ethics and politics.

While Confucianism came to Korea in ancient times—namely, before the Three Kingdoms—its influence dates to the beginning of Koguryŏ, when the *Extant Records (Yugi)*, a massive history of the early Koguryŏ, was written. Koguryŏ's establishment of the National Confucian Academy, or *T'aehak*, marks the wholesale acceptance of Confucianism.

In each of the Three Kingdoms, the acceptance of Confucianism brought the compilation of state histories, a noteworthy phenomenon suggesting that historical consciousness is a con-

firmation and manifestation of sovereign identity. More importantly, this was the initial posture for the acceptance of foreign thought.

Until the Unified Silla period, Korean Confucianism focused on the study and practice of filial piety and loyalty, core principles of Confucian ethics and political thought. In particular, acceptance of the concept of filial piety permeated every aspect of life, taking the form of Confucian rites, which came to characterize family morals. Acceptance of the concept of loyalty became a means of strengthening the power of the king domestically and promoting patriotism and the defense of the state against outside forces. Korea has benefited from its acceptance of these concepts since this period. Koryŏ was praised for its courtesy and practice of Confucian politics by the Chinese, and over the centuries, Koreans have withstood numerous foreign invasions on the strength of their fierce loyalty to state and nationality.

From the Koryŏ period, filial piety was legally enforced through a system of punishments and rewards. Under the Chosŏn Dynasty, it was further systematized in the *Family Rites of Zhu Xi (Chuja Karye)* and enhanced within the framework of the Three Bonds and the Five Moral Disciplines of human relations (*samgang oryun*) laid out in three texts: *Conduct of the Three Bonds (Samgang haengsilto)*, the *Five Moral Disciplines (Oryundo)* and the *Lesser Learning (Sohak)*.

The metaphysical foundation of filial piety may lie in a theory of human nature advanced by Yi Hwang, Yi I and other Neo-Confucian scholars in the 16th century. Filial piety was, along with ethics, worshiped and considered a ritual absolute on par with criminal law. We should remember that in the Neo-Confucian climate of that time, ritual filial piety was a prescription for individual behavior and at the same time a mode of politics and the grounds for factional strife.

Originally the Confucian definition of *ye*, or rites, was not restricted to ethics. This broad sense of ye was to be expected, however, when we realize the Confucian political ideal implies

During the Chosŏn period, the coming-of-age ceremony (left), weddings, funerals and ancestral rites were prescribed by law. They became an integral part of daily life, serving as a basis for maintaining order in one's life and household.

government through rites and the governing principle of the Chosŏn Dynasty was Neo-Confucianism.

On the other hand, monarchism, based on the concept of loyalty, developed from very early times, perhaps because of the developing relationship between Korea and China and Koreans' maturing national consciousness. The question of how loyalty should be put into practice was, beginning with the Three Kingdoms, considered from the point of view of maintaining and strengthening the monarchy, rather than establishing it anew. For this reason, the monarch's duties, qualifications and governing skills were also considered important. In other words, as the Confucian political ideal—governing through rites and benevolence—was embraced from the Three Kingdom period, people began to discuss politics inspired by the exemplary practice of rites and benevolence by the king himself.

This was particularly true of Wang Kŏn, the founder of the Koryŏ Kingdom, who ascended the throne amid an atmosphere of dynastic revolution and clearly recognized the political temper of the age—that is, the trend toward rule through rites and benevolence. In his agriculture-first policy and tax reductions and exemptions, Wang Kŏn gave more concrete form to the practice of rule by the people and for the people. This spirit was carried on by the Chosŏn kings.

With improvements in the bureaucratic system following on the promulgation of a government examination system at the beginning of Koryŏ, royal despotism was restricted, and as the bureaucratic system matured in the Chosŏn period, kings were increasingly asked to consider public opinion, and were sometimes threatened with expulsion or regicide if they did not rule properly.

On the other hand, bureaucrats were held to strict standards of loyalty. Thus, by the 16th century, toward the middle years of the Chosŏn Dynasty, loyalty did not simply mean loyalty to the king, but rather extended to a love of country and love of the people. The spirit of high-level scholar-officials became synonymous with a spirit of conscientious public service, which, reinforced by the Neo-Confucian value system, solidified in a spirit of self-sacrifice, sometimes at the risk of one's own life. This is why we see a succession of virtuous officials, *sŏnbi*, or scholar-officials without government positions, patriots and heroes during this period. They were born of the growing spirit of public service.

Korean thought is not limited to Confucianism, however; it includes Shamanism, Buddhism and Taoism. In the past, most Confucians rejected other bodies of thought because they believed Confucianism had more to offer the Korean people. But what makes Confucianism superior? We must illuminate its positive points if we are to compare it with other bodies of thought and evaluate its contributions to Korean culture.

Korean Confucians did not actively criticize Shamanism and Taoism for they thought the two belief systems did not constitute serious rivals to Confucianism. Rather, Yi I (1536-1584), Pak Se-dang (1629-1703) and other Neo-Confucian scholars borrowed elements from the beliefs of Lao-zi and Zhuang-zi—although they did not believe in Taoist thought—in an effort to reinforce their Confucian beliefs. Criticisms of Shamanism and Taoism were limited to appeals to the king made by Ch'oe Sŭng-no, a Koryŏ administrative reformer (927-989), and Cho Kwang-jo, a Chosŏn era reformer (1482-1519).

Ch'oe Sŭng-no argued that shamanistic rituals to wandering spirits were little more than ineffectual appeals for good fortune, and Taoist rites to natural spirits actually reflected disrespect for those spirits and were a waste of the energy and resources of the common people. Cho Kwang-jo echoed Ch'oe's concerns. He contended Taoism's fundamental theories were vague and frivolous and called for the closure of the Sogyŏksŏ, the National Taoist Temple, which was, in fact, abolished in 1518. Ch'oe and Cho rejected Shamanism and Taoism because they believed they were overly superstitious and harmed the people.

In Koryŏ, Buddhism was embraced as the state religion and came to be seen as a potent enemy by adherents of Confucianism. A model Confucian, Ch'oe Sŭng-no stepped up his criticisms of Buddhism at this time. He argued that frequent Buddhist ceremonies harmed the people and drained the national coffers. Buddhism was also suspect for it was concerned with the afterlife rather than the present. According to Ch'oe, the answers to life's questions—especially the problem of developing principles for gov-

Respect for ancestors being one of the basic teachings of Confucianism, every step of a funeral, including carrying the coffin to the grave site (right), was conducted with utmost solemnity. Next page and opposite: The sons of the deceased wore clothes and head coverings of hemp cloth. On behalf of the nation, court officials of Chosŏn performed rites to the gods of earth and harvest at the Sajik Altar (right).

erning the nation—were in every case to be found in Confucianism.

Some Confucians of the late Koryŏ period fervently opposed Buddhism, urging the burning of temples and slashing of monks' throats. The theoretical grounds for their rejection of Buddhism was not significantly different from that of Ch'oe Sŭng-no, however.

The Chosŏn scholar-official Chŏng To-jŏn (1342-1398) also rejected Buddhism, arguing it neglected family and national life in the present and undermined ethics and national values. He criticized what he saw as Buddhism's weak ethical sense and lack of governing values—in other words, its rebuff of filial piety and loyalty.

Neo-Confucianism, on the other hand, guided society, through filial piety and loyalty, toward a fruitful and ideal life in the present. For Chŏng, filial piety meant the Three Bonds and the Five Moral Disciplines. He went so far as to call Neo-Confucianism "practical learning," or *sirhak*. Accordingly, he advocated Neo-Confucianism as the governing principle and state religion, a status once enjoyed by Buddhism.

In the 17th century, Chosŏn Confucians rejected Catholicism for being as heretical as Buddhism, if not more so. The introduction of Catholicism was a shock to Neo-Confucian circles, although some Confucians, including Yi Sŭng-hun (1756-1801), Yi Pyŏk (1754-1786) and Chŏng Yag-yong (1762-1836), willingly embraced the new thought system in the 18th century. These intellectuals sided with proponents of Western technology, introduced to Korea by way of the Chinese Qing Dynasty, and contributed to the formation of the Practical Learning (*Sirhak*) movement.

A number of Neo-Confucian scholar-officials, including Yi Ik (1682-1764) and An Chŏng-bok (1712-1791) had already criticized Catholic thought by this time, however. This criticism reached its height with Yi Hang-no (1792-1868) and Yi Chin-sang (1818-1885) in the 19th century, and Yu In-sŏk (1842-1915) and Yi Sŭng-hŭi (?-1916), students of the two Yis and leading figures in the Righteous Army resistance to Japanese colonial rule.

Confucians condemned Catholicism not only for its contents and characteristics, including its view of God, but, more importantly, for its heretical ethical values, so clearly expressed in the Catholic believer Yun Chi-ch'ung's refusal to honor his ancestors in Confucian rites. The main reason for rejecting Catholicism was its ethical stance and blatant repudiation of the Five Moral Disciplines.

At this time Confucians viewed Buddhism as something that merely neglected the Confucian system of the Five Moral Disciplines without fundamentally denying it. Catholicism went further, however, completely denying the Five Moral Disciplines. One example is the Catholic notion that all humans are equal before the Lord. Although this notion is almost universally accepted today, it was the reason Confucians criticized Catholicism more forcefully than they did Buddhism.

Also we must remember that Catholicism was a Western thought system. Buddhism, on the other hand, was introduced by Asians. What is more, Buddhists came peaceably while the Catholics were equipped with firearms. Nineteenth-century Neo-Confucians attacked Catholicism because it was a foreign religion linked to the armed forces not only of the Western powers but of imperial Japan as well. At the end of the Chosŏn period, the rejection of

Catholicism was expressed in the "defending orthodoxy and rejecting heterodoxy" movement and came to be associated with the "anti-reconciliation" (ch'ŏkhwa) stance of the Chosŏn court under the Taewon'gun, King Kojong's father.

When we recall what happened after this—the takeover by imperial Japan and the loss of Korean sovereignty—the Confucians' interpretation hardly seems a frivolous exercise in ideology. Needless to say, the loss of national sover-

eignty was far graver than the collapse of the Five Moral Disciplines. On this point, we must not overlook the spirit of the patriots who fought against imperial Japan as an expression of loyalty. The moral sense of loyalty endorsed by Confucians in the face of foreign invasion was not devoted to the ruler alone; it was also a loyalty dedicated to national livelihood and the preservation of the Korean people.

In this sense, Confucianism served as a national belief system and can therefore be seen as a body of *Korean* thought. Korean Confucianism is closely related to the formation of a sense of national selfhood and to the establishment of a sense of sovereignty. In other words, although Confucianism was originally an imported thought system, it has become a Korean body of thought inasmuch as it has had a strong impact on Koreans' view of their national livelihood and their historical view of themselves as a people.

Confucianism has had a powerful influence on Korea's historical development. Korea was, however, bitterly humiliated by the loss of its national sovereignty to imperial Japan, and for this reason, one could question the historical function of Korean Confucianism. This argument is all the more persuasive when we remember that Neo-Confucianism was the governing principle of the Chosŏn Dynasty which collapsed under Japanese pressure. Korean Confucianism must, to a certain extent, be responsible for this historical fact.

Any historical evaluation requires consideration of relative merits and demerits, however, and we must remember that the Japanese colonial regime also embraced Confucianism as its governing principle. Thus, one could say responsibility for Korea's loss of sovereignty lies with those managing the country at the time, rather than with Confucianism itself.

We must also remember that Confucianism was the reason for Korea's reliance on China. A respect for Ming China and a rejection of the Qing simmered throughout the late Chosŏn period. This tendency to respect China and reject barbarians was born of the Koreans' respect for the moral sense endorsed in the Confucian canons, the *Spring and Autumn Annals.* Inasmuch as a reliance on a stronger country is inevitable for a weak country, we must recognize the existence at that time of a practical sense of national sovereignty among the Korean people. We must also realize that the trend toward a respect for Chinese culture and thought in fact proceeded against a background of armed intervention by the Qing regime, Western powers and Japan. The Ming

Dynasty, which Qing had succeeded, had by that time collapsed and its ruler was only a figurehead. Therefore, any "respect" for China was for appearances only. China had a stake in keeping the Korean people weak. Therefore, even though late Chosŏn Confucians, especially the faction that called for the defense of orthodoxy and a rejection of heterodoxy, described Korea at that time as a "Little China," they never lacked a sense of national sovereignty. In their own way they held fast to it. Their perceptions of the Chinese and Western "barbarians" suggest their sense of national sovereignty derived from the wisdom to maintain independence within the international order. The Three Kingdoms' compilation of national histories at the time Confucianism was introduced also suggests this.

Recognition of one's identity in terms of birth and parentage has been exacting since Korean Confucianism's earliest years. The rectification of names and personal identity reach far into the past because most Korean Confucians, including scholars such as Chosŏn's Yi I, believed the source of Korean Confucianism was Kija, the legendary founder of Kija Chosŏn, which succeeded Tan'gun Chosŏn—although Chŏng Yag-yong and others disagreed.

While there are many difficulties in proving this theory, it basically suggests that Korean Confucianism predated Confucius. The theory, then, seems to be that Kija was of the Chinese Yin people, who along with the Koreans were called "Eastern Barbarians," and by this token, Korean Confucianism, which originated at that time, is more advanced than that of China. In fact, the modern Confucian and journalist Chang Chi-yŏn (1864-1921) embraced this belief as his life philosophy, saying that Korea was the birthplace of Confucianism. His position reflects the pride and wisdom of Korean Confucians, who used the Confucian cultural order to serve their country. Therefore, when Korean Confucians called their country the "Little China," they did not mean Korea was subject to China; rather they meant Korea shared China's cultural character.

In this sense, Korean Confucianism clearly contributed to the formation of a sense of national selfhood and sovereignty and became an important force in the unfolding of Korean history. It has provided a universal cultural consciousness that has given rise to a value system directly related to a highly developed view of ethics and politics and has helped stimulate a unique national consciousness directly related to the existence and future prosperity of the Korean people. ◆

T'oegye Thought

Lee Ki-dong

Chosŏn philosopher Yi Hwang (1501-70) perfected the Neo-Confucian theories introduced to Korea from China in the latter part of the Koryŏ Kingdom. Yi, better known by his pen name T'oegye, was born in 1501 in Ongye-ri, Tosan-myŏn, Andong County, Kyŏngsangbuk-do province, the youngest in a family of seven boys and one girl. His father died when he was only seven months old, and Yi was raised by his mother who was very poor. He passed the preliminary provincial civil service examination with top honors at the age of 33 and continued his academic pursuits, while holding a number of government positions, until his death at 70. Yi Hwang is best known for the establishment of a philosophy widely known as T'oegye thought.

T'oegye thought recognizes the relationship among people as essentially interlocked and mutually dependent and sees the individual not as a separate entity but as an inseparable part of a greater whole. In T'oegye thought, one overcomes all difficulties arising from personal limitations and relativity and loves one's fellow man as one loves oneself.

The development of theories by which human beings can overcome the difficulties of everyday life is one of philosophy's most important tasks. It is hardly philosophical, for example, if a man commits suicide or becomes incapable of leading a normal life because of his unrequited love for a woman. A philosophical attitude would be to overcome the misfortune by asking questions such as "What is love?" "Why do I love her?" and "Is there really a reason to love her?" and thus realizing that love is but one part of life.

For the individual, life's gravest shock is one's own death and for society, destruction caused by the struggle for a share of its rewards and the selfish pursuit of profit. If we can solve these problems, everything is easy. Yi Hwang attempted to find solutions to these

Tosan Sŏwon, established by
Yi Hwang (T'oegye) in the mid-16th century

difficult problems.

Like Zhu Xi's Neo-Confucianism, T'oegye thought seeks a systematic and logical way to overcome the fear of death. Yi Hwang used Zhu Xi (also spelled as Chu Hsi) as an example: While ordinary people are apt to give up their studies upon hearing of a friend's death and become depressed by the cruelty of time, Zhu Xi studied even harder. His dedication reflects a system of logic by which the fear of death is overcome, for sorrow at the death of another reminds us that we too are destined to die. Overcoming the fear of death is an important objective of learning; therefore the perfection of learning must bring the greatest joy. Yi Hwang, in fact, said that learning is life's greatest joy.

T'oegye thought teaches that the body cannot be equated with our spiritual essence. The body grows from a tiny being whose life is endowed by its parents and fed on various nutritional foods. If we could take from our body what has been given or formed by others, nothing would be left. Yi Hwang seeks the essential being not in the body but in the mind, which he calls the master of the human body.

There are two minds: the constant mind and the changeable mind. The constant mind always works the same, regardless of time sequences, past, present or future. One example of the constant mind is the longing to see one's parents. The changeable mind is reflected in simple appetites, like the desire to have a cup of tea. The constant mind is shared by all men. In other words, the constant mind is identical with everyone else's constant mind. Yi Hwang meant the same thing when he said, "The human mind is the mind of the world, and my mind is the mind of ten million people."

A life governed by the changeable mind will be meaningless, while a life dictated by the constant mind will be without regret, transcend personal desires and overcome personal relativity and restrictions. If one's life is led by the constant mind, the fear of death can be easily overcome. Yi Hwang's life was a succession of introspections to see if he was led by this constant mind.

What does T'oegye thought say about the struggle and conflict in daily life? Yi Hwang once said: "All human beings share the same spiritual essence, so if I expand my constant mind and reduce my changeable mind until my fellow men and I are integrated into one being, I will experience the pain of others as if it were my own." If we can find the spiritual

In its simplicity and solemn air, sŏwon *architecture reflects the Confucian thought promoted by T'oegye.*

essence shared by all people, as Yi Hwang taught, and love others as dearly as ourselves, all conflict will vanish.

But what about real life, where competition is institutionalized? Suppose a friend and I take the same examination for a scholarship. Yi Hwang's logic would go as follows: If I concede to my friend, I would be sacrificing myself, and if I asked him to give up the scholarship, I would be sacrificing my friend. Both would not be appropriate solutions. The only way out, therefore, is to compete fairly. If I win the scholarship and my joy instantly turns to sorrow because of my friend's failure, my friend would sense my sorrow and any possible conflict would be minimized in a rational manner to achieve harmony.

Yi Hwang's thought is expressed in his major writings which include *Introspections* (*Chasŏngnok*), *A Summary of the Writings of Zhu Xi* (*Chuja-sŏ chŏryo*), *A Survey of Neo-Confucian Theories of the Song, Yuan and Ming Dynasties* (*Song gye Wonmyŏng ihak t'ongnok*), *An Introduction to the Science of Divination* (*Kyemong chŏn'ŭi*), *Commentary*

on the *Mahaprajnaparamita-hridaya-sutra* (*Simgyŏng huron*), *An Illustrated Introduction to Confucianism* (*Sŏnghak sipto*), *A Manual for Health* (*Hwarin simbang*), *Annotations on the Three Classics* (*Samgyŏng sŏgŭi*), and *Annotations on the Four Books* (*Sasŏ sŏgŭi*). He also educated more than 300 disciples, including Yu Sŏng-nyong (1542-1607), Kim Sŏng-il (1538-93), Cho Mok (1542-1607), Yi Tŏk-hong (1541-94), Kwon Ho-mun (1532-87) and Chŏng Ku (1543-1620), and the T'oegye school has continued to exert an influence on modern Confucian scholars.

T'oegye thought was introduced to both China and Japan. In Japan, it left such a deep impact that one could say it virtually launched Confucian studies in that country. Kang Hang (1567-1618), a scholar in T'oegye thought taken to Japan as a prisoner of war, was a mentor to Fujiwara Seika (1561-1619) who founded modern Japanese Confucianism. T'oegye thought continued to exert an influence on Japanese Confucianism down to the Meiji Restoration through scholars such as Hayashi Razan (1583-1657) and Yamazaki Ansai (1618-82). It also

Chŏn'gyodang Hall, the main building at Tosan Sŏwon (above), bears a signboard written by King Sŏnjo as a gesture of the monarch's respect for Yi Hwang. At right, a side gate leads to the verdant woods surrounding the academy.

contributed greatly to the development of Japanese culture.

In China, Liang Qi-chao (1873-1929) was so moved by Yi Hwang's *Illustrated Introduction to Confucianism* when it was published in his country that he composed the following poem.

You are as lofty as bygone teachers.
You have shown the way of truth
In just ten paintings.

You have studied Zhu Xi's teaching
over and over,
Adding luster to it.
And you have added luster to
the teachings of Lian Qi
All people love and follow
your teachings of three-hundred years.

Yi Hwang educated his students at Tosan Sǒwon, a Confucian academy in his hometown of Andong. He began building the academy in March 1557, and it was completed in 1573, five years after his death. Sǒnjo, the reigning king at that time, presented the academy with a sign board written in his own hand.

From its founding until the end of the Chosǒn period, Tosan Sǒwon was the center of the T'oegye School of Thought. Memorial services are still held there twice a year in the second and eighth lunar months, and incense is burned in honor of Yi Hwang on the first and fifteenth days of every month. ◆

A display of writings pertaining to Yi Hwang's life (below); the lake below the academy (right opposite)

120

Sŏwon Confucian Academies

Art Space

During the Koryŏ and Chosŏn dynasties, before the introduction of a modern educational system, state-run educational institutions consisted of the Kukchagam, or National Academy, the Sŏnggyun'gwan, or National Confucian University, the eastern and western *haktang*, or district schools, all located in the capital, and the *hyanggyo*, community schools found in the provinces. These schools taught the Confucian Four Books and Five Classics to prepare students for the *kwagŏ* civil service examination.

In addition to these state-run schools were private village elementary schools, known as *sŏdang*, and private academies which had their own ancestral shrines, called *sŏwon*.

The sŏwon and hyanggyo provided the basic Confucian education during the Chosŏn period. A number of sŏwon still stand today, dignified reminders of the nation's Confucian roots.

With the emergence of the Neo-Confucian literati as Chosŏn's new ruling class, Confucianism replaced Buddhism as the leading ideology, and education came to be of great importance, especially for those aspiring to join the civil service through the kwagŏ examination. State-run educational institutions, such as the Sŏnggyun'gwan, and the local hyanggyo, sŏdang and sŏwon were intended to educate the sons of the ruling class in Confucianism.

By the mid-Chosŏn period, a time of numerous literati purges, the hyanggyo were unable to carry out their responsibilities effectively. Local scholars established sŏwon in response to this deterioration of the hyanggyo, as a way of providing a proper education in Confucianism and fostering a healthy spiritual and moral environment for the demoralized literati.

Mandaeru, at the entrance of Pyŏngsan Sŏwon, is the largest sŏwon pavilion in Korea.

The sŏwon combined elements of private academies and shrines honoring respected Confucian scholars. They resemble the European universities of the Middle Ages in terms of their origins in religion. The sŏwon differed from the *chŏngsa*, or study hall, and the sŏdang because they had these shrines.

The sŏwon trained young men in Neo-Confucian ideology, manners and morals. They also served as centers for regional cultural development and overseers of the spiritual and moral development of the local literati.

Shrines honoring deceased Confucian scholars were built from the Silla period, but it was not until well into the Chosŏn Dynasty that academies and shrines were combined to form new institutions. Korea's first sŏwon was established in 1542 by Chu Se-bung, magistrate of P'unggi County. Chu's successor, Yi Hwang (T'oegye, 1501-70), petitioned the court for a hanging signboard written in the king's hand. The king complied, writing four Chinese characters, Sosu Sŏwon. The academy has been known by this name ever since. The king also donated copies of the Four Books and Five Classics and other Confucian texts.

After the establishment of Sosu Sŏwon, a number of sŏwon were built by local community leaders with their own funds or state subsidies. By the time of King Sukchong at the turn of the 18th century, there were 80 to 90 sŏwon in each province. The sŏwon gradually became economically and politically counterproductive, however, and in 1871, the Taewon'gun, King Kojong's father, closed all but 47 as part of his effort to centralize power under the throne. P'ilam Sŏwon and Musŏng Sŏwon in the Chŏlla region and Pyŏngsan Sŏwon, Tosan Sŏwon, Sosu Sŏwon, Todong Sŏwon and Oksan Sŏwon in the Kyŏngsang region were the most famous of these.

Here we will consider three sŏwon still standing in the Kyŏngsang region: Pyŏngsan Sŏwon, Tosan Sŏwon and Sosu Sŏwon.

Pyŏngsan Sŏwon is found in Pyŏngsandong, Andong County, Kyŏngsangbuk-do province. It was founded as P'ung'ak Sŏdang and given a generous gift of land and texts by Koryŏ King Kongmin who took refuge from Red Turban bandits in Andong during the late 14th century. Kongmin was impressed by the diligence of the students at the sŏdang.

P'ung'ak Sŏdang was moved to Pyŏngsan in 1572 by a respected scholar-official, Yu Sŏngnyong. Only 31 at the time, Yu changed the school's name to Pyŏngsan Sŏwon. After his

Behind two-story Mandaeru Pavilion at Pyŏngsan Sŏwon is a large garden (right) and a man-made pond said to resemble one of the sacred mountains of Chinese folk belief (above).

death, the local students built Chondŏksa, a shrine honoring him. Memorial services honoring him are held every spring and autumn.

Pyŏngsan Sŏwon faces southeast toward the Naktong River. Entering its front gate, the visitor climbs a flight of stone steps passing beneath Mandaeru Pavilion, said to be the largest sŏwon pavilion in Korea. On the other side, one must climb a few more steps to reach the lecture hall, Ipkyodang. In front of the lecture hall is a dormitory which stands parallel to the library. On raised ground behind Ipkyodang is a gate leading to the shrine honoring Yu Sŏng-nyong. A storage room for woodblocks stands to the west of this shrine, and a memorial service preparation office and duty officers quarters stand to the east.

The two-story Mandaeru Pavilion commands a fine view of the surrounding area. A man-made pond near the wall to the west of the pavilion is said to resemble Fangzhangshan, one of three sacred mountains in Chinese folk belief.

A pair of stones supported by pillars stands in front of Chondŏksa. These stones are believed to be the site where a bonfire was built to illuminate the shrine during nocturnal memorial services. Similar stones have been found at Todong, Oksan and Tosan Sŏwons.

The largest extant sŏwon is Tosan Sŏwon in T'oegye-ri, Andong County, Kyŏngsang buk-do province. Yi Hwang (T'oegye, 1501-70), often called Korea's Zhu Xi, taught and developed his ideas here. It began as Tosan Sŏdang and grew to become a sŏwon when Yi's disciples built a shrine honoring him as well as two dormitories and a lecture hall in 1574. The following year, the king gave the sŏwon a hanging signboard written by Han Sŏk-bong (1543-1605), the greatest calligrapher of the period.

Tosan Sŏwon faces southeast over Nakch'ŏn, a stream feeding the Naktong River. It is surrounded by mountains, which Yi Hwang once compared to a folding screen. The main buildings include the lecture hall where Yi taught and the shrine dedicated to him. Entering the outer gate one sees Yi's study. On the left is Nong'unjŏngsa, a dormitory. Nong'unjŏngsa is laid out like the Chinese character gong 工, reflecting Yi Hwang's devotion to a balanced development of the mind and body. Climb a few stairs and one finds Chindomun, the main gate. To either side of the gate is Kwangmyŏngsil Library. The two main dormitories, Pak'yakchae and Hong'ŭijae, stand facing each other. Passing between them, one climbs a flight of stairs to

The main gate at Tosan Sŏwon (above) opens onto a complex campus of dormitories, a shrine dedicated to Yi Hwang, the academy's founder, and a lecture hall where Yi once taught.

Sosu Sŏwon (top), the entrance to a **hyanggyo,** *one of many community schools found in the provinces (above), and Tosan Sisadan where examinations in the Chinese classics* *were held (opposite)*

Chŏn'gyodang Hall, the main building. To the east is Changp'an'gak, where books by Yi Hwang and other scholars as well as woodblocks for the *Twelve Poems of Tosan* (*Tosan sibigok*) are stored.

Yi Hwang's spirit tablet is enshrined in Sangdŏk Shrine behind Chŏn'gyodang. By the west wall of Chŏn'gyodang is Chŏnsach'ŏng where offerings for memorial services are prepared.

The storage hall for ceremonial wine and paraphernalia is reached through a small gate at the end of the west yard of Chŏn'gyodang. Okchin'gak, in which some of Yi Hwang's possessions are displayed, was built in 1970.

Sosu Sŏwon is located in Sunhŭng-myŏn, Yŏngju County, Kyŏngsangbuk-do province. In 1542, Chu Se-bung built a shrine dedicated to An Hyang (1243-1306), the Koryŏ scholar who introduced Neo-Confucianism to Korea. An was born and raised in Sunhŭng and studied in nearby P'unggi. In 1543, Chu opened

Paegun-dong Sŏwon, the forerunner of Sosu Sŏwon. Sosu Sŏwon means "Academy of Received Learning," a name suggested by Sin Kwang-han, an official in the Office of Special Advisors, to honor An Hyang .

Sosu Sŏwon was the first sŏwon to be honored with a hanging signboard donated by the royal court and was thus the first "royal charter" private academy. Until the Taewon'gun's crackdown in the late 19th century, the academies, whose number had increased to more than 100 by the turn of the 17th century, received government grants of books, land and slaves and were exempt from taxes and corvée.

Sosu Sŏwon stands in a grove of old pine trees near Chukkye Stream. Entering the main gate, the visitor faces Myŏngnyundang, the lecture hall. Four dormitory buildings—Chikpangjae, Ilsinjae, Hakkujae and Chirakchae—are located to the left and rear of the lecture hall. To the right of Chikpangjae

are shrines dedicated to An Hyang, An Chuk, An Po and Chu Se-bung, and the Chŏnsach'ong, where ritual vessels used in Confucian memorial services are housed. When building Sosu Sŏwon, Chu Se-bung used a Chinese academy founded by Zhu Xi as a model. He also adopted the curriculum and rules of conduct of that academy.

The portrait of An Hyang housed in the shrine here was commissioned by Koryŏ King Ch'ungsuk in 1318, 12 years after An's death. As an indication of his respect for An, the king had a Yuan Chinese artist paint the portrait from an original painted during the subject's lifetime. The An clan first enshrined the portrait in Sunhŭng Hyanggyo, but during the literati purge of 1457, they had it moved it to the family shrine. In 1543, it was enshrined at Sosu Sŏwon. The oldest extant painting in Korea, it is a realistic painting which is neither Buddhist nor Confucian in style. Because it was painted from an original portrait, it is

believed to be a faithful depiction.

Sosu Sŏwon is also home to a painting of Confucius and his 72 disciples. Confucius is seated on a throne while his disciples sit in rows before him. This work was among the paintings, ritual vessels and portraits brought from Yuan China at the instruction of An Hyang in 1303. The painting is said to have once hung in the main hall of the Sŏnggyun'gwan. It was later moved to Sunhŭng Hyanggyo, then enshrined in the portrait room of Sosu Sŏwon's lecture hall. The painting is important to the study of the introduction of Confucianism and Neo-Confucianism to Korea, although scholars are not certain it is an original.

A pair of stone flagpole supports stand in the pine grove to the right of Sosu Sŏwon's entrance. They once belonged to Suksu Temple which stood on this site before it was destroyed to make room for the sŏwon.

Sosu Sŏwon survived Taewon'gun's crackdown, but it was banned from carrying out any activities after that. In 1975, local Confucianists began repairing the academy, and a new exhibition hall was built.

These sŏwon stand with mountains to their rear and rivers in front. They provide the perfect natural environment for study. Tosan Sŏwon is exceptional for the beauty of its surroundings.

Although frequently criticized for fostering factionalism and academic conflicts, the sŏwon have been credited with a creative contribution to education and the promotion of Neo-Confucianism, the mainstay of Chosŏn culture. Because of the independence and spirit of equality it fostered, Sosu Sŏwon played an especially important role in the rise of the local Neo-Confucian literati, and the private sŏwon filled the educational gap created when state-run schools deteriorated under the devastating misrule of King Kwanghaegun in the early 17th century. ♦

Surrounded by old pine forests, the sŏwon provided the perfect environment for study. Clockwise from near right: the woods outside Sosu Sŏwon; the signboard marking the entrance of Pyŏngsan Sŏwon; Kyŏng'yŏnjŏng at Sosu Sŏwon; and a pair of stone flagpole supports near Sosu Sŏwon.

131

Sŏnggyun'gwan: Sanctuary of Korean Confucianism

An Byung-ju

Some Western scholars say Confucianism is dead, that it has gone the way of aristocratic society, but they are mistaken. Confucianism is still popular among a sizable group of Koreans. The 1985 census revealed that 2.8 percent of Korea's religious population is Confucian.

Twice each year, in the second and eighth lunar months, a ceremony is held at a shrine on the grounds of Sung Kyun Kwan

University to honor Confucius and some of his greatest Chinese disciples and Korean Confucian scholars. Korea is the only place in the world where this traditional ritual, Sŏkchŏnje in Korean, is preserved in its original form.

When you enter the gate to the university in downtown Seoul, you will find a cluster of traditional buildings to the right. These buildings have been known as Munmyo from early times. One of the buildings is the main shrine, Taesŏngjŏn, where the sacred tablets of Confucius and other sages are housed. The Sŏkchŏnje ritual takes place in the courtyard of this shrine.

The ceremony begins when all the officers, musicians and dancers have taken their positions. Confucian rituals emphasize ceremony over music and dance. Each time an officer makes an offering, eight rows of eight students dance rhythmically, bowing left, right and center. In the first part of the rite, the dancers hold a flute in one hand and a dragon-headed stick in the other. In the second half of the rite, they beat wooden hammers on wooden shields. Musicians play traditional musical instruments, including a graded set of 16 stone slabs (p'yŏn'gyŏng) and bronze bell chimes (p'yŏnjong) to accompa-

ny the reverent slow-motion bowing, the ritualized incantation of poems and the offerings of "divine wine."

The Munmyo Confucian Academy and shrine, designated a national treasure in modern times, was constructed in 1398 during the reign of Chosŏn's founder, King T'aejo. It was renamed Sŏnggyun'gwan in the early 14th century. (Sŏnggyun'gwan is the McCune-Reischauer romanization. However, the modern university uses its own spelling, Sung Kyun Kwan.)

The name was borrowed from the *Book of Rites (Yegi)*, one of 13 Confucian classics. The Confucian academy dates back to the early days of the Silla and Koguryŏ kingdoms but Sung Kyun Kwan University claims 1398 as the year of its official founding.

Despite numerous ups and downs, between 1398 and 1894, Sŏnggyun'gwan's basic curriculum focused on Confucian thought and values. From 1895, it was transformed into a modern university teaching a wide range of subjects.

The major buildings located on the grounds of Munmyo are Taesŏngjŏn (Main Hall), Tongmu (East Hall), Sŏmu (West Hall), Myŏngnyundang (Lecture Hall), Tongjae (East Dormitory), Sŏjae (West Dormitory), Chŏnggyŏngdang (Library) and Chinsasiktang (Dining Hall).

When Confucianism was in its prime, the sacred tablets of Confucius and 132 Chinese disciples and Korean scholars were housed in the Main Hall, East Hall and West Hall, but later 94 of these were withdrawn. Today the tablets of Confucius and 38 Chinese disciples and Korean scholars are enshrined in the Main Hall. The East and West Halls are empty.

After the collapse of the Chosŏn Dynasty and the institution of the Japanese colonial pol-

Rites honoring Confucius, his Chinese disciples and Korean Confucian scholars are held in the courtyard in front of Munmyo Confucian Academy's Main Hall (right and preceding page). Lectures were once held in Myŏngnyundang (below), and students lived in the dormitories (above).

icy aimed at obliterating Korean culture, Sŏnggyun'gwan, which had played such a vital role in national education and culture, was reduced to a private institute. When Korea was liberated from Japanese rule in 1945, Confucianists around the country consolidated the properties of 231 *hyanggyo* (local Confucian academies) and established Sung Kyun Kwan University to carry on the Confucian educational tradition.

Confucianism is deeply rooted in the Korean psyche. It is very difficult to tell what in life is truly Confucian and what is not. Koreans do not think of themselves as Confucians, though the Korean way of doing things is often Confucian. This tendency is reflected in social life, familial relations, interactions between generations, between men and women and between friends, as well as in Koreans' respect for the elderly, their thirst for education, and much more.

Critics say Confucianism is a system of subordinations: of son to father, of younger brother to elder, of wife to husband, of subject to central authority. They claim the concept has failed to keep pace with Korea's modernization. Confucianism, however, embraces a moral and ethical system, a philosophy of life and interpersonal relations, a code of conduct and a method of government all viable enough to have taken the place of more orthodox religious beliefs in China for thousands of years. The same held true in Korea for centuries.

Confucianism came to Korea around the same time as Buddhism and had a powerful influence on social and governmental institutions. It was not until the establishment of the Chosŏn Dynasty and its oppression of Buddhism in the late 14th century that Confucianism was elevated to the status of a state cult, a position left vacant by the suppression of Buddhism.

Education in the Chinese Classics, and especially the ethical and philosophical books of Confucius, became the sole basis of education. Erudition was the only path to social and political success. State examinations, which many failed and took over and over again for years while their families supported them, were the criteria for a scholar-official's advancement. Indeed, officialdom was the only career that a man of talent and breeding could honorably pursue.

Confucianism at best insured stability and security within the system but was deplorably inadequate in meeting challenges from outside, whether military, political or social. Korea thus became a "Hermit Kingdom" and remained one until the painful period late in the l9th century when the old system eroded under pressure from Japan and the Western powers.

It is encouraging to note that some Western scholars are studying the Confucian values still alive in the Chinese Classics and are seriously considering the reintroduction of Confucian philosophy in our modern world where ethics and morals have been shattered by individualism. At the same time, Korean Confucians are studying ways to make Confucian values more relevant to modern life, emphasizing harmony and discarding the system of subordination. ◆

Confucian rites emphasize ceremony; their dance and music are solemn. As senior officials make offerings (above), eight rows of eight students perform a slow, stylized dance (right).

Confucian Influences on Education

Park Sun-young

Korea's first public educational institute appeared in 372 when Koguryŏ established its National Confucian Academy (*T'aehak*) modeled after Chinese educational institutions. The establishment of the educational machinery for the inculcation of Confucian values, such as loyalty to the king, was essential to the development of a bureaucratic structure that could reinforce the sovereign's power.

Little is known about Paekche's educational system, but scholars have found considerable information on Silla's early educational efforts. From its early years, the Silla Kingdom had a youth training system, which eventually developed into the *hwarangdo*, a semi-official social educational system embracing elements from Shamanism, Confucianism and Taoism. The hwarangdo was basically a system for disciplining youth in Buddhist thought and martial arts. Inculcating loyalty and patriotism, it later served to unify the Silla people in their efforts to consolidate the peninsula.

Silla's territorial expansion following unification required more bureaucrats capable of governing under the authoritarian power of the throne. The National Confucian College (*Kukhak*), modeled after a Chinese public institute for higher Confucian education, was thus established in 682.

Thanks to an abundance of historic records, scholars know a great deal about the organization and operation of Silla's Kukhak. Its curriculum, which focused on the inculcation of loyalty to the monarch and filial piety to parents, was divided into three courses of study based on elective subjects including philosophy, history and literature. Upon graduation, students took a state examination in the Confucian classics and were appointed to public posts according to their scores. This was the first of a long tradition of state civil service examinations, which later came to be known as the *kwagŏ*.

Though Confucianism dominated formal education during the Three Kingdoms and the Unified Silla periods, its influence was, for the most part, limited to the socially privileged elite class. Culture at the grass root level was dominated by Buddhism, which had been assimilated through the native Shamanism. Buddhist monks were revered as preceptors. Many were respected teachers in politics, military tactics, philosophy and the arts. We can thus assume that Buddhism was the dominant element in informal education at that time.

Toward the end of a millennium of rule, Silla was increasingly beleaguered by unrest caused by its rigid social system and internal political strife. As the central government's power waned, the landed gentry in the countryside emerged as a powerful political and economic force. The individualistic doctrine of the then popular meditative school of Buddhism, in which all people were believed able to achieve the Buddha nature through meditation, provided an ideological basis for an assertion of political independence from the central government.

Silla thus crumbled and was eventually absorbed by Koryŏ, born of struggles among local powers. Koryŏ succeeded Silla in many ways, including its cultural and social structures. Spiritually, it relied heavily on Buddhism, while politically, it aspired to Confucian values.

Koryŏ's educational system was basically no different from that of Silla. A National University (*Kukchagam*) was established in the capital in 992, and local public schools (*hyanggyo*) were operated in the countryside. All were dedicated to the inculcation of Confucian ideals and precepts.

Kukchagam, the kingdom's highest educational institute, was similar to Silla's Kukhak; however, its curriculum included not only Confucian classics but also practical subjects such as law, calligraphy, accounting and, in later years, military tactics. By the early 12th

Chŏnju Hyanggyo, one of many traditional public schools found in the countryside

century, the National University comprised six separate colleges and, later with the addition of military studies, seven, classified by field of study and the students' social standing.

The National University in the capital took care of advanced education, while the hyanggyo taught mainly Chinese classics and history. In fact, the hyanggyo were much like today's middle schools. In later years, similar academies, known as *haktang*, were established in the capital.

Private academies and village elementary schools flourished during the mid-Koryŏ period as a number of well-known Confucian scholars founded schools. Twelve institutions, known as the "Twelve Assemblies" (*Sibi to*), distinguished themselves by offering a quality education that sometimes challenged the standards of the National University.

It is not clear when the *sŏdang*, or village elementary school, appeared on the Korean educational scene, though some scholars date it to the Koguryŏ period. Historical records indicate the sŏdang were common throughout the country by the mid-Koryŏ period. Curriculum and quality varied; some sŏdang taught only rudimentary reading and writing of Chinese ideographs while others offered advanced courses approximating college-level study.

Toward the late Koryŏ period, education in applied studies was systemized to produce a ready supply of low-ranking bureaucrats. The National University was reorganized to concentrate on advanced Confucian studies by removing law, calligraphy and accounting from its curriculum completely. These three subjects, together with seven other non-Confucian courses, including medicine, music, dance, foreign languages and astronomy, were taught at concerned government agencies where proficiency in such areas was needed. A similar system had existed from the Silla period.

The introduction of Neo-Confucianism from China was by far the most important event in the educational history of the late Koryŏ period. Throughout Koryŏ's early years, Buddhism and Confucianism coexisted without much conflict. In fact, Buddhism enjoyed precedence over Confucianism. Renowned Confucian scholars, who believed Confucianism was no match for Buddhism in philosophical depth, were always well versed in Buddhist texts. However, with the advent of Neo-Confucianism, which offered a metaphysical explanation for the origins of man and the universe, Koryŏ scholars began to reassess Buddhist thought from a fresh perspective.

By the late Koryŏ period, the Buddhist community was suffering from rampant internal corruption. Temple land holdings had grown to the point where they posed a grave threat to the national treasury. Neo-Confucian scholars began criticizing Buddhism's excesses and eventually masterminded the establishment of a new kingdom.

The Chosŏn Kingdom, founded in 1392, adopted Confucianism as its state doctrine and endeavored to ingrain Confucian values among its people, while repressing Buddhism. In China, where it originated, Confucianism changed with the times, but in Korea it remained static. Neo-Confucianism, intolerant of any revisions, formed the mainstream of Confucian studies and thought for five centuries.

Neo-Confucianism explains all existence in terms of two inseparable elements, *i* (*li* in Chinese), which might be compared to the Greek Logos, and *ki* (*qi* in Chinese), an energizing element. Actions, reactions and matter exist in the sphere of ki while the principles or laws behind them and the formative elements of matter exist within i.

Similar in some ways to Kant's Practical Reason, Neo-Confucianism asserts that the i side of human nature is endowed with four positive elements—sympathy, righteousness, humbleness, and wisdom—which separate right from wrong, while humanity's ki side is quite detrimental, being related to the material and self-centered desires.

In Confucianism, a man becomes a "sage" when he has sublimated his ki and achieved a state of i. A man striving to become a sage is called a *kunja*, or "great man." *Sŏnbi*, the literati so idealized in traditional Korean society, is another name for a great man. He strives to attain perfection of the i, and at the same time, to lead people in the right direction.

The first objective is achieved through learning and moral cultivation, mutually complementary processes. Learning without self-cultivation results in an accumulation of dead knowledge, while the practice of self-cultivation without learning often ends in tunnel vision. Correct leadership is achieved through education and good government.

In Chosŏn society, great men served in the bureaucracy so as to lead people through moral government. After retirement, they served as teachers. A *kunja*, or "great man" was, in short, a scholar, an introspective student, an educator, and a politician.

The literati were the ruling class in this Confucian-dominated society. Below them came the middle class, which included low-ranking officials, then the commoners engaged in farming, trade and crafts or industry. At the lowest level of the social strata were the low-born, slaves and outcasts.

The function of each class was clearly defined and observed with unquestioned rigidity. A literatus never engaged in manual labor; he was a student dedicated to self-cultivation. Likewise, a commoner must work hard at his trade and never indulge in books or study.

Confucianism's predominance brought forth an efflorescence of Neo-Confucian scholarship, surpassing that of China, but on the other hand, it stifled any possibility of scientific or technological development. It also gave birth to a general disdain for manual labor. The kwagŏ national civil service examination was institutionalized in the early years of Koryŏ as a means of recruiting government officials. During the Chosŏn period, the system took on even greater importance and was enforced with strict objectivity to ensure equal opportunities for members of the ruling class whose number had increased greatly. Success in the kwagŏ was regarded not only as a personal honor but also as a matter of great pride for the entire clan and the most desirable expression of filial piety. While promoting educational zeal and scholarly activities in general, this attitude tended to reduce scholarship to a means of preparing for the national examination.

The kwagŏ reflects a great deal about the educational system of the Chosŏn period. The state examination was conducted in three categories: civil, military and miscellaneous. The examinations were supposed to be held every three years but were administered more frequently in the form of special examinations commemorating important national events.

The examinations for civil service were conducted on two levels: the licentiate or lower level (sogwa) and the erudite or higher level (taegwa). The licentiate examination, a preliminary test determining candidates for the taegwa, was held at various locales throughout the country and was offered in two forms: the classics licentiate examination (saengwon'gwa) to test proficiency in the Confucian Classics, philosophy and history, and the literary licentiate examination (chinsagwa), which tested proficiency in composing various Chinese literary forms.

Candidates who passed the classics examination were called saengwon, while those who passed the literary examination were called chinsa. Both were qualified to apply for the higher level taegwa examination, to enter

Located on a hillside, the terraced Tosan Sŏwon is one of Korea's loveliest sŏwon. 141

Sŏnggyun'gwan, the National Confucian Academy in the capital, and were publicly acknowledged as a true sŏnbi. They were also given the choice of embarking on a civil service career.

The higher level examination was aptly called taegwa, literally the "Big Examination," for it was the gateway to high officialdom. Technically, all saengwon and chinsa were eligible to apply but those currently enrolled in the Sŏnggyun'gwan had a natural advantage. The candidates were tested in their knowledge of the Confucian Classics and literature and asked to write an essay on government policy.

Those who passed the taegwa had one more test to take, this time in the presence of the king. The palace examination (chŏnsi) was the final step by which a candidates was ranked and appointed to a government post.

Military examinations (mugwa) were also conducted in three stages: regional, central and palace examinations. Martial arts, including archery, marksmanship and riding, were the most important subject in the regional examination. The second examination at the capital consisted of three parts: the Confucian Classics, military science and an elective subject. The palace examination required a mastery in martial arts and comprehensive knowledge of military science. Candidates were generally from military families or low-ranking government officials.

Miscellaneous examinations (chap-kwa) covered subjects deemed less important in the Confucian sense. The use of the word "miscellaneous" (chap) reflects Chosŏn's Confucian disdain for anything less than Confucian studies.

These "unimportant" subjects included foreign languages, medicine, astronomy, law, geography and other technical skills. Examinations were conducted in two stages: first at the regional level and later at the capital. Most candidates came from the middle class.

The kwagŏ system reveals much about the educational patterns of the Chosŏn period. Public education was divided into two distinct categories: Confucian studies and the study of things not Confucianism. Confucian studies were carried out at public educational institutes, while other subjects were taught at workshops set up by concerned government agencies.

The public school system comprised four haktang in Seoul and one hyanggyo in each county throughout the country, both similar in function and educational level to today's high schools. The haktang operated as they had in the Koryŏ period, although their number was reduced.

Hyanggyo, on the other hand, were accorded great care and respect because their maintenance and operation were one of the seven major responsibilities of a county magistrate and thus were directly linked to his personal advancement.

The curriculum of the Sŏnggyun'gwan, haktang and hyanggyo consisted mainly of reading and understanding Confucian classics, literary writing and calligraphy. Students at the Sŏnggyun'gwan were encouraged to cultivate their learning through lively discussions and were graded in five distinct categories.

Sŏnggyun'gwan, the only national university, was housed in magnificent buildings complete with a library, a Confucian shrine and auxiliary facilities. The shrine housed memorial tablets of Confucius, his disciples, and Korean and Chinese Confucian sages. Confucian academies were not simply institutes of learning but sacred grounds where Confucian rites were held. The haktang in the capital, however, did not have Confucian shrines because their students attended the Sŏnggyun'gwan rites.

Sŏnggyun'gwan students were accorded great privileges and considerable autonomy. They were allowed to voice their ideas on national policies and joined in collective protest.

Two kinds of private educational organizations prevailed in the Chosŏn period: sŏwon and sŏdang. Sŏwon, private academies which had their own shrines, had long been in existence in China. They were introduced to Korea during the early Chosŏn period by Chu Se-bung, magistrate of P'unggi County, who established an academy modeled after the Chinese prototype. Paeg'un-dong Sŏwon (later Sosu Sŏwon) consisted of a shrine honoring An Hyang (1243-1306), the Koryŏ scholar who introduced Neo-Confucianism to Korea, and a lecture hall for educational activities.

Encouraged by the attention Sosu Sŏwon received from the court, numerous private academies with shrines dedicated to deceased statesmen or Confucian scholars, sprouted up across the country. The sŏwon differed from Sŏnggyun'gwan or hyanggyo in that they had private shrines and functioned as educational

Confucian scholars line up to perform rites to Confucius, some of his greatest disciples and Korean Confucian scholars at Munmyo Shrine on the campus of Sung Kyun Kwan University.

institutes at the same time. Their curriculum consisted of the Confucian Classics, Neo-Confucian commentaries, and training in literary composition. Unlike public schools, they were usually located in scenic places, far removed from residential areas, and their students were allowed to pursue their studies in a relatively liberal atmosphere.

Local literati centered their scholarly activities around the sŏwon, and as a result, the schools were often the starting point for philosophical movements that affected policy-making in the central government. As time passed, the system deteriorated, fueling factional strife. In 1868, the Taewon'gun, King Kojong's father, ordered taxes levied on the sŏwon, and in 1871, he drastically reduced their number to 47.

The sŏwons' success had contributed to a deterioration of the hyanggyo and the Sŏnggyun'gwan. Soon a movement aimed at establishing a fixed training program for candidates who had passed the taegwa was launched. The sŏwon were rated a step lower than the Sŏnggyun'gwan, but some were rated more highly than the national university.

Sŏdang, the village schools, already ubiquitous during the Koryŏ period, were even more common under the Chosŏn regime. Every village of 20 to 30 households had at least one, if not two. The sŏdang operated in various forms. Some were set up in private residences, where the master of the household taught a few village children. Others were established by ordinary villagers who pitched in to hire a teacher for their children.

Though its main purpose was preparing children for advancement to the hyanggyo or haktang, the sŏdang curriculum was not always elementary. Depending on the academic achievements of the teacher, it sometimes extended beyond training in rudimentary Chinese ideographs to cover the Confucian Classics at the middle school level. Students ranged in age from five or six to adulthood.

In a typical class, the teacher read and interpreted the Confucian text written in Chinese ideographs. Students repeated after him and practiced at home until they memorized the text. They were not allowed to advance to the next lesson if they could not recite the text perfectly.

Chosŏn's Confucian-oriented society was a patrilineal system of extended families ruled by a strict patriarchy. The relationship between men and women is graphically exemplified by the traditional custom of referring to men as the "outside" and women as the "inside." Men resided in the outer part of the house while women stayed in the inner part of the building. Men were concerned with business outside the home; household affairs were below them. The family economy and management thus fell to the women. Confined to the innermost part of the house, they were not allowed to take an interest in things outside the home. Indeed, they rarely went outside, except on very special occasions.

It was women's job to serve men. Academic achievements were completely unnecessary, even dangerous for they might jeopardize the feminine virtue of obedience to men.

Women were thus excluded from all schools, private or public. Their education consisted of home training in womanly manners and virtues, skills needed to carry out household chores, such as cooking, laundry, sewing, embroidery and preparations for gatherings and family ancestral rituals.

According to Confucian norms, four virtues were essential to a model wife and mother: chastity and loyalty to her husband, discrete manners and quiet speech, an unadorned yet clean appearance, and proficiency in home management skills.

To instill these virtues in women, the government published vernacular collections of admonitory episodes and biographies of exemplary women. Parents wrote admonitions for their daughters of marriageable age to bear in mind. Some literati taught their daughters the *Lesser Learning* (*Sohak*), a Confucian ethics textbook that described the etiquette and disposition required of ideal "inside" persons. However, women's academic education seldom extended beyond the vernacular *han'gŭl* script and rudimentary Chinese ideographs.

In short, women's education during the Chosŏn period was irregular at best and conducted at home, or more accurately, acquired naturally through everyday experience. If there was a conscious effort to educate women, it was with the intention of instilling in them the "virtues" required of women in male chauvinistic Confucian society.

It was only in the late 19th century, the final years of the Chosŏn Kingdom, that women began to be recognized as independent human beings.

The infusion of Confucian values in the minds of the people was one of the major responsibilities of the local magistrate. He did this by circulating vernacular publications on ethical codes and manners for women as well as educational materials on farming, sericulture and other professional skills, also in han'gŭl. The local magistrate was also responsible for educational activities in his jurisdiction. He was directly or indirectly involved in the operation of hyanggyo and disciplinary programs led by village elders. Hyanggyo occasionally printed books on ethics and manners for children and women and offered special morals courses. The teacher at the local sŏdang was always revered for his learning, and his counsel was often sought by the villagers.

The sŏdang were essential to the operation of the *hyangyak* village code, a system of local self-government. The hyangyak system originated in China and was refined by Zhu Xi. It was introduced to Korea during the Koryŏ period together with Neo-Confucianism. Several attempts to put the hyangyak system into effect had been made by the government and literati-officials from the early years of Chosŏn. However, it was not until the mid-Chosŏn period that it spread throughout the country under the influence of Yi Hwang and Yi I, champions of Neo-Confucian thought.

The hyangyak code was basically a mode of neighborhood self-government infused with a spirit of community justice and mutual assistance and enforced by respected village elders.

In Chosŏn's Confucian society, everything was evaluated from a moral perspective. Throughout its 500-year rule, statesmanship and education focused on instilling moral values in the general populace. These moral values meant a certain order in human relationships, an order realized through rules of propriety governing details of etiquette and ceremonies and, in a broader sense, proper attitude and expression. Morals defined the role of every member of the society: fathers and mothers, husbands and wives, sons and daughters, teachers and students, ruler and subjects.

The rectification of names and responsibilities was the paramount creed of life for the Chosŏn people and especially for the sŏnbi. This cultural tradition lives on today. Modern Korean society is in many ways caught between this tradition and the industrialization process.

Education on names and the responsibilities they entail was extremely thorough in both theory and practice. Neo-Confucianism was structured on the basis of rigid class distinctions and male-centered values. The tendency toward authoritarianism, sexual discrimination and an aversion to manual labor is a Confucian legacy still very much felt in educational sectors today.

This educational tradition has caused the Korean mind to become inflexible and less understanding. Even today, an uncompromising person is seen as a man of integrity, not an extremist.

On the other hand, Confucianism has provided Koreans with a rational way of thinking, a strong moral sense and a zeal for education. The Confucian precepts and educational tradition to which Chosŏn society adhered with such unmitigated thoroughness are not entirely negative. There is much to be developed and perpetuated. ◆

Surrounded by forests and streams, the sŏwon provided a quiet, peaceful environment conducive to thought and study. Pyŏngsan Sŏwon in Andong stands on a mountain slope facing the Naktong River.

Confucian Rites

Art Space

Chongmyo Royal Ancestral Memorial Rites

The royal ancestral memorial services of the Chosŏn Dynasty are still performed each spring at Chongmyo, the royal shrine in downtown Seoul. In 1995 the rites, their accompanying music and dance and the shrine buildings were added to UNESCO's World Heritage List in an effort to preserve such irreplaceable cultural assets. The most important government events of the Chosŏn calendar, the rites are complicated and often ponderously slow, but they offer an invaluable glimpse at Confucianism in practice. The rites consist of bows and offerings of wine and food by senior officiants, interspersed with performances of court music.

The Chongmyo rites are governed by exacting rules. Costumes, music, dance, sacrificial offerings and the utensils used to hold offerings are strictly regulated by Confucian concepts of courtesy. The rites, held once a year in modern times, have been simplified in recent years but continue to play an important role in the preservation of traditional music and dance genres as well as Confucian values.

149

Sŏkchŏn Rites

Biannual rites honoring Confucius, his Chinese disciples and eminent Korean Confucian scholars are held at the Munmyo Shrine on the campus of Sung Kyun Kwan University. The Sŏkchŏn ceremony, literally "rites offering libations," consists of offerings of food and drink before the spirit tablets of Confucius and other sages. The highly stylized rites, no longer performed in China where they originated, serve to foster Confucian values of loyalty and filial piety.

Classical court music, performed on traditional instruments such as the hun, *a globular flute made of clay (below), and* Ilmu, *a line dance (right), are integral parts of the Sŏkchŏn rites.*

The ceremony is conducted by a head official who addresses the spirits and directs the musicians and dancers. Offerings to the spirits include wine, raw meat and various grains. In the courtyard of Munmyo Shrine are two old trees symbolizing the Three Bonds and the Five Moral Disciplines (clockwise from top).

VILLAGE RITES

The ritual significance of Korea's village rites has been diluted in modern times, but they remain potent reflections of the Korean people's traditional reverence for the power of nature. Today village rites are generally celebrations of life, tools used to promote community. By studying them, we can learn a great deal about traditional lifestyles and thought patterns.

As Professor Chang Chong-ryong notes, the term "village rite" is a sweeping expression, referring to ceremonies and rituals linked to a single community. He, and other contributors, look at the different kinds of rites, creating a colorful mosaic of spiritual life in rural society.

Village Rites:
A Rich Communal Heritage

Im Dong-kwon

Koreans venerate their gods, of which there are legions, in many ways according to their personal needs and the unique powers of each god. Household gods, such as the birth god, land god, and kitchen god, are invoked when needed by families or individuals, whereas village tutelary deities are invoked on a regular basis with all residents of the village participating in the rites. On occasion, however, individuals make personal offerings to village deities.

More than 500 traditional rituals are practiced in Korea today. The vast majority honor communally revered deities, known by different names in different regions. Among these, 114 honor mountain deities, 109 village tutelary deities, 68 tutelary deities, 23 mountain and river deities, 23 ancestral deities, 11 tree deities, 11 land deities, and 164 other miscellaneous deities. Mountain deities clearly dominate the list.

Why do Koreans worship mountain spirits and village tutelary deities? If the entire community participates in these rites, they must bind the villagers together somehow. By looking at the rites and the reasons behind them, we can learn much about Korean beliefs and traditions.

Historical records attest to the Korean penchant for the worship of mountain and river spirits. According to Tang Chinese sources, the people of Silla and Paekche held rites to these spirits. The *Memorabilia of the Three Kingdoms* recounts a heavenly god's descent to Mt. T'aebaek, and tells of Tan'gun, the founder of the Korean nation, who became a mountain spirit after his death. It also states that spirits of great mountains appeared and danced at the courts of the Silla kings Hŏn'gang and Kyŏngdŏk.

Mountain worship was important in the Koryŏ period as well. Local officials and resi-

dents held rituals to the mountain spirits at many great mountains, and records indicate the court dispatched female shamans to four major mountains—Mt. Tŏkchŏk, Mt. Paeg'ak, Mt. Song'ak and Mt. Mongmyŏk—to officiate at the rites.

Korea's foundation myths attest to the Korean people's reverence for spirits living in mountains. Mountains were a source of food—fruit, wild vegetables and game—and other daily necessities. However, hunting and gathering food in the mountains were dangerous enterprises. There were many wild animals and other perils. Mountains were places of mystery and danger, where people needed divine protection. Perhaps this was why people believed in mountain deities and performed rites honoring them.

With the gradual development of agriculture, Koreans' dependence on the mountains for their livelihood diminished. They went into the mountains less frequently, and as a result, they had to move their protective deities closer to home. Hence, the shrines of the mountain deities were relocated to the villages. Appeals to the mountain deities indicate that villagers were mainly interested in preventing disaster, enjoying a good harvest and general prosperity. Because of their limited ability to defend themselves, people looked to the mountain spirits for protection. They designated the mountain to the north of the village *chinsan*, or guardian mountain, and believed that the deity residing there would protect the village and all its residents.

Sŏnang is a tutelary deity believed to dwell at the entrance of a village or on a nearby hillside. It protects the village from evil spirits, disasters and epidemics. The shrine to the sŏnang is called *sŏnangdang*. It is usually a large pile of stones, an old tree with a rope tied loosely

*Spirit poles (*sottae*) are worshiped during community rites appealing for village welfare and a bountiful harvest or catch. The poles are often topped with wooden or stone birds thought to ward off evil spirits.*

Village rites bring communities together,
promoting a sense of common destiny and cooperation.
This scene from communal rites in Ŭnsan,
Ch'ungch'ŏngnam-do province,
suggests the level of community participation.

159

around the trunk, or a combination of the two. When passing a sŏnangdang, it is customary to add a stone to the pile or tie a straw rope on the tree.

Rites to the sŏnang are held on behalf of the entire village. Women perform the rites on the First Moon, whenever the village is experiencing difficulties, or when the villagers have a special request. The rites often stretch on for several days, as in the case of Tano rites held in Kangnŭng in Kangwon-do province beginning on the fifth day of the Fifth Moon.

These rites are officiated by shamans and local officials. They involve "escorting" the male sŏnang of nearby Taegwallyŏng Pass to the shrine of the female sŏnang in Kangnŭng. The Taegwallyŏng sŏnang is believed to have great influence over the village, and is often invoked in prayers for a good harvest on both land and sea and to request safe passage for travelers crossing the rugged mountains to Seoul.

In some villages, mountain spirits are considered village tutelaries. The rites honoring them are referred to as village rites. Shrines to them are similar to those honoring other village gods.

The shrine to a village tutelary deity is found at the foot of a hill behind the village or near the entrance to the village, although in some places it is located in the village itself. The shrine usually consists of an old tree, a group of trees, a pile of rocks, a large rock, almost anything natural. There is often a pair of spirit posts (*changsŭng*) or spirit poles (*sottae*), or both, nearby.

Most village rites are held on a regular basis, at the beginning of the new year and on other significant occasions. Rain rites were only held in times of drought. Koreans were an agrarian people, generally farming rice, so drought meant crop failure and starvation. The whole country suffered. Even the king participated in rain rites. During the purification period prior to the rite, the king refrained from visiting his lady's chamber and ate frugal meals. Taking responsibility for his lack of virtue, the king promised to lead a frugal life and ordered the number of side dishes at royal meals reduced to a bare minimum. Clean water was brought from rivers or wells to wash the altar area, the market was temporarily relocated, and all impure activities that might enrage the heavens were prohibited.

Village rites are also held in honor of the Dragon King, ruler of the waters. Shrines to the water deity are usually held near a river or a stream or on top of a mountain. As part of the

Spirit posts (**changsŭng**) are found at the entrances of many villages.
After erecting the posts, villagers offer bows, prayers and gifts of food and drink.

rite, a large bonfire is built at the top of a mountain so the flames will reach the sky.

Village rites honor deities revered by all villagers, so it is only natural that all villagers participate. Before a rite, a number of villagers are selected as officiants, for example, the master of ceremonies, the chief cook and so or etc. They must be of impeccable reputation and respected by everyone in the village. They also should not have attended a funeral during the past year. Their duties include preparations for the rite, such as preparing the food offerings, and the actual performance of the rite.

For a set period prior to the rite, the officiants must purify their minds and bodies through prayer and cold baths. This period of purification actually applies to all villagers. Certain rules and taboos must be observed. For example, they should not look at a corpse, visit a family in mourning, kill an animal, or

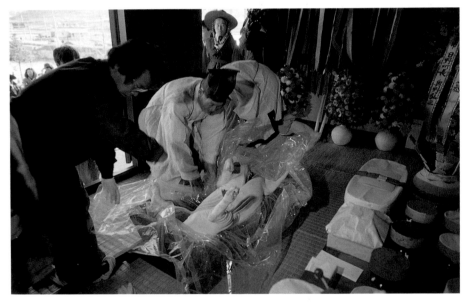

The villagers pool their resources, in cash or kind, to provide offerings of food and drink (above) and to pay for the services of a nong'ak *farmers' band (right).*

contaminate the well from which the water for the rite will be drawn. They must also be careful of what they say and do. Anyone who has traveled in other areas and seen a corpse or butchered an animal is prohibited from entering the village until the rite is completed.

The vessels used to hold food for the ritual must be new and all food freshly prepared. A great deal of food is needed. For a large rite, a cow is slaughtered, for a small one, a hog. The villagers contribute according to their means, either in cash or in kind. Sometimes the village *nong'ak* (farmers' music and dance) troupe goes from house to house collecting funds. Either way, the expenses are shared.

The rite itself is usually held at night, beginning just after midnight. First, a bowl of wine is

offered to the deity, then the officiants bow. Next, an invocation is read, and the paper on which it is written is burned. Food and wine are offered to other deities, such as the earth god. Next, the food table is removed from the altar, and the officiants sit down together and partake of the food and wine that was offered to the gods. When they have finished, they ring a bell to let the villagers know the rite, and with it the taboo period, is over.

The next morning at daybreak the villagers gather in the village plaza or at the house of one of the ceremonial officials to celebrate with much feasting, singing and dancing. This celebrating is an expression of their gratitude to the deities who protect them, their satisfaction at having rewarded the deities, and their hopes for continued protection. While the ritual itself was conducted by a small group in the wee hours of the morning, all the villagers joyfully participated in the eating and drinking of the food offerings in the days that follow.

Everyone participates, even if he or she is too poor to have contributed to the ritual expenses. Packages of food and drink are also sent by messengers to elderly shut-ins. Thus the entire village shares in the feast.

After the villagers are fed and have had plenty to drink, the singing begins to the accompaniment of a farmers' band. Mask dances also follow the ritual as part of the effort to comfort the deities. In fact, many traditional mask dances originated in local rituals. The longer the village tradition, the bigger the rituals, and the more pronounced the folk art forms. The frequency and intensity of these regular village rites has made an important contribution to the development of traditional performing arts.

Communal rites manifest a profound belief in a multiplicity of spirits. The ancients believed almost everything, animate and inanimate, embodied a spirit which influenced human life. They thus worshiped mountains, valleys, rivers, wells, rocks, trees, the sun, the moon, the stars, thunderstorms, wind rain, and land. They worshiped deified ancestors, kings, generals, sages and great men, dragons, tigers and birds. Even insects had their place in the traditional pantheon. One historical source says the Koryŏ people "did not take medicine but appealed to the gods when ill." This indicates the Korean people's strong belief in the power of their gods.

Of course, the belief in such gods has diminished greatly with the introduction of modern education and science and the influx of Western civilization and culture. Nevertheless, many remote villages still hold rites to tutelary gods, and villagers dare not remove or damage the soil, stones or trees around their village shrines.

The ultimate purpose behind any folk rite, be it a private ceremony or a village ritual, is the realization of *subok kangnyŏng*, "longevity, good fortune and well-being." People want to be happy. They want to live a long time. But living a long time with disease is painful and hardly enjoyable. Therefore, they want to be healthy. But if they are poor, they will not be happy living their long, healthy life. So they want to be wealthy too.

Our ancestors believed personal fortune was controlled by good and bad spirits. Thus, they believed in a variety of deities who could prevent or eliminate misfortune and protect them from evil spirits. Of course, the best way to avoid misfortune was to prevent it from occurring. Hence, village rites were held, exorcisms were conducted seasonally, sacrifices were offered frequently, and the shrines of the tutelary deities were kept clean and neat.

When calamity did strike, rites were held to appease the gods. If the calamity was deemed the work of an evil spirit, an exorcism was performed by a shaman to persuade the spirit to leave the village or to actually drive it out. Villagers sometimes tried to frighten spirits away with swords, arrows or lances.

A life free of disaster and illness is an absolute precondition for happiness. The village rituals are meant to achieve this most basic of human needs. The villagers' cooperation in the ritual process reveals just how important the rites are. Their common yearning for happiness has kept the tradition alive through the centuries.

Village rites are a community activity. These people share the same interests, the same goals. They till the same land, gather firewood from the same mountains, intermarry and exchange labor. Cooperation is a means of survival. No one can deal with life's dangers alone. Village rituals provide the villagers with a sense of common destiny and oneness, promoting friendship and the essential cooperative spirit. ◆

The head officiant of any community rite is always a respected village elder, known for his upright character and uncontaminated by impure thoughts or actions.

The most important motivations for any community rite are the expulsion of evil, realization of a bumper harvest, village harmony and prosperity through prayer. This ideology is closely linked to Silla's P'ungnyudo. Sŏnang worship may also have stemmed from the Taoist belief in Sŏnwang, the King of Immortals.

Unlike household rituals held in individual homes, village rites defy a simple explanation. They are diverse in character, type and function. Let us consider their intrinsic attributes by citing a few examples.

Rites to Female Deities

Rites to the sea spirit are held in fishing villages along the east coast in Kangwon-do Province. The sea spirit is a female figure who migrated to this area from another place. She is often the spiteful ghost of someone who has died an undeserved death, but, when appeased by the villagers' veneration, she becomes a patron of the village and its inhabitants. A similar deification of female figures is found in southern China and Taiwan.

The female deities venerated in Kangmundong in Kangnŭng and Simgok-ni in Myŏngju, both on the east coast, are also said to have come to these fishing villages from elsewhere across the sea. A popular myth about the Simgok-ni deity tells of the appearance of a beautiful woman in the dream of an aged villager named Yi some 200 years ago. After introducing herself as having come from Hamgyŏng-do Province, the woman said she was drifting near the Buddha Rock between Simgok and Chŏng-dong and asked him to rescue her. The next day Old Man Yi rowed out to the rock and found a casket, containing the portrait of a woman, caught between the rocks. He enshrined the portrait in the village, and from then on, the village fishermen enjoyed bumper catches. To this day, the villagers pray to the spirit before setting out to sea and hold a community rite on the first full moon and on Tano, the fifth day of the fifth lunar month.

Chumunjin, also on the east cost, is home to another female deity, the spirit of a woman victimized by bureaucratic corruption. According to local legend, a woman named Chin-i committed suicide rather than submit to the lascivious overtures of the magistrate of nearby Yŏn'gok. After her death, the village suffered from epidemics, and its fishermen had poor catches until another magistrate held a village rite to appease her

bitter spirit. The village enjoyed bountiful catches after the institution of regular rites.

Inland villages honored maidens from heaven. For example, Ongnyŏdang in Yŏngyang, Kyŏngsangbuk-do Province, is a shrine to Ongnyŏ (Jade Maiden), daughter of the Jade Emperor of Heaven. Ongnyŏ descended to earth as the daughter of the local magistrate and was worshiped after her death. The goddess of P'yŏng'an-ni in P'yŏngch'ang, Kangwon-do, was also a heavenly maiden before she rode to earth on a cloud and settled here. Villagers believe these maidens use their powers to ensure a bumper harvest if they are pleased with village rites.

Phallicism

Phallicism, transmitted from generation to generation in its primal form, is believed to have developed from fertility rites, a desire for male heirs and geomantic concepts. Villagers in the coastal village of Sinnam-ni in Kangwon-do, carve phalli from juniper wood and dedicate them to the Sea Maiden on the first full moon and the "Horse Day" of the tenth lunar month. The tradition, said to have been practiced for over 400 years, began after a village girl drowned while gathering seaweed. Villagers hold the rite to appease her unrequited spirit and to pray for a bumper catch.

Manggae Village in Kosŏng, on the northern coast of Kangwon-do, holds a community rite on the first full moon every year to appeal for a bountiful catch. The rite involves the carving of an alder wood phallus which is fit into a groove in a sea rock.

Phallic worship and female spirits are obviously related. While wooden phalli are offered in rites praying for rich fishing harvests in villages along the east coast, inland villagers use stone phalli to expel evil spirits and strengthen underground forces which, according to geomancy, are believed to effect their communities.

Horse Rites and Tombs of Tiger Victims

In legends and myths, horses are attributed magical powers. Community rites honoring horses have been common in Korea since ancient times. The *History of Koryŏ*, written in the 15th century, refers to seasonal rites venerating horses. *Notations of Korean Music* (*Siyong hyang'akpo*), compiled at the turn of the 16th century, includes a song entitled "King of War Horses," which is believed to have been sung at horse rites during the Koryŏ period.

Several factors could have motivated the veneration of horse images in village rites: outright horse worship, a desire to prevent or eradicate horse diseases, or simply to enhance respect for the primary object of the rite, such as the *sansin* (mountain spirit) or *sŏnghwang*, who would no doubt ride a horse. Traditionally ironmongers and roof-tile makers enshrined an iron or earthenware horse in their shops and held regular rites to the animals. In some cases, a horse image was enshrined to protect the village from man-eating tigers.

Pictures enshrined in village *sŏnang* shrines (*sŏnangdang*) often feature maimed horses, suggesting that the injury was caused in fights with tigers, which the horse, of course, won. Horse rites, which depict the horse as the victor over the tiger, embody the villagers' desire to be protected by the occult power attributed to the horse.

Iron horses are the most prevalent horse images used in village rites. In Kangwon Province alone, more than 20 mountain villages have shrines in which iron horses are consecrated. Stone or wood horses are also found in some villages. For example, two wooden horses representing the horses of the Koryŏ General Ch'oe Yŏng are enshrined in a village shrine in T'ongyŏng, Kyŏngsangnam-do Province.

The people of Sŏngma (Stone Horse) Village in Kosŏng, Kyŏngsangnam-do, carved two stone horses and adopted them as their tutelary deities to protect them from tigers. Rites honoring the animals are held on the first full moon of the New Year. The rites include an offering of a full bushel of beans.

In many mountain villages in Kangwon-do, one can still find *hosikch'ong*, tombs where the cremated remains of villagers killed by tigers are buried under a stone mound. At the time of burial, a rice cake steamer was placed upside down on top of the mound. An iron bar was then stabbed through the steamer into the mound in the belief it would prevent further harm from tigers. There are more 70 *hosikch'ong* in T'aebaek, Chŏngsŏn, Yŏngwol, Samch'ŏk and Myŏngju along the T'aebaek Mountain Range where reports of tiger maulings were common as recently as the early 20th century.

In ancient times, tigers were a grave threat. *The Annals of the Chosŏn Dynasty* refer to reported maulings of no less than 100 people in Kangwon-do and Kyŏngsang-do alone during the second year of King T'aejong's reign in the early 15th century. Horse rites and rites held at tiger victims' graves are thus believed to have originated as a religious defense mechanism against tigers.

Stone Mounds and Rock Spirits

In some village rituals, rocks are venerated as the embodiment of a deity. The rocks are often unusually shaped, unnaturally round, erect or oversized. Stone grottoes, man-made stone images, stone pagodas and stones in the shape of the Taoist *yin-yang* are also revered. Stones piled in round mounds are known as stone tombs, while conical piles are called stone pagodas (*tolt'ap*).

Essential implements for hunting and farming in ancient times, stones are believed to have become religious objects because of their solidity and durability.

Unlike those found at Buddhist temples, the stone pagodas venerated in folk belief are erected by a village as the abode for the tutelary deity, the village guardian. The pagodas are believed to be endowed with various powers, such as the ability to reinforce the earth's energy which, according to geomancy, influences village prosperity and peace, the ability to enrich the soil, the ability to ensure the procreation of humans and animals and control over seasonal changes. Pagodas are also believed to embody the mountain spirit, the earth deity, the sŏnghwang, and the deity of birth and fertility.

Stone pagodas are found throughout .the country. In T'ap-dong (Pagoda Village), Myŏngju, Kangwon-do, villagers have built stone pagodas at three locations to balance their boat-shaped village which, according to geomantic theory, is off-balance. These pagodas are venerated in community rites. Villagers of Taebanggol in Samch'ŏk, Kangwon-do, believe their stone pagoda "Lord Sinyu" guards their village. Ch'owon-ni Village in Hoengsŏng, Kangwon-do, and Ŏsi-ri Village in Sunch'ang, Chŏllabuk-do Province, are both home to "Grandfather" and "Grandmother" pagodas which are venerated on the first full moon. T'ap-ni and Ansan-ni, two neighboring villages in Kŭmsan, Ch'ungch'ŏngnam-do province, have pagodas to protect the villagers from harm. Stone pagoda worship is especially notable in Taeryang Village, Namhae, Kyŏngsangnam-do, where the annual rite to the village pagoda has been carried on for more than 350 years.

Stone pagodas are sometimes accompanied by *changsŭng* (spirit posts) and *sottae* (spirit poles) in a syncretic representation of diverse cults. Villagers have a great affinity for these guardians because they are at the lower echelon of the divine hierarchy and closely associated with daily life. Stone pagodas and individual stones do not constitute especially important deities but are honored for the timelessness represented by the stones.

Some natural stones, such as the one representing the *sŏnang* in Hwalgi-ri, Samch'ŏk, Kangwon-do, are also worshiped as village guardians. Kwanp'o-ri villagers on Kŏje Island off the southern coast of Kyŏngsangnam-do have enshrined not one but a family of six stones in their local shrine. They hold a rite to the stones twice a year, on the first and tenth full moons. Local legend tells of a village patriarch who dreamt an old man instructed him to go to the beach and find six deities who would bring good fortune to the village if the villagers held a rite to them. The next morning the old man went to the beach and found the six stones worshiped today.

Stone worship is especially common on Cheju Island, famous for its abundance of rocks. A bride sometimes takes a stone from her village shrine to her new home to set up a branch shrine. Villagers of Sinyang on the eastern coast of Cheju Island worship a rock which represents the sea deity. They pray to it for good fishing and the safe return of their boats.

Stones, whether singular or in pagodas, as seen here at Horse Ear Mountain in Chŏllabuk-do province, are worshiped for the timelessness they represent.

Sottae and Changsŭng

A sottae often stands with changsŭng at the entrance of a village. The spirit pole is an object of worship venerated during community rites praying for village welfare and a bountiful harvest.

Known as *chimdae* in some regions, sottae are made of wood or stone and have wooden birds or bird-shaped stones on top. The birds are believed to protect the village from evil spirits by pecking at them.

In some regions, especially Kangwon-do, the chimdae are topped with wooden ducks. The poles are carved in dragon and snake patterns, an expression of dragon worship, which is believed to bring the rain so essential for farming.

A chimdae in Murim-ni, Koch'ang, Chŏllabuk-do, is topped by wooden ducks to prevent fire. The water birds represent a Taoist belief in the yin-yang and the five elements by which water surmounts fire. The chimdae in Songjŏng-dong, Kangnŭng, has the same function. The ducks on spirit poles not only signify agrarian society's affinity for water but also symbolize fertility and prosperity.

Villagers in Naeryuk-ni, Puan, Chŏllabuk-do, venerate a granite pole which they call *chimdae hanassi tangsan*. On the first full moon, they dress the pole in ropes and hold a rite praying for a good year. A similar rite is held in Nodong-ni, Koksŏng, Chŏllanam-do province, which has three wooden chimdae.

The word sottae, onomatopoetically understood as a "soaring pole," can be traced to *sodo* which the "Account of the Eastern Barbarians" describes as a sacred area where a tall wooden pole was erected for religious ceremonies in the ancient Samhan period. A prototype of the sottae can be seen on a shield-like bronze artifact excavated from a site in Taejŏn's Koejŏng-dong. The object is believed to have been used in religious rituals.

The word chimdae appears in a Koryŏ poem "Green Mountain Song" (*Ch'ŏngsan pyŏlgok*) and again in *Song of Return to the Western Paradise* (*Sŏwangga*) by the monk Naong. It is believed to refer to a carrying pole.

Together with sottae, changsŭng serve to protect a village from evil spirits and ensure its peace and prosperity. A graphic representation of Korean folk beliefs, changsŭng are common fixtures in the countryside, woven into the fabric of village life through the *changsŭngje*, a rite venerating them.

Changsŭng are made of wood or stone. The stout stone changsŭng in Chungnim-ni, Puan, Chŏllabuk-do, looks like a jovial neighbor with his hat, toothy smile and bulging eyes.

Chŏnch'igok-ni Village in Ch'unch'ŏn, Kangwon-do, is famous for its rite honoring the community's wooden changsŭng. The rite, known locally as kŏritche ("street rite"), is part of the annual ritual held on the third day of the third lunar month. Each year a new pair of changsŭng and sottae are erected. The titles "Great General Under Heaven" and "Great Underground Woman General" are written in black on each of the changsŭng, and the inscription "300 li to Seoul, 40 li to Hongch'ŏn, 15 li to Tongsan" is painted on the lower part of the posts, turning the changsŭng into milestones. Offerings of food are spread in front of the changsŭng and sottae, and the officiant of the rite dresses the changsŭng in skeins of silk thread decorated with folded mulberry paper and dried pollack. Incense is burned, then the villagers bow to the changsŭng and make offerings of wine. After the officiant reads an invocation, the paper on which the prayer is written is burned.

Planted firmly at the entrance of a village, changsŭng are at once village guardians and protectors, boundary markers, milestones, and friends to wayfarers. One still finds many villages called Changsŭngbaegi, literally "a place with changsŭng," evidence of the strong belief in and abundance of changsŭng in the old days. Though incorrectly deemed a symbol of idol worship by some Western theologians, changsŭng are actually integral elements of the Korean psyche.

Mountain Rites

The worship of the mountain spirit, or sansin, is one of the oldest and most widespread folk cults of Korea. The sansinje, a rite venerating the mountain spirit, is still a major part of village festivals across the country. Some scholars believe the mountain spirit is a personification of heaven, the absolute and supreme being.

Numerous historical records indicate mountain spirit worship has existed since ancient times. The Memorabilia of the Three Kingdoms states Tan'gun, a mandeity, founded the Korean nation and became the Mountain Spirit of Asadal after his death. The ancient Yemaek people deified tigers and venerated them as totems. A Chinese source describes the Silla people as fond of rites to the Mountain Spirit.

The ducks atop spirit poles symbolize prosperity and fertility and are indicative of agrarian society's affinity for water.

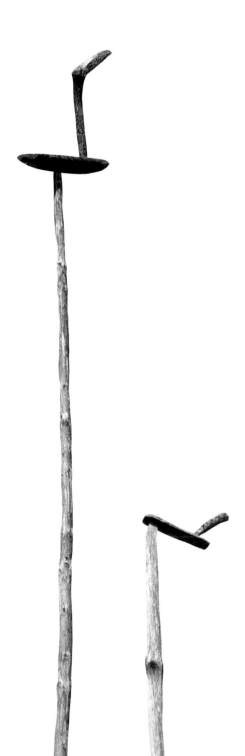

The Kangnŭng Tano festival, a local folk rite designated Important Intangible Cultural Property No. 13 in 1967, begins with a rite honoring the Mountain Spirit at Taegwallyŏng Pass on the fourth full moon. A description of the rite in a 1611 collection of stories by the Chosŏn writer Hŏ Kyun (1509-1618) indicates the people of Kangnŭng believed the Taegwallyŏng Mountain Spirit was the reincarnation of General Kim Yu-sin who unified the three kingdoms of Koguryŏ, Paekche and Silla in the seventh century.

In his "Chilly Tales from the Autumn River" (Ch'ugang naenghwa), the early Chosŏn writer Nam Hyo-on (1454-92) described a Mountain Spirit rite in the Taegwallyŏng Pass area:

> One of the customs of this region is to hold a rite to the Mountain Spirit with shamans on a day in the third, fourth or fifth months. People bring food offerings—the rich carrying them on their horses and the poor on their heads—and pile them on the altar. For three days and nights they drink, eat and dance to the music of flutes, drums and lyres before returning home from the mountain.

Even today the Mountain Spirit shrine on Mt. Chillak in Kŭmsan, Ch'ungch'ŏng-nam-do, hosts a never ending stream of visitors hoping to hold a rite to the Mountain Spirit. Rites are conducted at sansindang, shrines to the Mountain Spirit, on virtually every well-known mountain in Korea, reflecting the Koreans' undying dependence on their mountains.

Rites to the Mountain Spirit are also meant to "defend against the mountain," the mountain here indicating the tiger, lord of the mountains. Residents of villages deep in the mountains who often fell prey to tigers resorted to religious means, such as the so-called sanmaegije rite, to protect themselves. In the sanmaegije rite, a specially made rope is hung on a tree in the forest. The rite is a manifestation of the belief that mountain villages could be protected through the magical powers of the Mountain Spirit.

The people of Samch'ŏk and Myŏngju, Kangwon-do, refer to their sanmaegije rites as "feeding the mountain" for the word can be interpreted in that way. Selecting a day

172

in the third, fourth or fifth lunar months, the villagers head to the mountain with food offerings. After making offerings, they hang a sanmaegi rope or a long strip of hemp cloth on a pine branch to pray for the welfare and prosperity of their homes and families and for the well-being of their domestic animals.

In Tojik-ni and neighboring Simgok-ni, Myŏngju, women go to the mountain to conduct the sanmaegije rite on Tano. However, in no less than 41 villages across Samch'ŏk County, people head to the mountain en masse accompanied by professional shamans to perform formal exorcisms, or *kut*.

The sanmaegi rope is made of ordinary rice stalks. Prior to use in a rite, it is hung in a kitchen in a loose V-shape for a year. The meat of the first chicken or another domestic animal slaughtered that year is hung from the rope. On the day of the sanmaegije rite, the rope is taken down and carried to the mountain together with the food offerings.

Rites to Heaven and Tree Spirits

In ancient times, Koreans worshiped heaven and the sun as a symbol of heaven. Because the sun symbolizes brightness, the rite to heaven (*ch'ŏnje*) was first held on Mt. Paek, a white (and thus bright) mountain. In Korea's foundation myth, Hwanung, the father of Tan'gun who founded the Korean nation, descended to a sacred tree on top of Mt. T'aebaek, the "Mountain of Great Brightness," with a legion of some 3,000 followers. Obviously the Mountain of Great Brightness was the altar for the rite to heaven.

The rite to heaven was held on top of Mt. T'aebaek from the Samhan period. According to the *History of the Three Kingdoms*, Hyŏkkŏse, Silla's founder-king, set up a sacred area where he built an altar for rites to heaven. The chronicle also tells of King Ilsŏng's trek to the north in the tenth lunar month to hold a rite to heaven on Mt. T'aebaek, and of a similar rite held by Wonsul, a *hwarang* warrior, before he vanquished the Tang Chinese army.

According to the *Augmented Survey of the Geography of Korea* (*Tongguk yŏji sŭngnam*), a rite was held every spring and autumn at Ch'ŏnwangdang, a shrine to the Heavenly King on top of Mt. T'aebaek. An ox was tethered at the shrine, and when the ritual participants departed, they never looked back for fear of inviting retribution from heaven. Within three days, the officials of Samch'ŏk would return for the ox in a ritual called "withdrawal of the ox."

Mt. T'aebaek has been the hallowed site for rites to heaven throughout history. Sin Tol-sŏk, a "righteous army" leader in the late Chosŏn period, is said to have won all his battles because he offered a white horse to heaven in a rite at the altar on Mt.

T'aebaek. Rites are still held there today.

As indicated by the sacred tree in the Tan'gun myth, Koreans have a deeply rooted belief in the power of trees. The tangible object of veneration in many village rites is an old tree where the tutelary deity is thought to reside. Trees are worshiped not for their species but for their age. Koreans have long believed that animate and inanimate things of great age have spiritual powers.

The villagers of Munong-ni, Changsu, Chŏllabuk-do, hold a rite to their tutelary tree on

the second day of the first lunar month. In Ch'ilsŏk-dong, Kwangju, an 800-year-old ginkgo tree is honored each year with prayers for village welfare. The tree is carefully protected because any damage to it, even a broken twig, would invite punishment from the tutelary deity. Many old trees designated as Natural Monuments are venerated as tutelary deities by residents in the surrounding areas.

Through these village rites, Koreans experience a communion with divine beings and enhance communal solidarity and social bonds. Village rites also serve a political function by resolving issues of common interest through community cooperation. In fact, these rites are not simply religious rituals but folk festivals that have made considerable contributions to the development of folk arts such as farmers' dance and music, mask dances, shamanistic rituals and all kinds of folk games and plays.

In today's changing world, the traditional village rite is facing extinction. Only with increased public awareness of traditional culture and active restoration efforts will village rites be handed down to future generations. ◆

The tangible object of veneration in many village rites is a very old tree where a tutelary deity is thought to reside.

Village Festivals: Echoing Life's Rhythms

Choe Chul

What is life but a combination of work and recreation? Work means using our bodies and minds to sustain life, to benefit from production and creation, while recreation means using our bodies and minds for pleasure and fulfillment, as in the appreciation of art, religion, leisure and rest.

Human history is a chronicle of work and recreation. The two elements resemble our body and soul in that they cannot be separated. They are mutually dependent, coexisting to fulfill complementary roles. As the old saying goes, "All work and no play makes Jack a dull boy." People cannot live by work alone nor can they survive for long on constant entertainment. Human beings must work and engage in recreation.

Recreation is by nature both collective and successive. Humanity's pursuit of order and harmony, the search for uniqueness, the craving for the imaginative, and the human capacity for logical thinking, the desire to relieve tension, the pursuit of and longing for eternity and the belief in the powers of an absolute being are all related to a certain recreational creativity and reveal humanity's religious yearnings.

Traditional festivals reflect many elements of recreational culture. Here I use the term "festival" to refer to large-scale celebrations or the performance of sacrificial rituals. A festival is a community activity. Celebratory feasts and sacrificial rites involving producers and laborers are performed on the basis of group ties or shared blood lines. They may be performed by the residents of a village, a clan, a tribe or a nation. Festivals, by their very nature, reveal elements of collectivity, realism, spiritualism and masquerade. Festivals are never private affairs; they involve the participation of a group. They embody the collective consciousness and joy of a community.

In Korea, festivals or rites are usually held at the beginning of a new year, a change of season, after planting and harvesting, or on the occasion of the birth or death of a family member.

Festivals recreate a sacred past by turning the clock back to a time when gods and ancestors created the world. They reveal time-honored beliefs and customs, offering modern beings a different perspective on daily life.

The site where a festival is held must be a sacred and transcendental place. Perhaps this is why Korean festivals usually center around revered mountains, swamps, large rocks or trees, altars to tutelary deities and tombs. Only in such places can the gods and revered ancestors manifest themselves.

Some annual festivals are held on set dates during specific periods, or at a change in season. These include regular village festivals, clan celebrations and shamanistic rituals performed on specific days each year.

Festivals can also be categorized by participants: farmers, fishermen, city dwellers, workers or students. The content of the festival varies according to the needs and goals of the participants. Fishing communities pray for bountiful catches. Farmers pray for a good harvest. College students pray for democracy or wise school administration.

And thus, festivals are also classified by purpose. Some address the needs of the community. Others are meant to venerate ancestors, to entertain, to appease gods or spirits or to solidify the foundation of one's home. Festivals can also be differentiated by format or the sex of the participants.

One of the most conventional forms of recreation that reflects the seasonal aspects of a Korean village festival is the *chuldarigi*, or tug-of-war, held immediately before and after the first full moon of the lunar calendar. The chuldarigi is an agrarian ritual, in which the participants pray for, and sometimes foretell, good harvests. Such rituals are quite common in Korea, China, Japan and the rice-growing nations of Southeast Asia. In Korea, this game is most popular in the southern regions where ricefarming prevails. The outcome of the game is believed to forecast the year's harvest; a victory by the team from

Learning folk music and dance is becoming increasingly popular with young people.

the west means a rich harvest, a win by the eastern team, a bad harvest. The practice originated from the belief, promoted by the ruling class, that the dragon was a god of procreation. The two teams thus represent male (east) and female (west) dragons at play.

The tug-of-war of Changhŭng in Chŏllanamdo Province is held on a grand scale. It begins on the eleventh full moon with a small tug-of-war for young children and ends with a grand competition between two teams of villagers on the first full moon of the next year. Changhŭng's tug-of-war is unique for the dazzling red and blue cloth lanterns adorning the rope and the dozens of torches that accompany the two teams as they carry their enormous ropes to the playing field. Young men dressed as dandies and women wearing the costumes of the *kisaeng*, traditional female entertainers, ride the rope, waving their arms and singing. As they approach the center of the town, they bow to the head of the village, then continue to the playing field. The bright lanterns on the rope, boisterous singing, and pounding drum of the colorfully dressed farmers' band add to the festiveness of the occasion.

Ssangyong nori, the "Twin Dragon Game," is actually a play based on a fable about two dueling dragons that has been passed down for generations in a village in Kimje, Chŏllabuk-do Province. It is a unique practice in which dozens of villagers climb inside a huge dragon mask and dance, making it appear alive. The play consists of four acts and is accompanied by much singing and dancing. In the first act, the village dam crumbles, and the local people fetch a repairman. In the second and third acts, a blue dragon and a white dragon appear and a fight ensues. The violent-tempered blue dragon wins and threatens to destroy the dam with a rainstorm. The dragon has a change of heart, however, when Tan-yak, the daughter of a minor official, volunteers to sacrifice herself to save the village. The fourth act consists of Tan-yak dancing and the villagers and local officials enjoying themselves. This game expresses the villagers' hope for a bountiful harvest and protection against the natural disasters.

Yongma nori, the "Dragon-Horse Game," is part of the local festival in Namwon, Chŏllabuk-do. The villagers are divided into northern and southern teams. Each team makes a painted "dragon-horse," which it carries in a colorful parade to the "battlefield." A "general" carrying

The traditional game ch'ajŏn nori *has helped promote village unity and military preparedness for generations in the Andong area.*

a dragon flag in one hand and a horse flag in the other escorts the dragon-horse. The battle begins when the two teams, on orders from their generals, send their dragon-horses crashing against each other. The team that smashes or seizes the opponent's steed is the winner and earns the right to parade around the village, basking in glory.

Kossaum nori is a fast-paced ramming game played with enormous straw rope "chariots." The practice has been passed down and is best preserved in Kwangsan, Changhŭng, Namp'yŏng and Kangjin in Chŏllanam-do Province. After a rite honoring the tutelary deity, the village is divided into eastern and western teams. Young men control the large loops at the front of the chariot, and women control the end of the rope. Following the orders of the leaders who sit astraddle the large loops, the teams ram their chariots against each other in an effort to push the opposing team to the ground. The outcome of this game is believed to directly affect the year's harvest so the participants always compete with great vigor.

Soemŏri daegi is a mock battle that originated in the village of Yŏngsan in Ch'angnyŏng, Kyŏngsangnam-do Province. The villagers are divided into two teams, one from the east and one from the west. Each team carries a straw and wooden structure shaped like a cow's head (*soemŏri*) on top of which the team leader stands. The object of the game is to topple the other team's head. The losers provide food and drink for the participants and spectators, and the whole village joins in the celebration.

These games played at the beginning of the year are directly linked to traditional customs and beliefs. They have several purposes—to bring about a rich harvest, ward off misfortune and bring good luck—and their essence lies not in the winning but in the spirit of communion they foster.

Of the games played during *Tano*, the fifth day of the Fifth Moon, women's swinging contests, men's wrestling matches and *Hanjanggun nori* are the best known. There are swinging contests in which women swing alone and contests in which two women swing together. The women stand on a swing, which consists of a thick rope hung from a wooden scaffold or tree branch. The winner is the person, or team, who goes the highest in the shortest time.

Traditional wrestling matches, known as *ssirŭm*, are held throughout the year in some regions, but mostly on Tano. Each wrestler binds his loins and his right thigh with a white cotton sash called a *satpa*. The two wrestlers kneel down on the ground face to face, clasping their opponent's satpa. At the referee's signal, they stand and begin to wrestle. After much pushing and pulling a victor is determined when one wrestler forces his opponent to touch the sand with any part of his body.

Hanjanggun nori, the "General Han Game," is centered around the legend of a general who dressed up as a beautiful woman and, with his sister, performed a dance that so charmed their enemies that his soldiers, disguised as farmers, were able to circle and kill them. In this practice, two children, dressed as women and wearing round floral wreathes, dance together while dozens of people dance in a circle around them. Then a shaman, who has performed an exorcism prior to the game, and the onlookers become "soldiers" and, at the command of "General Han," encircle the dancers in a mock capture. In Kangnŭng, on the coast of Kangwon-do Province, a masked dance-drama about officials and slaves is performed without the "General Han" character.

Of the Tano festivals celebrated today, the village festival of Kangnŭng is the best preserved. The festival includes wrestling, tug-of-wars, swinging, exorcisms and masked dance-dramas. Through the festival, the residents of Kangnŭng pray for a good harvest and for peace throughout the year. The principal deity revered at the Tano festival is the Sŏnghwang of Taegwallyŏng Pass. A special shamanistic rite is held for him.

Han'gawi, the "Harvest Moon" and fifteenth day of the eighth lunar month, is marked by a number of time-honored festivals and folk practices, including kanggangsullae, a circle dance for women, and the t'apdori dance of Pŏpchu Temple in Poŭn, Ch'ungch'ŏngbuk-do Province.

There are several theories on the origins of the kanggangsullae circle dance. One suggests the dance originated in the 16th century when Admiral Yi Sun-sin deceived a fleet of Japanese invaders into believing their target was well-defended by ordering several groups of women to dance around fires at night. Another theory asserts the dance was originally part of thanksgiving rituals practiced during the Mahan period. Most likely the dance was performed as an expression of thanks to the gods and ancestors for an abundant harvest.

Kanggangsullae demonstrates the active role women have played in village festivals. The dance is performed by several dozen women. They hold hands and circle a woman singing a folk song, Kanggangsullae. The dancers join in the refrain. The circle symbolizes the full moon, a symbol of feminine productivity and a confirmation of a good harvest.

A shaman performs a cleansing rite during the Tano Festival in Kangnŭng, Kangwon-do province (above). A masked dance is a prominent feature of the village rite performed in Hahoe, Kyŏngsangbuk-do province (right).

T'apdori, like lantern-lighting ceremonies, is a folk game derived from Buddhist rituals held on the Buddha's birthday, the eighth day of the fourth lunar month. It began as a purely religious ritual expressing a longing for enlightenment achieved through endless prayer and meditation, but gradually developed into a festive celebration linked to the Buddha's birthday. The participants gather around a pagoda and pray for a rich harvest and a peaceful year with offerings of thanks to their ancestors and songs praising the Buddha. As the full moon rises, the participants begin to circle the pagoda, stopping in front of the pagoda at each rotation to bow and pray.

The folk practices of coastal villages express the local people's desire for a bountiful catch and are quite different from those of farming villages. Perhaps this is because fishermen spend so much time at sea, and fishing is less dependent on seasonal changes.

In the "Fishermen's Game" of the Suyŏng neighborhood of Pusan on the southern coast, villagers act out fishing scenes to the accompaniment of music, using many colorful banners calling for a good catch and a variety of fishing equipment. The *sisŏnbat nori* of Inch'ŏn portrays the joys of a hold full of fish when the croaker are in season off the west coast. In one version set on a fishing boat, the fishermen erect dozens of colorful banners to show they have hauled in many fish and sing a folk song called *paech'igi*. Another version is set in a fisherman's home.

Many folk practices are associated with funeral rites. The most famous is the *tasiryegi* of Chindo in Chŏllanam-do Province. In this practice, performed the night before a burial, participants carry an empty coffin around the village. The tasiryegi is unique for it tries to alleviate the bereaved family's grief through humor.

In summary, we find most festivals are held on or around the first full moon, Tano, the fifth day of the fifth lunar month, and Han'gawi, the Harvest Moon. The games and folk practices performed during these festivals vary from region to region and are, of course, quite different from those played by individuals, children's games or year-round games.

As lifestyles change in modern times, many traditional games and folk practices face extinction, but several group games have been revived as people become more conscious of their cultural roots. These practices cannot survive on the good intentions of a few, however. They must be made a vital part of community life. Hence, there is a need to promote and develop these traditional forms of recreation so that they may be carried on and enjoyed by future generations. ◆

Changsǔng: Friendly Guardians

Lee Sang-il

Sometimes grotesque, sometimes humorous, the traditional spirit posts, or *changsǔng*, usually have bulging eyes and queer smiles revealing ugly teeth. It is hard to tell how long these poles, most frequently made of tree trunks but sometimes of stone, have guarded village entrances and the paths leading to temples. Intermediaries between earth and the beyond and guardians of good fortune, changsǔng have been a unique feature of the rural landscape for centuries.

The faces of these primitive village guardians, often found in pairs, one male and one female, appear angry at first glance. But look closer and you will find their expressions are remarkably varied and sometimes even change with the light and angle. Some look austere and dignified, some warm and gentle, and some are even amusing. They seem to have an affinity with traditional masks, known for their comic smiles, and the languid tigers of old folk paintings. Sometimes, they resemble the demons that embellish traditional roof tiles, both humorous and horrifying.

Whether of wood or stone, changsǔng are usually crude and simple, displaying few traces of refined artistry. For centuries they have been carved by nameless villagers inspired by upcoming communal rites. Once the objects of serious worship, the poles remain part of the unsophisticated folk arts that have survived from generation to generation in villages across the country.

The origin of these sacred poles is not known, but they are generally thought to have developed from *sottae*, towering prayer posts erected in an area believed to be ruled by spirits that influence village fortune. Sottae may be traced to the worship of trees, a form of animism which was widely practiced among the primitive peoples of East Asia.

The changsǔng's shape and the materials of which they are made vary from locality to locality. Wooden poles are common in the central region, while stone changsǔng predominate in the southern areas. The wooden poles of the central provinces are often inscribed with names such as *Ch'ŏnha Taejanggun* ("Great General Under Heaven") and *Chiha Taejanggun* ("Great Underground General"), or sometimes *Chiha Yŏjanggun* ("Great Underground Woman General").

The spirit posts are also called by different names in different parts of the country. Changsǔng is commonly used in Kyŏnggi-do province, *susal* in the Ch'ungch'ŏng region, *poksu* in the Kyŏngsang region and the Chŏlla region, and *harubang* on Cheju Island. The purported function of these poles is complex, though it was primarily to stand guard over the village and ensure the peace and prosperity of the inhabitants by expelling evil spirits.

Traditionally, villages conducted periodic rites to honor the spirit of their guardian poles. In some villages, they are still held. Special communal rites called *pyŏlsin-gut*, held at specific intervals of three or ten years, include special sessions devoted to the changsǔng. New posts are erected and old ones replaced in the lunar leap months which occur every four years. The posts are usually well cared for because they are believed to be sacred. The village would suffer great misfortune if they were damaged. Of course, it has always been taboo to cut one down.

In Ŭnsan, Ch'ungch'ŏngnam-do province, where a pyŏlsin-gut is still held every three years, a village meeting is convened on the third day of the first lunar month to elect a ritual officiant and attendants. The meeting is followed by jubilant music and dance performed by the village band, and by the collection of donations. A rite honoring the mountain spirit is observed on the 15th day of the first lunar month. A rite in which the new changsŭng are raised is usually held before the 20th day of the same month on a day judged auspicious by the head officiant.

At twilight on the day for this rite, exhilarating music is played on drums and gongs, and colorful flags are hoisted on new changsŭng poles erected on the four cardinal directions of the village square. Special foods are placed on candle-lit altars set before each pair of poles. Prayers are offered to the changsŭng spirits, and drinks are served three times before the paper on which the prayers are written is burned. When the ceremony is over, the villagers enjoy the ritual food together.

Unlike changsŭng in many other areas, the poles in Ŭnsan do not have female partners. Instead, the four poles in the village square are named for the dancers in the traditional exorcist "Dance of Ch'ŏyong" and appear in robes of four different colors, symbolizing the spirits of the four cardinal directions. The poles bear inscriptions identifying them as the "Blue Emperor and Great General of the East," the "White Emperor and Great General of the West," the "Red Emperor and Great General of the South" and the "Black Emperor and Great General of the North."

The elaborate rites at Ŭnsan are said to have originated to appease the spirits of local Paekche soldiers who fought in the final battles against the victorious Silla forces in the seventh century. Once the rites were performed on a regular basis, the villagers are said to have no longer suffered from the rampant disease and disasters that had plagued their region. The rites were revived with government support in the 1960s when they were designated an "intangible cultural property," but earlier in the century, they were not held for lack of funds. There also was a period when tree-cutting was prohibited by law and only a simple ceremony was observed before paper scrolls bearing handwritten names of the poles.

In fact, the Ŭnsan rites begin with the felling of four 3-meter-tall oaks. The head officiant and attendants dress in ritual costumes and march to the woods to cut the trees for

183

communal rites, called pyŏlsin-gut, observed in the first lunar month every year or every third year, the mountain spirit is first honored, then the sottae and changsŭng poles are worshiped. Three days before the rites are held, the area surrounding the posts is cleaned, yellow mud is spread over the ground, and ropes are placed around the poles to keep people off the sacred area. The ropes are removed on the day of the rites before the altars are set up and special foods put in place. Then the shaman prays for the peace and prosperity of the entire village.

The head officiant is selected from among the villagers who are believed to have good luck and have not seen a dead body or the blood of an animal. The head officiant and the rest of the villagers must strictly observe a number of taboos before the rites. The head officiant, in particular, has to keep his body clean and is not allowed to leave his house. The persons chosen to prepare the ritual foods also must not have committed impure deeds. The foods usually include dried pollack, a pig's head, white rice cakes and three different colored fruits. Liquor is indispensable at all rites.

The changsŭng are believed to originally have been simple wooden poles or stone pillars. Later, grotesque faces with fierce eyes were carved on them. The more grotesque changsŭng have three or four bulging eyes, and many are painted red to symbolize their magical powers. When they appear in pairs, they often wear the hats of Chosŏn aristocrats, and the red paint is confined to dots on the cheeks of the female changsŭng. Poles made in later years generally have more gentle expressions, some resembling stone images of the placid Maitreya, Buddha of the Future. With time, the poles were often erected simply to help measure the distance between villages.

Traditionally changsŭng were well looked after, but today most have been destroyed, either by the elements or nonbelievers. Approximately 50 are confirmed to exist, although some scholars estimate there are really about 250. The oldest known changsŭng is a stone post at the entrance to Sŏ-oe-ri in Puan, Chŏllabuk-do province. It was erected in 1689. Other famous posts are located at Unhŭng Temple in Naju, Chŏllabuk-do, Silsang Temple in Namwon, Chŏllabuk-do, and T'ongdo Temple in Yangsan, Kyŏngsangnam-do province. ◆

184 the new poles. This act in itself has ceremonial significance. The folklorist Son Chin-t'ae gives an interesting account of these rites in *A Study of Changsŭng* (1932).

On the night of the 15th day of the first lunar month, the farmers place ropes around the sacred bodies of the changsŭng and sottae. They then prepare special foods for the spirits of these poles and play music on drums and gongs and dance in groups ... During the

185

SHAMANISM

The roots of Korean Shamanism are buried deep in Korea's ancient myths, but the religion lives on in the arts, religion and spiritual consciousness of the modern Korean. Korean Confucianism, Buddhism, Taoism, Christianity and hybrid religions, which have developed over the past century, have all been profoundly influenced by shamanistic beliefs and rituals. In modern times, many have denounced the religion as superstitious and irrational.

Shamanism is gradually being rejected in favor of modern science and technology. Efforts are being made, however, to preserve the rich traditions of Shamanism, the dance, music and art, for they have played such an important role in the development of a uniquely Korean culture.

The Role of Shamanism in Korean Culture

Yoon Yee-heum

Complex by nature and found in many diverse forms around the world, Shamanism is difficult to define. Indeed, it is this complexity and variety that has caused so much confusion and debate among its students both in Korea and abroad.

What is Shamanism? The answer depends on one's point of view. Some scholars define it in terms of folklore while others emphasize cultural norms, social structure or the spiritual ethos and the magic-religious context of a given culture. Clearly, the complexity of the topic makes a precise definition and unified understanding difficult as does the diversity of shamanistic practices found in cultures around the world. It is no wonder that confusion and controversy are common in the study of Shamanism.

Korean Shamanism is no exception. Over the years, the topic has been the subject of many studies varying in intent and content. For example, literary scholars have reconstructed previously unknown areas in the history of Korean literature through an examination of shamanistic rites. Historians have achieved a better understanding of ancient society through the analysis of clues found in Shamanism.

Since the 1960s, Shamanism has been seen as a unique key to interpreting Korea's traditional culture. Some scholars have convincingly argued that all new Korean religions find their spiritual roots in Shamanism. Others claim Shamanism has been the unique religious tradition of the Korean people since ancient times. And of course there are those who insist Shamanism is nothing more than a hodgepodge of superstition and irrational thinking.

Shamanism's influence on Korea's traditional culture is well-recognized thanks to the efforts of Korean studies specialists active since the 1960s. It has been the agent through which epics and myths have been preserved and archaic songs and dances have been conveyed to the contemporary performing arts community. Many people believe Shamanism is the most dynamic factor in Korean culture today, influencing such major spiritual forces as Buddhism and Christianity. The widespread performance of *kosa*, a simple shamanistic ritual, reflects the enduring importance of Shamanism in our modern society.

No one can be certain how many Koreans believe in Shamanism today for few people are willing to admit they are believers and so have never been counted in national religion surveys. A national shamans' organization recently published statistics indicating that they have some 40,000 dues-paying members. If this is true, the organization is much larger than any of the other indigenous religions extant today.

Shamanism is clearly a mighty cultural institution with vast hidden power, but how is it related to other religious traditions, such as Confucianism, Taoism, Buddhism and Christianity? In order to probe the interaction between these traditions, we must first examine the meaning of Shamanism and then review the history of religions in Korea.

Any study of Shamanism requires an organized framework of understanding. The term is generally used in two ways: broadly speaking, it refers to primitive or magic-religion; and, in a narrow sense, it indicates the distinctive religious tradition of northern Asia. In this study, I use the term in the latter context.

Shamanism is closely related to the shaman's spiritual experience. A shaman is a religious professional who has direct experiences of possession and ecstasy. When in a state of possession and ecstasy, a shaman is believed to be able to communicate with a deity or discern the deity's wishes. Thanks to these powers, the shaman is capable of telling fortunes. Thus the first and most important characteristic of Shamanism is a shaman's personal and direct experience of the deities.

The second fundamental characteristic relates to function. The purpose of Shamanism is the fulfillment of practical human needs. People engage the services of a shaman for pragmatic reasons: to restore or enhance health, to promote

A shaman performing a knife dance in a kut from the Hwanghae region

conception, to acquire wealth or power, and so on.

This practical and worldly element is called *kibok*, praying for the fulfillment of worldly desires. Korean Shamanism has blended mystic and worldly attitudes for thousands of years and has·been the central force in the maintenance and dissemination of this mystic-worldly attitude in Korean society. It is the matrix for the expression of the common people's practical needs. As such, it has had an enormous influence on established religions such as Confucianism, Buddhism, Taoism and Christianity.

Two major cultural shocks have influenced the history of religion in Korea: first, the introduction of the three Oriental religions, Confucianism, Taoism and Buddhism, and second, the arrival of Christianity and Western culture.

Historians are uncertain when Confucianism first came to Korea. Some evidence indicates that it was introduced, along with Chinese writing, during the Warring States Period in China (B.C. 403-221). The adoption of Confucianism by Koreans is evidenced by Koguryŏ court's establishment in A.D. 372 of a Royal Academy for the training of future government officials in the Confucian tradition.

Buddhism reached the Korean peninsula in the summer of 372 during the reign of Koguryŏ's King Sosurim. Confucianism and Buddhism have coexisted since then and remain the two major official religions influencing Korea's traditional culture. As in China, Taoism was rarely considered as an official religion and remains a minor tradition in Korea.

Confucianism, Buddhism and Taoism were fully developed by the latter part of the fourth century at which time thoroughly refined metaphysical systems and processes for logical discourse were already established.

Korea was home to many indigenous religious traditions prior to the introduction of these three religions, however. An ancient inscription claims that one of Korea's indigenous religions had a far more profound spiritual message than the three classical religions combined. Contemporary scholars generally believe that indigenous religion was Shamanism.

Shamanism was the most powerful belief system found among the indigenous religious practices in Old Korea and has played a central role in the transmittance of kibok, down

During the Kangnŭng Tano Festival, a shaman in a state of possession "drinks" from a brass bowl filled with money offered to the spirits in an appeal for good fortune.

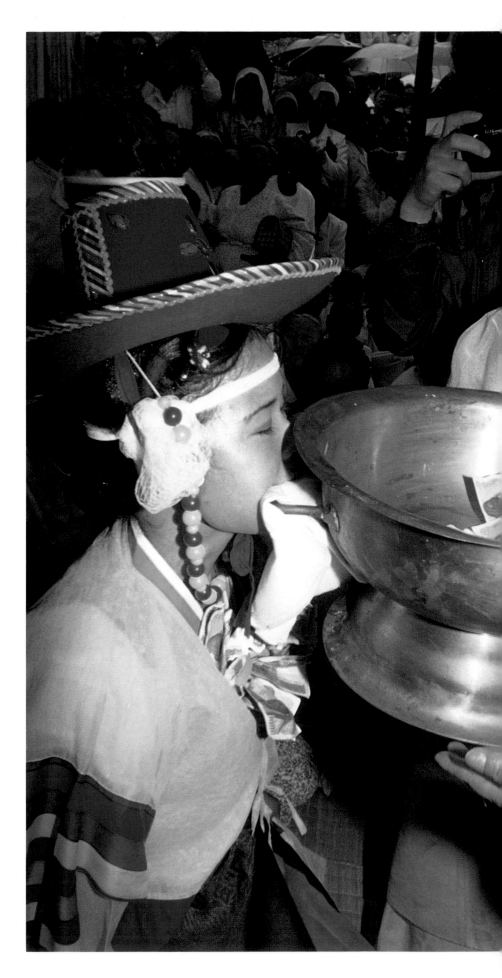

through the year to the present. Unlike the established belief systems, Shamanism has provided the Korean people with a way of expressing their daily needs. In principle, Confucianism provides a vision for a noble order of social life, and Buddhism offers believers the wisdom to understand the meaninglessness and emptiness of earthly things. However, neither religion offers an immediate response to the most basic needs of the common people, that is, the direct alleviation of the misery of everyday life.

For this very practical reason, Confucianism and Buddhism have incorporated elements of Shamanism into their own religious systems. Confucianism has never excluded the shamanistic viewpoint on life and death. In fact, Confucian ancestral services have always been conducted within the context of a shamanistic belief system.

Korean Buddhism has also accepted Shamanism as a means of satisfying popular needs. Neither *Kyo*, the study of the Buddha's teachings, nor *Sŏn* (Zen), the meditative tradition, can satisfy these basic needs, so Mahayana Buddhism gave birth to Tantrism, an amalgamation of the classic Buddhist belief system and popular shamanistic beliefs.

Shamanism mingled much more easily with Taoism because Taoism by its very nature was born of the interrelationship of classic philosophy and popular folk beliefs.

Although Shamanism has been excluded from the ranks of Korea's official religions, it has been a persistent influence on both Confucianism and Buddhism, and its influence on Christianity has been equally great.

Of the non-Western nations, Korea is the most successfully Christianized: Christians constitute 20-25 percent of the total population. Koreans were relatively receptive to the Christian faith from its initial introduction because the concept of a personal deity and man's direct experience of divine grace are familiar spiritual concepts. History suggests that churches that emphasize the direct experience of God, regardless of the form that experience takes, and the divine guarantee of the fulfillment of worldly desires grow most rapidly. Churches also flourish if they emphasize the mystic-worldly attitude that has prevailed in the shamanistic belief system since early times.

A perusal of Korea's religious history clearly indicates that the religions introduced to Korea from abroad soon became associated with Shamanism in one way or the other. In fact, the relationship between Shamanism and the major religions has been much stronger and more prominent than the relationship between Confucianism, Buddhism and Christianity. The three major official religions tend to compete with each other since each asserts its own absolute superiority. Each is based on what its believers assert is a perfect belief system with its own refined metaphysical outlook and logical basis. Mutual accommodation between perfect or absolute systems is impossible since an absolute cannot accept influences from outside. Instead, accommodation has taken place through indirect relations, that is, through Shamanism, a channel for expressing popular needs.

Unlike the official religions, which are based on an organized belief system with refined metaphysics and logical uses, Shamanism is an attitude played out in everyday life, a primal survival impulse responding to the harsh conditions of human existence. Historically, Shamanism has never developed a belief system advanced enough to constitute an official religion. It has remained a primal religion, a latent function and a powerful cultural undercurrent. Unlike more systematic dogma, Shamanism can, as a potentially latent and hidden attitude, interact easily with the official religions without threatening their underlying principles.

We have noted above the dual role that Shamanism has played in Korea's religious history: first, as a durable channel for the expression of distinct popular needs and, second, as a conduit for the interrelation of the various official cultural systems. From these two functions springs Shamanism's third major function: the preservation and perpetuation of popular culture. Korea's cultural history clearly indicates that Shamanism has been the means by which traditional culture has been transmitted to new generations.

Shamanism's three major functions are founded in the mystic-worldly attitude, man's natural and primitive survival response to adverse living conditions. This primal impulse is combined with the mystic experience of possession and ecstasy within the context of shamanistic beliefs.

Shamanism will survive in one form or another as long as Koreans are faced with the challenges of human life and the mystic experience of possession. Similarly, the official religions will continue to associate with shamanistic practices as long as they are confronted with the historical demands of popular life. As long as Shamanism remains a part of our culture, history will require us to carefully scrutinize the selfishness that underlies the mystic-worldly attitude and to search for a harmonious accommodation between classical wisdom and the needs of the common people. ◆

Shamanism and the Korean Psyche

Rhi Bou-yong

One summer back in the late 1960s I was asked to lecture on Shamanism at a gathering of Korean students in West Germany. At the time I was studying at the C.G. Jung Institute in Zurich and in the midst of writing my dissertation on Korean Shamanism. After being away from home for so long, I was happy for the chance to get together with other Koreans. On the eve of the seminar, there was a dinner party with lots of dancing and singing—quite a change after several years living among the rational Swiss.

The following day after my lecture on Korean Shamanism and its psychological implications, one of the students asked if Shamanism still played a role in Korean society. The previous night's festivities popped into my mind immediately.

"Oh yes, Shamanism's still important," I said. "After watching you last night, I'm sure you all have the makings of wonderful shamans. That party proved Shamanism lives on inside of every one of you!"

The audience burst into laughter, but it was true: those singing Koreans were masters in ecstasy, what Mircea Eliade has referred to as the unique characteristic of Shamanism.

I began my study of Shamanism reading the essays of Ch'oe Nam-sŏn, Yi Nŭng-hwa's studies on Chosŏn Shamanism, and Akiba Takashi's field work on Korean Shamanism in the 1920s and 1930s. My first encounter with Siberian Shamanism came in 1959. That was when I began to feel a strange sense of inspiration growing within me.

The feeling intensified later when I began reading Eliade's writings while studying in Europe. It was a new world for me, a dark and distant world that frightened me and yet made me curious, that strangely mad world, an unreal world, an irrational world. My initial research goal was determining whether *sinbyŏng*, the shamanistic initiation disease, was a culture-bound syndrome. However, I soon realized that my psychopathological approach was off the mark and so began approaching the question from another angle: did Shamanism, as the underlying foundation of Korean culture, constitute the basis of the Korean psyche?

I chose Korean Shamanism as the topic for my dissertation because I felt an internal desire to find the roots of the Korean people's consciousness. I felt Shamanism was Korea's most authentic cultural legacy, but it had been forgotten in our Westernized lives.

I had dreamt about elements of Shamanism before I began writing my dissertation, and as I wrote, the dreams grew more vivid. Thus, my study of Shamanism was not so much an attempt to investigate the psyche of the Korean people as a whole as it was a personal bid to revive the primordial experience of one particular Korean, that is, myself, while at the same time applying Jung's theory of archetypes, which asserted that this primordial experience was not limited to the Korean people but rather was a feature shared by all mankind.

A scholar's choice of discipline is influenced by a variety of factors, both external and internal. However, generally speaking, the choice of a particular field is influenced less by material or external phenomena than by psychological elements related to the scholar's unconscious complexes. This is especially true in the case of scholars who devote their lives to the study of one particular subject. In fact, it is not uncommon for scholars studying Korean Shamanism to rediscover lost elements of themselves in the course of their research and to begin a process of self-healing as they reintegrate those elements into their own consciousness.

Interestingly, in the 1960s and 1970s, the vast majority of the scholars active in this field were Christians or people with a strong background in Confucianism. There has been a tendency for these scholars to develop an ambivalent attitude toward their subject matter despite their strong attraction to Shamanism, although it varies with each individual.

Actually, the contemporary Korean's ambivalence toward Shamanism is only natural. Proponents of the "advanced" religions and rationalist modern men tend to feel a certain hostility toward the incantatory elements of Shamanism.

Music and dance are essential to shamanistic rites. At right, a newly initiated shaman performs a dance symbolizing her spiritual possession.

The brilliant colors, the boisterous drumming, the wild dancing, the shaman's apparent impudence and coarse language as he or she delivers the gods' messages can upset those who value rationalism and good manners. However, a closer look at the shaman's ceremony reveals a rich world of symbols that are found not only in Korean Shamanism but throughout modern society. In fact, these symbols constitute man's primordial experiences and serve as the fountainhead of modern society's spiritual life.

The outlook on human life portrayed in Jung's *Two Essays on Analytical Psychology* was decisive in my realization of this fact. After returning to Korea in 1968, I saw that, as a Jungian analyst, I could not understand my Korean patients without first understanding the symbolism found in Shamanism and other folk beliefs, which played such an important role in their dreams, and, by extension, their unconscious. Shamanism is much like a vessel in which all the archetypal images that form the basis for what Jung called "the collective unconscious" are contained. By understanding Korean Shamanism, transmitted through history relatively free of humanity's artificial intellectual embellishments, I felt I could achieve a deeper insight into the Korean unconscious.

In my work, I have found that the concepts of wholeness and a union of opposites are the most significant symbols in Korean Shamanism. In the state of ecstasy, the shaman links this world, the human world, with the other world. This process is identical to the psychological process used to break down the barriers between the unconscious and conscious. In the shamanistic initiation process, the shaman often meets spirits in his or her dreams.

The concept of uniting two worlds, of fusing opposites into one, is found in all advanced religions. Shamanism is unique in that this experience is linked to ecstasy, a state of intense emotion. The symbolic "world tree," found in the nomadic societies of Siberia, is an example of the concept of "oneness" realized through a state of ecstasy. In Siberian Shamanism, climbing the sacred trees signifies flight to the heavens.

In Korean Shamanism, the concept of a sacred tree exists in the form of *tangsan*, trees representing tutelary deities. However, the concept of the center of the world is weak in the Korean tangsan, which are always referred to in pairs, such as the grandfather and grandmother tangsan. Sacred bells, bird feathers and brightly colored fabric are often attached to the sacred tree, and when it is placed in the hand of the shaman, it is believed to be the route by which the spirits descend to earth.

The world view of the nomadic peoples of central Asia and Siberia is quite different from that of Korean Shamanism. In Korean Shamanism, the concept of a boundary between the outside world and the village is much stronger than the nomadic world-centered outlook. This is why we see a leveling out of the Siberian concept of a three-dimensional universe (the underworld, the world on earth, and the heavens) in Korean Shamanism. This is reflected in the Korean people's placement of guardian totem posts (*changsŭng*) bearing the titles of "General of the Underworld" and "General of the Heavens" at the entrance to many villages. The symbol of wholeness found in Korean Shamanism is expressed through the motif of harmony or a union of opposites, a reflection of the relationship between *yin* and *yang* (*ŭm* and *yang* in Korean).

This harmonization cannot be achieved without conflict or pain. This is why we find pain, death and resurrection in the shamanistic initiation process everywhere.

In Siberian Eskimo culture, the prospective shaman must live in a cave and wait without food for days in hopes of seeing a spirit. When a spirit appears, the novice shaman adopts it as a guardian spirit. In the nomadic cultures of central Asia and Siberia, the prospective shaman must endure a horrifying initiation rite involving dismemberment. The greater the pain one endures in the dismemberment process, the greater one's power as a shaman. For those of us in modern society, so eager to avoid pain at all costs, true Shamanism shows us how the state of wholeness found in ecstasy cannot be achieved without pain.

Immense pain is also an essential part of the Korean shaman's initiation process. *Kangsinmu*, shamans who receive their calling through spiritual possession, must undergo sinbyŏng, a physical illness born of a state of mental derangement, in the initiation process. Unlike the shamanistic initiations of central Asia or Siberia, sinbyŏng is a form of spiritual possession.

Occasionally we find examples of dismemberment in Korean myths and legends, but the concept is not present in shaman chants or ceremonies. In the Korean shamanistic initiation, the prospective shaman or *sin ttal* (literally "spiritual daughter") is initiated into the calling through the *naerim-gut* ceremony under the direction of the *sin ŏmŏni* (literally "spiritual mother"). Through this process, the "false master," the spirit which causes the illness, is driven out, and a benevolent helping spirit (*momju*) is enshrined in the new shaman's body.

Ecstasy is not simply the achievement of a

During the naerim-gut, *a senior shaman or "spiritual mother" initiates a younger woman into her calling. In many ways, the initiation ceremony resembles a traditional wedding.*

high state of emotion; rather, the newly initiated must be able to deliver a spiritual oracle (*kongsu*) while in that state. The naerim-gut initiation can go on for hours before the spiritual oracle is delivered, and when the shaman fails to produce an oracle, the rite is repeated on another day.

The ritual of dismemberment practiced in central Asian Shamanism reflects the unique nature of nomadic culture, while the concept of possession found in Korean Shamanism is characteristic of an agrarian culture. However, both cases vividly reveal the importance of suffering to the process by which the initiated achieves the power to mediate between this world and the other world. One can only become a great healer after overcoming the pain of initiation.

The harmony motif is also a factor in the *kut* rite as a whole. Kut are generally composed of 12 acts, or *kŏri*, each act a distinct unit involving possession by a different deity. Each deity's personality is unique—the *taegam* deity is greedy and crude while the Buddhist-influenced *posal* is mild-mannered and pious. The appearance of these different deities over the course of the 12-act kut reflects the full range of human emotions.

In each act, this world is linked to the other world through confrontation and emotional assimilation. The reconciliation of the living and the dead is not achieved easily; it requires a process of emotional confrontation. The kut begins with a flurry of complaints and threats from the deities in the form of the oracle, but by the end, the living manage to extort the deities' forgiveness and blessing after considerable squabbling.

In the *chosang kŏri* (the ancestors' act) and the *chinogwi*, in which the angry spirits of deceased ancestors are appeased, the dead express their resentment through the shaman, and the living voice their grievances in return. This practice of *nŏkduri*, the expression of grievances and resentment by the living and the dead, has various psychotherapeutic implications.

Perhaps most revealing is the *paridegi* portion of the chinogwi act. Paridegi is a dramatic portrayal of the myth of Pari Kongju, who was abandoned by her parents at birth. The act is performed through song, dance and narration. It constitutes the initiation of Pari Kongju into the ranks of the shamans and, to a certain extent, represents an effort to overcome the pain and discrimination suffered by women in Korea's patriarchal society.

Korean Shamanism, and Shamanism in general, stress the significance of suffering and embody the concepts of the accommodation of pain, the harmonization of opposites and the existence of a single world that embraces this world and the world beyond the living. What is the relationship between these concepts and the Korean psyche?

The Korean psyche is more closely linked to the emotionality of Shamanism than to its doctrine. The Korean people are ecstasy-oriented, whether on an overt or covert level. They may seem very individualistic and independent on the surface, but once they discover a doctrine or object with sacred force that transcends the individual, they unite with religious intensity. In many ways, Koreans seem to be constantly searching for that sacred force, whether it takes the form of the Olympic Games, an export quota, a great leader or a revival meeting. This is why the ecstasy phenomenon is so vibrant in Christian churches today. The minister activates the archetypal elements within the believers, causing them to experience the sacred force and thus

curing their illnesses. However, this emotionality can degenerate into a spontaneous festival of emotion, devoid of insight. That is to say, it can end in a sort of ego inflation, much the way the nŏkduri allows for the expression of grievances, without ever advancing to the level of understanding or forgiveness found in the Pari Kongju section of the kut.

Specific manifestations of Korean Shamanism do not play an especially important role in the Korean people's consciousness or unconscious. That is to say, shamans or elements of the kut do not appear in modern Koreans' dreams on a regular basis, and if they do, they usually have a negative connotation. This is because in everyday life modern Koreans tend to hold Shamanism at a respectful distance or ignore it altogether.

The Korean psyche is a product of history, subject to the effects of time and regional differences, and therefore is difficult to define in a simple phrase. However, I have always felt that Korean Shamanism is one of several important subcultures that contribute to the formation of the Korean psyche. Buddhism, Confucianism, Taoism, and other religious elements influence the unique nature of the Korean character together with Shamanism. In fact, they play a decisive role in determining the Korean psyche. Throughout history, Confucianism and Shamanism have been in conflict with each other. Confucianism is based on intellectualist, aesthetic and patriarchal values while Shamanism tends to construct a new order in the unconscious through religious spontaneity, emotional experience, maternal tolerance, and a breakdown of society's ethical norms.

Confucianism was adopted as the official philosophy during the 500-year reign of the Chosŏn Dynasty, however, and modern Koreans continue to embrace this tradition, maintaining Confucian human relations sprinkled with touches of Buddhist, shamanistic, Taoist, or Christian beliefs. In recent years, however, we have seen an increase in the number of Koreans for whom Confucian elements are relatively weak compared to shamanistic elements. In these cases, a number of uniquely shamanistic behavioral types appear in the form of what we could call "shamanistic human relations." Unlike the uniquely shamanistic elements linked to the ecstasy phenomenon, these behaviors seem to be the result of the influence of history on Korean Shamanism. For example, the relationship between deities and humans in the kut is remarkably similar to that between our society's ruling elite and the common people. The authority of shamanistic deities is not absolute; rather they reign as relative entities who bargain with humans. The delivery of the deity's oracle in the kut is in many ways a dialogue between the deity and the human participants. The humans resist the deity's threats and use all manner of tricks and flattery to win the deity over to their side. This "bargaining" is very much like what we see in the marketplace everyday. Indeed, this give-and-take is a common feature of Korean human relations, a feature quite removed from traditional Confucian ethics in which vertical relations are strictly maintained.

The bawdy language and blatant references to worldly and sexual desires found in kut contrast sharply with the Confucian value system, which promotes self-control. At times, these particular aspects of Korean Shamanism reflect the repressed unconscious of those thoroughly indoctrinated in Confucian culture. By freely expressing what lies deep in the unconscious of the

Kangsinmu, *shamans who receive their calling through spiritual possession, must experience the descent of a spirit after a long "spiritual" illness. This shaman has just completed the initiation ceremony.*

Confucianized Korean, Shamanism provides a shock to the existing value system, thus promoting a reconstruction of those values.

Where do we find Shamanism in today's society? Right in the hearts of the Korean people. Shamanism is the world of our ancestors, the world of the dead, the foundation of our consciousness. It is universal and primitive and thus not restricted to the Korean people alone. In the West, there may be no sorcerers or shamans, but ideologies born of the ecstasy phenomenon, something which could be called a shamanistic complex, are found in many forms.

Korean Shamanism is a synthesis of this general shamanistic complex and a variety of elements absorbed over the course of Korean history. It reflects one side of Korean human relations.

It clearly plays an active role in the Korean psyche. However, it is not the only factor. Shamanism functions in tandem with other religious cultures to create the Korean people's unique character. During the Three Kingdoms period, the Korean people's world view was a combination of Shamanism and Buddhism, while from the latter part of the Koryŏ period through the Chosŏn period, the Confucian world view dominated. From this time onward, Korean Shamanism generally served as a mechanism by which human resentment brought on by the cultural gap between everyday life and Confucianism was relieved. In contemporary society, shamanistic elements have moved beyond the kut to play a role in everyday human and social relations.

It is difficult to say whether Shamanism plays a positive or a negative role in the Korean psyche. The psyche is composed of a number of contrasting elements—the rational and the emotional, the masculine and the feminine, the phenomenal and the super phenomenal. Korean Shamanism tends to activate the latter elements in these dichotomies, bringing a special vibrancy to Korean life. ◆

The Kut in Contemporary Shamanism

Hwang Rushi

People generally think of Shamanism as a relic of the distant past but, in fact, it remains an active part of the Korean consciousness today. Folk beliefs have been the target of repression since the Japanese colonial period, but the number of people searching for solutions to life's crises through the services of a shaman has increased in recent years. There are 40,000 registered shamans in Korea today. I would put the present number at over 100,000, however, as the 40,000 estimate has not increased over the last decade, despite the many initiation ceremonies that have taken place. Clearly many shamans have avoided registration.

Whatever the actual number, we can be certain of one thing: A substantial portion of the population embraces folk beliefs. However, while Buddhism, Confucianism, Christianity, Won Buddhism, the Chŭngsan Sect and other

This rite performed aboard a fishing boat on the western coast of Korea honors tutelary deities and appeals for the safety and prosperity of local fishermen.

"new" religions are covered in government-sponsored religious surveys, Shamanism has been excluded. As a result, no one can be certain of its present status in Korea.

Some people say this is justified because, in their view, *kut*, shamanistic rites, and fortune-telling do not constitute a religion. But what is religion? If the coexistence of three factors—a priest, a ceremony and a community—constitutes a religion, then Shamanism most certainly is one. The shaman is the priest (or priestess), the kut is the rite, and the hefty share of the Korean population that believes in Shamanism is the community. There may be no written scripture or systemized doctrine for religious scholars to study, but believers find the answers to life's questions in the songs and words of the shaman. What more do they need?

There are no permanent temples or churches in Korean Shamanism. Rites take place wherever the kut is held. In a seasonal village kut, the community designates a site for the regular performance of the ceremony. The site can have a variety of functions. Sometimes it is the site of the shrine used in the worship of the village's guardian deities. Sometimes it is the local meeting place where issues of community interest are discussed. And often it is a central part of the village's economic life, a sandy beach, for example, where villagers gather to mend nets or clean fish. This physical link to the village's economic life demonstrates the inseparability of shamanistic ritual and the cycle of daily existence in traditional society.

Such is the fundamental basis of Shamanism. But who are these shamans, and what is a kut?

The shaman (generally referred to as *mudang*) is an intermediary who communicates between the gods and human society, relaying humans' desires to the gods and revealing the gods' intentions to the humans. The shaman mediates through the kut, in which a variety of songs, dances, and dramatic vignettes, as well as stories and legends, are performed. Far more than a simple fortuneteller, the shaman is a priest (or priestess) overseeing a religious ceremony, just as the Christian or Buddhist clergy perform rites in their religions.

Traditionally, Korean shamans have been classified into two categories: *kangsinmu*, shamans who receive their calling through possession by a deity, and *sesŭpmu*, hereditary shamans who inherit their calling from their ancestors.

Kangsinmu are most common in the area north of the Han River and west of the T'aebaek Mountain Range, that is, Seoul and the northern part of Kyŏnggi-do Province, Hwanghae-do, P'yŏng'an-do and Hamgyŏng-do provinces, and the western portion of Kangwon-do province.

They usually experience the descent of a shamanistic spirit or god (*sinnaerim*) after a long "spiritual" illness (*sinbyŏng*) bordering on mental disease or after experiencing great emotional pain, such as the collapse of a marriage or family business. These individuals formally receive their shamanistic calling through an initiation ceremony known as the *naerim-gut* in which the deity is enshrined in the body of the shaman. It is at this time that the shaman acquires his or her prophetic skills.

To become a professional mudang, the shaman must practice the kut. It can take anywhere from two to ten years to fully acquaint oneself with the intricacies of shamanistic practices. The newly initiated shaman should establish a teacher-student

relationship with the shaman who performed his or her initiation ceremony, serving as an apprentice to the senior shaman.

Hereditary shamans are most common to the south of the Han River and in the region east of the T'aebaek Mountain Range. These shamans, all female, have been responsible for the preservation of the mudang tradition in Chŏlla-do and Ch'ungch'ŏng-do provinces, southern Kyŏnggi-do and in southeastern Korea. Men serve as musicians, performing the music for the kut and accenting the performance with witty comments and sarcasm.

Kut performed by experienced hereditary shamans are rich in artistry and reveal the true skills of the Korean mudang. Of course, one does find some kangsinmu in this region, but they are generally little more than fortunetellers and cannot perform kut. This, I believe, reflects the firm social organization of the hereditary shamans.

Since the establishment of Confucianism and Buddhism as the dominant religions in the Koguryŏ and Paekche kingdoms, Shamanism has, for the most part, been the belief of the common people, quite removed from the lives of the ruling class. During the Koryŏ period, Shamanism coexisted with Buddhism in the form of state rituals such as the *p'algwanhoe*, the "Festival of the Eight Vows," honoring the Celestial King and five famous rivers and mountains, but shamans were reduced to *ch'ŏnmin* status, the lowest social station, following the adoption of Confucianism as the official ideology of the Chosŏn Dynasty.

As the elaborate system of social status deteriorated in the latter years of the Chosŏn Dynasty, the number of hereditary shamans began to decrease rapidly. There was no longer any reason for these people to put up with the degrading treatment they had been subjected to in their villages. However, they remained highly skilled in the performing arts such as *p'ansori*, a narrative form of musical drama, acrobatics, farmers' music (*nong'ak*), and various folk dances. In fact, most p'ansori masters today are descendants of hereditary shamans from the Chŏlla region.

Hereditary shamans are nearly extinct today. It is difficult to find any under the age of 40, even on the east coast where they have been most active. On the other hand, the number of kangsinmu is increasing. However, they rarely serve as apprentices to their elder masters as was the custom in the past. Generally, these unskilled shamans, or *sŏnmudang*, simply tell fortunes and perform lesser ceremonies such as the *p'udakkŏri*, a rite for simple healing purposes. They lack a true understanding of the kut and are incapable of passing on the world view or value system inherent in shamanistic rituals. Also, their narrow focus on the interests of individual clients has caused a general deterioration in shamanistic beliefs.

The life of a shaman is no different from that of ordinary people. They marry, have children, and live in houses like anyone else. Kangsinmu worship various deities at shrines in their homes, but hereditary shamans do not. The hereditary shamans of the Chŏlla region do not even have any special ceremonial clothing; they simply wear white *hanbok*, Korea's traditional costume, when they perform a kut.

In some rites, fire is used to purify the ritual site and people involved in the ceremony.

Kim Soo-nam

201

Most shamans are poor, uneducated and female. They are looked down upon by society, much as they were during the Chosŏn period. In fact, only those born to the calling or selected by the gods embrace Shamanism as an occupation, and then only reluctantly. In effect, society's least privileged citizens, women, play the role of religious cleric. This is one of the main reasons why Shamanism has not been treated as a respected religion. How can uneducated women possibly be the leaders of a religion? What could their believers possibly learn from them?

However, religion is not a means of transmitting knowledge. The purpose of religion is to provide solutions to life's unanticipated problems and solace in times of suffering. The shaman lives humbly at the very bottom of society and thus is the religious leader most familiar with the lives of the common people, most sympathetic to their economic woes, social concerns, and emotional hardships. This solidarity with the common people has been the driving force behind Shamanism for centuries.

Ceremonies

The ceremonies that form the core of Korean Shamanism can be divided into three categories according to size. The most rudimentary is *pison*, literally the rubbing of hands. This simple rite is usually performed to protect a family member embarking on a trip, to cure minor illnesses, or to improve marital relations. An offering of food is placed in the main room of a household or on the terrace where the soy sauce and bean paste pots are kept. The shaman then performs a simple prayer by rubbing her hands together. In some cases, the housewife will perform the prayer herself.

Kosa and p'udakkŏri are rites performed on a slightly larger scale. Kosa is generally performed in the tenth lunar month at harvest time. P'udakkŏri is performed throughout the year to drive away miscellaneous spirits (*chapkwi*) when a household faces misfortune, such as the illness of a family member or economic difficulties. In both rituals, one or two shaman visit the client's home and convey the humans' wishes to the deities through song, dance, and musical performances on the *changgo* (hourglass drum) and *chegŭm* (small cymbals). These ceremonies are relatively simple affairs lasting three or four hours at the longest. In recent times the kosa ceremony has been even further simplified. It is often limited to a few bows in front of a plate of rice cakes.

The largest and most important shaman ceremony is the kut. The kut is a composite of many different elements: offerings of food and liquor, paper flowers, lamps, boats, and other decorations to attract the gods, dances by several shamans to special music performed by professional musicians, singing, prayers, acrobatic stunts, witty banter, and the like.

As in any religion, an understanding of rites is essential to an understanding of Shamanism. In fact, this is especially true of Korean Shamanism because, as I mentioned above, there are no established scriptures or doctrine. Only in the kut can we find the essential elements of Shamanism merged in a cohesive unit.

Kangnŭng's Tano Festival offers some of the finest
examples of traditional folk culture.
At right, shaman dance during a Tano rite

202

Kim Soo-nam

In the nŏk-kut, *the souls of the dead are guided to the other world. Above, a spirit enters the shaman through a spirit stick.*

For the sake of simplicity, I will categorize kut in terms of the people who initiate the ceremony, that is the shaman's clients, and the purpose of the kut.

First of all, there is the village kut already mentioned. These ceremonies are generally held on a regular basis, although in some cases the ceremony is held at intervals as long as ten years. The purpose of the village kut is to pray for village harmony and prosperity.

Kut are also initiated by individuals. These center around the family unit and can be divided into two basic categories: *chesu-gut* to promote the welfare of the living, and *nŏk-kut* to guide the spirits of the dead to the other world. The chesu-gut is best understood as a smaller version of the village kut. *Chinogi,* a ritual to appease the angry spirits of the dead, *sumang-gut,* a rite performed for drowned fishermen, and *ssitkim-gut,* a cleansing

kut, are examples of nŏk-kut.

The naerim-gut, or initiation ceremony, in which a spirit is enshrined in the body of a kangsinmu, or possessed shaman, is one of the more commonly performed kut today. Kangsinmu also perform the *sin-gut,* a rite held on a regular basis in which the shaman and his or her believers honor the deity who has possessed the shaman. Hereditary shamans do not perform this rite.

Nŏk-kut

Religion has always dealt with the issue of death. For this reason, it is no surprise that the nŏk-kut, a ritual in which the spirit of the dead is guided to the other world, is the most commonly performed kut.

In Shamanism, there is no concept of heaven, hell or a world beyond the grave. When one dies, one simply leaves this world (*isŭng*) for the other world, the world of the dead (*chŏsŭng*). The boundaries of life and death are clearly delineated.

Not everyone can give up life in this world so easily. It is human nature to want to live as long as possible, and for people who feel slighted or unjustly treated in this life, it is only natural that their souls are reluctant to go on to the other world, even after their bodies have died. Someone who has died at an early age, without marrying perhaps, harbors a great deal of resentment and unfulfilled wishes, *han*, a concept crucial to an understanding of the Korean psyche.

These disgruntled souls lead a pathetic existence, caught between the world of the living and the world of the dead, and can be dangerous to the living. By performing a nŏk-kut, a shaman can send these spirits to the other world, protecting the living and offering peace to the dead. The nŏk-kut thus reveals an essential element of Korean Shamanism: the concept of salvation from without. No matter how virtuous and moral one is in life, a kut is the only way a soul can be assured of peace in the other world.

While nŏk-kut vary from region to region, their basic structure is almost always the same. It begins with the oral narration of the Pari Kongju myth, the epic tale of the seventh daughter of an ancient emperor, Pari Kongju, who was abandoned by her parents at birth. As punishment for their actions, her parents fell victim to a fatal disease and passed on to the other world. Being a filial daughter, however, Pari Kongju searched for a magical medicine to cure her parents and ultimately was able to bring them back to life. In the kut, the shaman asks Pari Kongju to guide the dead to the other world.

In the second act of the kut, known as *hanp'uri* (literally "relieving the han"), the resentment of the disgruntled spirit is alleviated. If a kangsinmu is performing the kut, the spirit of the deceased enters the shaman's body. It speaks through the shaman, describing all its frustrations and lingering attachments to the world of the living.

When a hereditary shaman performs this kut, the hanp'uri is performed with a spirit stick made from a pine branch or bamboo pole. The shaman focuses her attention on the stick, and the spirit enters it, causing it to shake violently. The shaman thus becomes the soul of the departed for a brief moment during which she shares its sadness with the grieving family.

In the Chŏlla region, the nŏk-kut is called ssitkim-gut, or "cleansing kut." The hanp'uri portion of the kut is known as *kop'uri*, the "unraveling of the knots." In kop'uri, nine lengths of cotton fabric are tied in seven knots looped around the deceased's rice bowl. These knots, symbols of life's hardships and resentments, are unraveled in the course of the shaman's dance. Kop'uri is the most highly developed and artistic of the hanp'uri performed by Korean shamans.

The final act of the nŏk-kut marks the spirits' departure from the human world. After the hanp'uri, the spirit is free from all lingering attachments and ready to depart for the other world. A Buddhist chant is performed as long strips of cotton cloth, symbolizing the road from this world to the other world, and linen cloth, symbolizing the entrance of the other world, are stretched across the kut site. The mudang performs a dance along the length of the cloth "roads," carrying a model boat for

the departed spirit to ride into the other world. When a kangsinmu performs the kut, the shaman rips the cloth, symbolizing the departed's salvation through a complete break with this world.

The nŏk-kut not only relieves the resentments harbored by dead souls but also eases the pain of the living. The sight of the shaman unraveling the knots one by one in the kop'uri segment allows the spectators to experience the freeing of the spirits from the bonds of the human world.

Death severs the relationship between the living and the deceased in a fleeting instant, and all communication is broken off. This is why death is such a painful blow to both the living and the dead.

A kut is our only opportunity for reuniting the living with the dead. Through the kut, life and death can be reconciled. We often say that the shaman speaks in the voice of the dead, but in fact, the shaman also serves as the voice of the living, giving them an opportunity to repent and resolve their own pent-up resentments.

Thus the nŏk-kut performs two functions: sending the dead souls to the other world and liberating the living from that death. The nŏk-kut gives the living an opportunity to say farewell to their loved ones while at the same time allowing them to express their common grief, resolve their own differences, transcend their loss, and begin life anew.

Village Kut

The village kut is a communal rite promoting village harmony, health, and prosperity. It also serves as a village festival since it includes a variety of entertainments such as tightrope walking, rock-throwing contests, various team games, farmers' music, mask dance, and clowns. Everyone in the village comes out for the kut, and the crowds attract a throng of peddlers, craftsmen and minstrels ready to take advantage of the festival atmosphere.

In traditional society, the village kut performed an important social function, promoting village pride and a sense of community. The kut always focused on the village's productive activity. Thus in fishing villages, the tutelary deity of the kut was the god of the seas, while in a farming village the tutelary deity represented the land.

Both fishing and farming depend on cooperation. The village unit was the lifeline of the individual, so by helping others, one was really helping one's self. The kut served to reinforce this collective consciousness and contribute to the well-being of the village as a whole.

However, it was precisely because of this social function that Shamanism and the village kut were suppressed during the Japanese colonial period. Following liberation in 1945, the traditional village unit was destroyed by the Korean War and the social chaos caused by the division of the Korean peninsula. As a result, many village kut have disappeared. This process of decline was further exacerbated by the Saemaŭl (New Village) Movement promoted by the Park Chung-hee regime. Many of the remaining village shrines were destroyed as part of the movement's campaign against superstition.

Korea's rapid urbanization has also been an important factor in the decline of village kut. The strong emotional bond linking people with similar lifestyles is lacking in urban life, and, as a result, there is little common ground for a community kut, even among people living in the same apartment building.

Few village kut survive today. The tradition remains relatively strong along the east coast and on Cheju Island, as well as in a few of Seoul's older neighborhoods. Also a number of village kut such as the Kangnŭng Tano rite and the Ŭnsan *pyŏlsin-gut* have been preserved as intangible cultural assets by the government.

While community-oriented kut are disappearing, p'udakkŏri rites performed by shamans unskilled in the more advanced rituals are increasing at an unprecedented rate. The problem with these ceremonies and simple rites performed by housewives at shamanistic shrines deep in the mountains is that they are exclusive and narrowly focused on personal desires. Traditional kut were open to the greater community. Anyone could participate. Whether a village kut or a family kut, the rite was performed in the spirit of the common good. It was a way of life that brought people closer together, offering them answers to life's questions through the meeting of gods and humans. However, the secret performance of p'udakkŏri at secluded mountain shrines is a selfish, individualistic activity. While this trend away from village and community-oriented kut does not necessarily reflect the disintegration of Korea's traditional communal culture, it clearly reveals a growing propensity for self-centered individualism in society today. ◆

Village kut *bring communities together, promoting pride and solidarity.*

Shamanism's Influence on Traditional Society and the Arts

Kim Tae-gon

The *kut*, rituals performed by professional shamans, expresses the basic thought pattern of Korean Shamanism—a combination of philosophies embracing deities, the universe, spirits, the afterlife, and shamanistic songs. These songs, chanted at rituals, are the verbal expression of Shamanism. At present, some 1,000 songs from across the country have been collected and recorded.

Some are ritualistic chants used to purify the kut site and participants, or to invoke and send off gods, but most express the suppliant's reverence for his or her ancestors, and the desire for many sons, a long life, good fortune, protection from bad luck, health, and a comfortable afterlife.

In short, a shamanistic ritual is an expression of the human aspiration for the eternal continuation of one's existence, for abundance rather than poverty, for strength over weakness, and life rather than death. The shamanistic logic of reversal—that is the concept of transforming the definite to the indefinite, delimited reality to unlimited eternity, death to life, and nothing to something—is beyond the reason of modern man, who would dismiss it as irrational and unrealistic.

Modern man only trusts phenomena of the physical world, but a shamanist, equipped with a multidimensional view of existence, accepts both the natural and the supernatural worlds and places greater importance on the latter.

This dual mind-set stems from Shamanism's arche-pattern philosophy which has all beings of the universe originating from chaos, a nonspatial, nontemporal state of confusion and disorder that preceded the emergence of the cosmos. The term "arche-pattern" expresses the search for the source—the "arche"—of all existence. When viewed from modern man's perspective of reason and logic, life and death and existence and nonexistence are diametric opposites separated by an unbridgeable chasm, but from the viewpoint of the shamanistic arche-pattern, they share a common origin coming from a primordial chaos which precedes the emergence of the cosmos, or from the separation of the cosmos from chaos.

To believe in gods and the existence of spirits is to believe in intangible, eternal beings beyond the limits of time and space. They are part of a nonspatial, nontemporal chaos. Shamanism is based on a belief that man owes his birth to God, that when he dies, he returns in the state of a spirit to the other world where he will either continue to live in immortality or assume a human body and return to this world. Man can "commute" between the two worlds because they are still embraced in chaos, not separated.

Shamanistic rituals are based on this inclusive arche-pattern. They are manifestations of humanity's eternal circulation beyond the limits of the cosmos to the eternal realm of chaos and back.

The concept of an arche-pattern, however, is not exclusive to the shamanistic tradition. It underlies all Korean folk philosophies, including folk beliefs and seasonal customs, oral traditions, paintings and arts, although it is not as evident in these as it is in Shamanism.

With its multidimensional view embracing both the real but transitory world and the unreal but eternal world, Shamanism appeases man's aspirations for eternal circulation more effectively than other religions and thus has much broader appeal. The belief in eternal circulation is not simply a religious phenomenon; it also has made a profound influence on traditional society and the arts in general.

Shamanism influences society in three basic ways. First, shamanistic ritual is a means of perpetuating social orthodoxy. Most traditional Korean villages have shrines to their tutelary deities and hold periodic community rituals to pray for village welfare and prosperity. These rituals, often called *tanggut* (shrine kut), take place every year or every three years depending on the size of the village and its religious fervor. By repeating the ritual in the same form and manner over hundreds of years—thus passing down the "pattern" of their ancestors' lifestyle—the villagers reconfirm their sense of

community and traditional values. Thus the ritual perpetuates traditional customs and orthodoxy.

Second, we must note Shamanism's contribution to the promotion of psychological bonds and solidarity within a community. Since the village kut is a communal event, the whole village is involved in its preparation. The villagers observe taboos together and they avoid impurities together. The taboo period is usually 21 days; however, in some coastal and island areas, it can stretch from 100 days to a year. Since the villagers share the belief that lax observation of taboos risks a poor harvest or fishing catch, epidemics and other misfortunes, the entire population unites in observing the taboos. They also contribute as much cash or grain to the ritual expenses as they can afford.

The day after the village kut on the eve of the first full moon by the lunar calendar, the villagers play a game of tug-of-war. The game usually pits two neighboring villages against each other, and, in some regions, the men against the women. It is traditionally believed that the winning side will enjoy a bumper harvest, so villagers take the event quite seriously.

The village kut is an essential rallying point for the villagers, a centripetal force promoting community solidarity and a sense of belonging. Active involvement by the entire community is encouraged from the earliest preparatory stages to the rite itself and maintained through the ensuing activities, such as the tug-of-war and other games.

Shamanism's third major contribution to society has been its influence on democratic development. The procedures and details of the community kut are traditionally determined at a village meeting. Villagers meet around the 20th day of the last month of the lunar year to elect the officiants, estimate expenses, and establish how funds will be raised. These decisions are reached democratically with the opinions of every villager reflected in one way or another.

The morning after the kut, villagers gather again and partake of the foods that were offered on the altar during the kut. Expenses are accounted in detail, the results are posted, and the balance, if any, is put aside for future use in community expenses. Other important village affairs, such as the building of bridges or dams or the widening of roads, are also discussed and settled at these meetings. The kut meetings thus serve as forums promoting democracy in traditional society.

Shamanism has had an undeniable influence on the performing arts, including folk music, drama, dance and literature, especially in the

208

genre of oral tradition and folklore. In fact, one could say shamanistic rituals are an aggregate of all folk arts.

The kut is composed of music, dance and drama from start to finish. The shaman sings, dances and performs an extemporaneous drama by alternately acting out godly behaviors and supplicatory gestures. While it would be difficult to differentiate each element of music, dance and drama as an independent artistic genre within the kut, the ritual is clearly the source from which these art forms have developed.

Shamanism holds an important place in the history of Korean art because it has influenced the development of almost all art forms. Paintings of Shamanism's many deities were the first religious paintings in Korea, just as shamanistic sculptures were the forerunners of subsequent sculptural genre. Paper flowers, lanterns and boats used in the kut promoted the development of paper crafts, and the ritual costumes worn by shamans are an excellent source of information for the study of sartorial development in Korea.

The *pŏm-gut*, a tiger mask dance-drama included in the *pyŏlsin-gut* performed in some coastal areas of the Kyŏngsang-do region, is for all intents and purposes a religious drama. The masks employed in the *t'al-nori*, or the mask dance and drama, are also related to Shamanism.

T'al-nori was traditionally performed after a village kut during the New Year season. The performances held around the first full moon in T'ongyŏng, Kosŏng, Suyŏng and Tongnae are believed to have originally been performed following the community kut on the eve of the first full moon. Inasmuch as the community kut is a celebration of the new year, the performance of the t'al-nori in the "chaotic" transitional period between the old and new years is quite pertinent, especially because the masks symbolize shaman spirits. Thus mask dance drama is not simply a recreational program for the holiday season but the embodiment of the idea of universal circulation in which an old world ends and a new one begins.

Nong'ak, or farmer's music, is closely linked to shamanistic rituals. The musical instruments used, including the *kkwaenggari* (small gong), *ching* (gong), *puk* (drum), *changgo* (hour-glass drum), *hojok* (wooden oboe), and *sogo* (small drum), are indispensable to the *chisinpalpki*, a New Year's celebration in which kut officiants and musicians dance through the village, visiting every house, to appease the earth god (*chisin*). Clearly Shamanism has done much to promote nong'ak.

Shamanism has made a comparable contribution to the development of dance for dance is a natural part of any shamanistic ritual.

The *changsŭngje*, another New Year celebration program held to erect guardian spirit posts (*changsŭng*) at the entrance of the village, could be called Shamanism's contribution to the development of Korean sculpture. The spirit posts are reerected every three years during the New Year season in the lunar leap year. Standing sentinel at the entrance of a village, these grotesque spirit posts have a special place in Korean sculpture.

Shamanism's influence on literature can be traced to the songs chanted during the kut. Shaman songs have been passed down in the form of epics, lyrics, drama, and narrations. The epics deal with shamanistic mythology, from which most of Korean mythology is derived. They are also the starting point for Korea's oral tradition.

These epics depict the lives of heroes in three parts: birth, deeds and death. This biographical structure is repeated throughout Korea's founda-

tion myths, legends, traditional novels and modern novels.

Shamanistic epics are believed to have provided a platform for the development of a broad oral tradition including folklore and *p'ansori*, dramatic mono-opera. P'ansori originated in Shamanism and later developed into the traditional novel form.

A study of some 1,000 shamanistic songs supports the theory that they originated as religious myths in the epic style but later developed into narrative songs as epic elements were eliminated in the course of oral transmission. On the other hand, we can also assume that, with the loss of the epic theme, the mythical religious motif was revived in a lyrical style and further developed into a narrative style. This narrative style can, in turn, be seen as a transitional mode developed in the process of restoring the mythological epic style.

How do these three styles differ? Shamanistic mythology of the epic mode establishes an individual god as its hero and features an objective portrayal of his life in three stages: birth and growth; achievements and service to society; and death and deification. In short, the epic is a three-part biography of a shaman deity.

Lyrical songs, on the other hand, have neither dramatic story lines or heroes. They are arbitrary prayers dealing with everyday needs and wishes which a shaman expresses to a deity on behalf of human clients. Most extant shamanis-

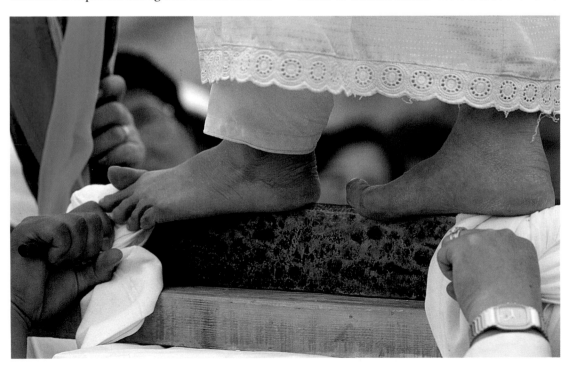

In some rites, the shaman walks on razor-sharp fodder blades (above). Injuries are rare as the shaman is in a deep trance. At right, a male shaman carries a spirit stick in preparation for the spirit's appearance.

tic songs fall into this category.

Shamanistic narratives have no heroes, and although they sometimes have plots, they generally lack consistency and objectivity. They are usually a statement of facts about the universe and human relationships, a shaman's narration to a god about the clients' wishes, or a narration to humans about the deity's thoughts and judgments.

The latter is best exemplified by the charismatic shaman's oracle, or *kongsu*, in which the shaman claims the spirit of the dead speaks through her. However, kongsu cannot be classified as a separate genre of shamanistic songs.

Narratives, in which man's needs and wishes are relayed to a god, are often confused with lyrical shamanistic songs. However, they are simply meant to inform the deity of human situations and are not actual prayers.

Some shamanistic songs are dramatic with consistent plot development. These songs can be divided into two categories: songs with dialogues for individual players and songs with dialogues adapted from a plot by the shaman during her kut performance. Neither, however, can be considered an independent drama because in the first case, the song is often part of a shaman epic, and in the second case, the song is essentially a spontaneous narrative in which the shaman relies heavily on her own resourcefulness. It does not have a consistent plot or developed story line.

Shamanistic songs are a form of primitive literature composed of a mosaic of styles that are still developing into independent literary genres. For this reason, we cannot apply the literary standards we use to analyze modern literary works.

In summary, Shamanism constitutes an effort by humanity to achieve its aspirations through the kut, a shamanistic ritual based on a philosophy of eternal circulation in which poverty can be transformed to wealth, illness to health, a short life to a long life, unhappiness to happiness, and so on. This eternal circulation is in turn based on the shamanistic arche-pattern, a multidimensional view of the universe in which chaos is thought to have reigned prior to the emergence of the spatial and temporal order of the cosmos.

The arche-pattern philosophy and the shaman ritual are interrelated. When the kut is a community ritual, it serves a social function, promoting solidarity and perpetuating village orthodoxy. When the rite simulates divine behavior, it is a conglomeration of various arts, from which individual genres such as dance, drama, music and literature develop. ◆ 211

The Implements and Costumes of the Shaman

Kim Kwang-on

The shaman flings her fan open and shouts: "Don't you realize who I am? I'm the dignified, the heroic, the wonder-working General Ch'oe!"

"Oh yes!" the villagers cry, rubbing their palms together as they bow.

"Who gives you the clothes you wear, the things you use, the food you eat? Is this all you've prepared for my feast? I should slice open your bellies and cut your throats! Do you realize how you've sinned?"

"What do we stupid humans know?" the villagers respond. "We may eat our rice with spoons, but we're no better than dogs or pigs. Please forgive us and accept our humble offerings. We already owe you so much, but please grace us with more of your great wisdom ..."

The villagers bow once more. Only then does the enraged general, embodied in the shaman, relent and bestow good fortune on them.

The above is the third act (kŏri) of a traditional 12-act community rite (sansang-gut). In this act, the village guardian deity, represented by Ch'oe Yŏng, a famous Koryŏ general from the 14th century, is invited to the ritual site. The shaman wears an indigo coat and colored horsehair hat, a costume modeled after traditional military uniforms, and carries a falchion in one hand and a trident in the other. At various points during the rite, she wields these tools proudly to reflect the dignity of the spirit that inhabits her. The villagers gasp in awe as the ferocious general seems to come to life.

The falchion, or ch'ŏngnyŏngdo, consists of a 50cm-long curved blade and a 70cm-long wooden handle. The prongs of the samjich'ang trident measure approximately 30cm in length and are connected to a long wooden handle. When in a state of ecstasy, the shaman drives the trident into the ground and balances the head of a pig or cow on top of it. If the trident stands erect, the shaman is thought to be truly possessed and the deity is believed to be partaking in the rite.

Folding fans are essential shamanistic accessories. They are named for the colorful paintings that decorate them. Among the most common are sambul-sŏn (three-Buddhas fans), ch'ilsŏng-sŏn (seven-stars fans), and irwŏl-sŏn (sun-and-moon fans).

But who is this General Ch'oe Yŏng so widely worshiped in Korean Shamanism? A famous military officer known for his upstanding moral character, Ch'oe served as commander-in-chief of the Koryŏ army in the late 14th century but met a tragic death at the hands of his deputy commander, Yi Sŏng-gye, during Koryŏ's campaign against Ming China in 1388. Yi then turned his troops against the Koryŏ king and staged a coup d'état to found the Chosŏn Dynasty.

Over the centuries Ch'oe has been revered for his bravery in battle and undaunted loyalty to the Koryŏ court. He was also a man of rare integrity, setting a model for the honest official. Along with General Im Kyŏng-ŏp of 17th century Chosŏn, Ch'oe is one of the most widely worshiped figures in Korean Shamanism, a benevolent god capable of dispelling evil spirits and bringing happiness.

In view of General Ch'oe's reputation as a great military leader and loyal subject, it may seem strange that he should complain, through the vehicle of a shaman, about the food offered to him during a shamanistic rite or kut. However, this simple fact reveals a fundamental characteristic of Korean Shamanism as well as of the Korean people's outlook on life in general: for Koreans, the world of the spirits is governed by the same rules as the human world. The old saying—"The spirits pay for the food they eat"—indicates how hard life was in the old days. People believed even the great General Ch'oe could be moved to grant his blessings if offered opulent sacrifices.

Shamans use fodder cutters, or chaktu, to demonstrate the mysterious power of the spirits they embody. A pair of iron blades, each

The costumes of the shamans account for much of the visual excitement of a kut.
Shamans change costumes and headgear to personify the various deities that appear during the kut.

Kim Soo-nam

213

about 80cm long, are placed parallel to each other, about 20cm apart. I have watched shamans dance barefoot on these razor-sharp blades on two occasions, but both times without the slightest injury.

Preparation for this awe-inspiring feat is a meticulous rite in itself. The shaman hones the blades on a whetstone until they are sharp enough to cut through a tree branch with ease. The sharpening of the blades is an important procedure because the shamans believe the spirits will be angered by improper preparation of the blades.

The freshly honed chaktu are placed on a precarious platform made of several stout ceramic jugs. With people on either side holding the blades firmly in place, the barefoot shaman mounts the chaktu. The spectators hold their breath in amazement. I actually closed my eyes, and when I opened them, the shaman was dancing on the fodder blades, swinging her arms. No one could doubt the existence of supernatural beings at that moment.

Shamans also use sacred swords known as *sink'al* in their rites. The sink'al are actually iron or bamboo sticks draped with long strips of white paper. At the beginning of the rite the sink'al are waved back and forth to chase away unwanted evil spirits. They are used again at the end of the rite to disperse any minor spirits that may have gathered near the ritual site.

Other tools of the shaman's calling include *myŏngdo*, round brass plates, and *myŏngdari*, long strips of cloth used in prayers for newborn children.

The myŏngdo (also known as *myŏngdu*) is a convex brass mirror engraved with inscriptions of the sun, moon, the fortuitous "seven stars," and Sanskrit lettering. At several times during the kut, the shaman places the myŏngdo on a pile of glutinous rice and offers a prayer. She then lifts it up to see how many grains of rice have stuck to the back. An odd number of grains indicates good fortune while an even number signifies bad luck.

In certain regions of central Korea, myŏngdo reflect the status of the shaman. A senior shaman (*sin ŏmŏni* or "spiritual mother") hands over her myŏngdo to one of her apprentices (*sin ttal*, "spiritual daughter") as a sign of the latter's formal appointment as successor.

Myŏngdari, or "life strips," are long pieces of silk or cotton, on which the names, dates of birth and addresses of the children of shaman clients are written in ink.

As late as 1945, the average Korean life span did not exceed 40 years due mainly to the high

This ritual altar reveals the many implements of the shaman: lotus lanterns, brass bells, concave mirrors, fans, folk paintings, incense, candles and numerous offerings of fruit and grain.

infant mortality rate. Many women gave birth at home in unsanitary conditions. Indeed, most Korean women over the age of 70 today gave birth to as many as ten children, but in many cases more than half of the babies died in infancy. Thus it is only natural that Koreans of this period resorted to Shamanism to pray for their offspring's health and longevity.

The shaman becomes a baby's adoptive mother when its parents present her with a myŏngdari and pay her for regular rites held at her household shrine. During these rites, the shaman calls out the baby's name as she dances about with the myŏngdari in her hands.

The number of myŏngdari entrusted to a shaman is an indicator of her popularity and the breadth of her influence. Shamans known for their skill are entrusted with many myŏngdari, and the strips are handed down to their sin ttal when the senior shaman retires. When a shaman moves, she may even sell her myŏngdari to another local shaman. The strips are replaced with new fabric after a certain period of time.

Bells are an indispensable tool to the Korean shaman. The spirits are said to be lured to the ritual site by the sound of the shaman's bells. However, the speed with which the spirits respond to the ringing depends on the individ-

ual shaman's skill. Cho Yŏng-ja, a shaman who lived in Yangju County in Kyŏnggi-do province during the 1960s, was actually called the "Bell Mother" because the spirits responded to her bells as soon as she picked them up.

Some scholars believe the name of the legendary founder of the Korean nation, Tan'gun, may be associated with the word tan'gol or tanggol, which means either customer or patron, or a favorite shaman in the vocabulary of Korean Shamanism. Some even contend the Buddhist monk-historian Iryŏn (1206-89) invented the name, Tan'gun, when he transcribed the pure Korean word tan'gol into Chinese characters for his *Memorabilia of the Three Kingdoms.* This book contains the oldest known reference to Tan'gun.

Tan'gun is believed to have been the shaman monarch of the first kingdom to rule Korea. In the Chŏlla region of southern Korea, shamans are still called tanggol or *tanggul.* Some scholars also contend the three heavenly treasures brought by Tan'gun's father when he descended to earth were the sword, myŏngdo and bells used by today's shamans.

Music is an essential part of any shamanistic rite. In the central regions of Korea, instrumental music has an especially important role in the kut. It accompanies all the shaman's songs and

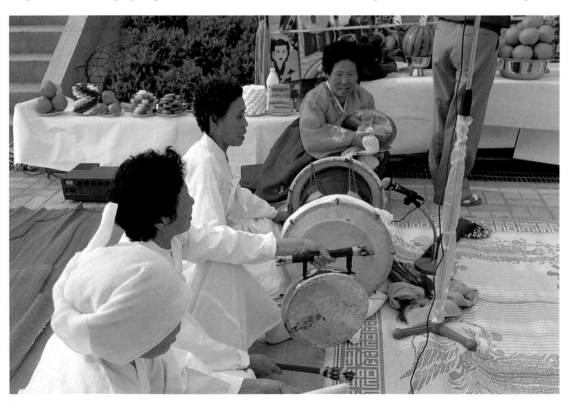

Music and dance are part of all shamanistic rites. Above, village women accompany a rite on the chegŭm *(cymbals), an hourglass drum and a* ching *(gong). At right, a shaman performs a knife dance while in a state of possession.*

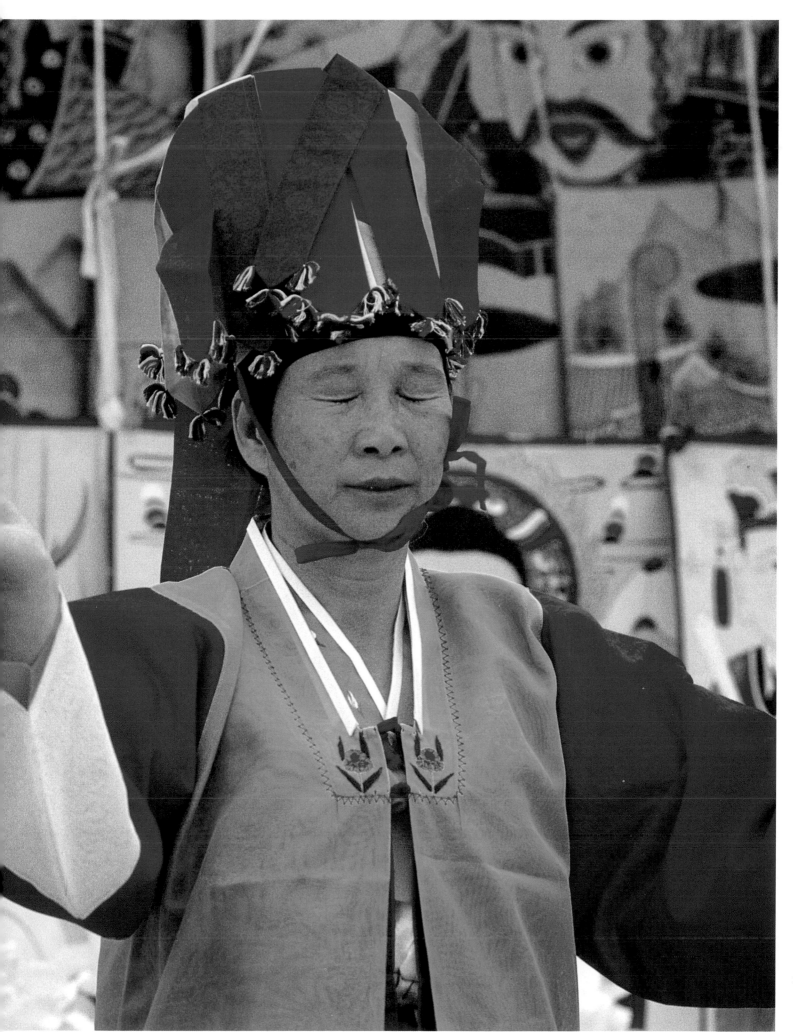

dances.

Among the many musical instruments played in shamanistic rituals, the hourglass drum, or *changgo*, is certainly the most important. It accompanies the articulation of the deities' blessing while the other instruments remain silent. The changgo's unique sound derives from its special construction: one head of the drum is covered with ox leather while the other is covered with horse or dog leather.

Shamans carry their own gongs (*ching*) and small cymbals (*chegŭm*), but other instruments such as the *p'iri*, a short bamboo flute, the *chŏttae*, a longer flute, and the *haegŭm*, a two-stringed fiddle, are usually brought by the musicians, or *chaebi*, who are often the husbands of the shamans. These men travel to ritual sites with their wives, perform odd jobs in preparation for the rites, and play the accompanying music. Large rites require several shamans, so the husbands make up a team of their own. In rites performed in fishing villages along the eastern coast, these musicians are called *hwaraengï*, a term that hints of a connection to *hwarang*, or "flower knights," talented young men of aristocratic birth who served the Silla Kingdom.

In large rites, the musical ensemble is made up of six musicians, two p'iri players and one person to play each of the other four instruments, the haegŭm, the chŏttae, the changgo, and the *puk*, a small single-barreled drum. Smaller rites are generally accompanied by a duet consisting of one p'iri and a haegŭm, or a trio of one p'iri, one haegŭm, and one chŏttae.

A variety of different implements and materials are used for shamanistic divination. Coins are one handy device used for fortunetelling. First the shaman reads her prayer, holding seven or nine coins in her hand. She then throws the coins on a table to see how many land overlapped. An odd number indicates good fortune while even numbers are considered unlucky.

This numerical concept holds true for divination using grains of rice as well. A pile of rice measuring 3 *toe* and 3 *hop* (1 toe equals 18 liters or 10 hop) is placed on a table. The shaman reads her prayer, calling out the name, birth date and address of the person whose fortune is being told. The fortune is revealed by the number of grains of rice scattered around the pile.

Bamboo strips inscribed with signs are also used for fortunetelling. A set of 60 strips, 0.5cm wide and 12cm long, are kept in a cylindrical container. The shaman shakes the container as she says her prayer and then selects one strip, which reveals the fortune of her client.

The shaman's implements and costumes account for much of the mystery and power of Korean Shamanism.

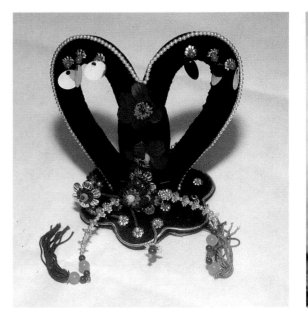

The costumes of the Korean shaman account for much of the visual excitement of the kut. Shamans originally from Hwanghae-do province (now part of North Korea) change their costumes for nearly every act in the 12-kŏri kut. Costumes from this region are by far the most colorful in Korean Shamanism. In 1963, a shaman from Hwanghae-do brought six bags of costumes for a four-day kut held in Inch'ŏn. I know of no shamanistic tradition in the world that can compete with Hwanghae-do when it comes to colorful costumes.

Shamans from the central region, including Kyŏnggi-do and Ch'ungch'ŏng-do, change costumes to personify the various deities that appear during the kut. Shamans from the Chŏlla region in the south wear the same simple white *chŏgori* jacket and *ch'ima* skirt, the traditional dress of Korean women, throughout the rite.

The costumes of the central region typify Korea's shamanistic ritual wear. The basic outfit consists of a long indigo skirt and a light blue jacket, a traditional dress that could be worn by any ordinary woman. The shaman wears a coat, known as *kugunbok*, fashioned after the uniform of a Chosŏn era military officer, over this dress when she embodies the spirit of a deceased general. The kugunbok is black and has narrow red sleeves. The back is slit at the center to facilitate the shaman's energetic movements as she performs in a trance.

Another traditional military uniform used by the shaman is the *chŏnbok*, a long blue vest with deep slits at the side and back.

The *namch'ŏllik*, a long blue coat, was worn by military officials of the third rank or higher during the Chosŏn period. The coat has a straight neckline and is pleated around the waist. The sleeves touch the ground and have white bands along their edges.

Even more colorful is the green coat with rainbow-colored sleeves worn during the act honoring the spirit of a deceased entertainer, or *ch'angbusin*. This coat is slit up the sides to the armpits, and the panels in front and back extend only to the knees.

The shaman's colorful horsehair hat was also part of the military outfits of the Chosŏn era. Of all the headgear worn by Korean shamans, the most ostentatious is the *pŏnggŏji*, part of the uniform of ranking military officers during the Chosŏn period. The hat is made of cloud-patterned silk with a bright indigo lining. It is decorated with colorful tassels and a peacock feather. When a shaman wears this hat cocked slightly to one side, she personifies the rich sartorial tradition of Korean Shamanism. ◆

RELIGION IN MODERN TIMES

Few countries can boast as rich a religious spectrum as modern Korea. Traditional thought systems, such as Confucianism and Buddhism, remain strong in the face of the widespread popularity of Catholicism and Protestantism, relatively new imports. And we must not forget the myriad of indigenous religions, such as Ch'ŏndogyo and Won Buddhism, which incorporate elements of traditional religions and modern nationalist historical interpretations.

In this final section, our contributors tell of religion and philosophy in modern Korea. The story echoes the instability and hardships of Korea's modern history. Foreign invasions, both military and cultural, rock the country as never before. Rulers experiment with isolation, but in the end, Korea opens up to new ideas, wholeheartedly embracing some and carefully selecting others.

Adapting to Historical Circumstances

Chung Chin-hong

From time immemorial, people have asked what it means to be human and what makes life worth living. These never-ending queries reflect the many problems of human existence and, at the same time, show that the search for answers is the essence of culture, the sum total of human life.

Religion, a cultural phenomenon, is the most specific and direct manifestation of this aspect of human life. It could be called a "symbolic system of answers" to humanity's existential quest. Every culture has its own doctrine of salvation. This is a universal characteristic of all religions.

Korean religions must be considered within this context. From a simplistic progressive historical perspective, traditional culture is often thought primitive. It is sometimes labeled backward or wrong from the viewpoint of major world religions. We must examine the validity of these claims within the context of universality because preconceptions undermine a true understanding of Korean religion and thought.

I will attempt to describe Korean religion and thought in a historical context, considering the ethos of native religions, how imported religions—Buddhism, Confucianism and Christianity— were grafted onto the native belief system, and how they have interacted to produce the current religious atmosphere.

Korea's native doctrine of salvation has been handed down in two forms: the symbolic system of answers that is either inferred from the experience of a "god" or presented by a "god," and Shamanism, the search for a divine force through the medium of a priest.

Korea's foundation myth, which describes the birth and legendary life of Tan'gun, is a narrative form of traditional religious thought. The founding father, Tan'gun, is described as a descendent of a heavenly god. From earliest times, Koreans believed in a supreme being symbolized by the sky or heavens. This belief is clearly evident in the religious ceremonies of all three early Korean kingdoms: *Yŏnggo*, the "spirit-invoking" drum ceremonies which the Puyŏ people performed to honor heavens, the *Tongmaeng* ancestral worship ceremony honoring the founder-king of Koguryŏ, and the *Much'ŏn* "dance to Heaven," a form of worship to heavens practiced by the Yemaek people. While these ceremonies are no longer performed today, modern Koreans continue to recognize and revere the existence of a supreme being expressed as the "heavens" or a "god."

Shamanism is Korea's most vibrant traditional religion because its basic purpose, rites and mode of expression remain intact. It is premised on the existence of a certain power, or god, capable of solving problems faced in everyday life. The prayers of the shaman, a medium between the supreme being and humans,

bring that power to the service of believers. Attendance at a *kut*, a rite presided over by a shaman, is central to this religious life. Through this rite-oriented religious practice participants can experience transcendence and the sacredness of the supreme being. While Shamanism did not develop as an orderly doctrine or give birth to an organized religious community, it does provide direct and practical answers to life's questions and is familiar to all Koreans.

The traditional reverence of heaven and the tendency toward Shamanism have at times been congenial and at other times have been in conflict. The dual structure of Korea's doctrine of salvation has shaped indigenous religious practices through the centuries, while at the same time providing a favorable environment for the accommodation of non-Korean religions.

Buddhism, which came to Korea from India in the fourth century, was, from a cultural point of view, decidedly foreign. Buddhism was embraced, however, despite cultural differences between India and Korea. Its explanation of human suffering as a cycle of birth, aging, sickness and death described the realities of life everywhere, and the answers derived from its many questions were accepted as providing a blueprint for an ideal way of life, however foreign the religion's claims or doctrines might have been.

Buddhism's influence was felt in many ways. It provided a foundation for the polishing of Korea's traditional doctrine of salvation within a mystical framework. The Buddhist experience of enlightenment, Nirvana, the Pure Land and the many ceremonies held at temples allowed Koreans to expand their experience of religious salvation to include a broader orthodoxy which could not be found in native religions. Buddhism offered a mystical narrative form, or mythos, reflected in the theories of all-encompassing harmony advanced by Wonhyo, the noted Buddhist master (617-686). For Wonhyo, harmony and generosity were practical tools for everyday life.

Korean Buddhism is interesting for the choices Koreans made as they embraced the religion. Their traditional faith in a supreme being resulted in a preference for Maitreya, the Future Buddha, and their experience in Shamanism caused them to favor Avalokitesvara, the bodhisattva of compassion, who embodied the belief in the power of salvation from without.

Buddhism enriched the religious vernacular and thought patterns, broadened the culture's religious horizons, and helped Koreans experience inexplicable mysteries in their everyday lives.

No one is sure when Confucianism arrived in Korea. Quibbling over the exact date of its introduction is meaningless

because Korean culture had long been under the influence of the Chinese writing system and Chinese culture, which took the Confucian value system for granted. Koreans' predilection for Confucianism is evident from the Confucian-inspired educational systems of the Three Kingdoms period and the 500-year history of the Confucianist Chosŏn Dynasty.

More important is the question of how Confucianism enriched Korea's religious life. Confucianism is generally divided into the study of the Classics, the study of the "Way" (*to*), or ethics, the study of the *Book of Changes*, or divination, the study of rites, and the study of Practical Learning, or *sirhak*. Among these, the study of the Classics and the study of rites were most

influential in Korea.

The native religious tradition did not have a rational norm for logical deduction. Koreans discussed mysticism and transcendence, but they lacked the concepts or logic needed to explain these states. While its fundamental principles were not necessarily equal to the ideals of Buddhism or native religions, Confucianism provided a rational framework for religious experience. The development of Neo-Confucianism revealed a brilliant new culture, namely logos—the Confucian logical orthodoxy—within the context of indigenous religious thought.

This rational philosophical framework also provided governing principles for individual behavior, relationships and commu-

nity life. It offered a clear-cut structure for all manner of human rites, and helped place familial ethics and political morality in a more specific and practical context. In Confucianism, traditional customs and rites found their theoretical foundation.

It was within this religious context that the ruler was accepted as a supreme being, as a priest who provided answers through the wielding of power. The heads of all communities, including the head of the household, were accepted as symbols of this religious function. In other words, the indigenous religious tradition was actively represented within the Confucian framework.

While Catholicism and Protestantism arrived at different points in Korea's history, both represented profound cultural shocks because they were more unfamiliar than other religions. Christianity has, however, been successfully transplanted to Korea.

Christianity's success owes much to the timing of its introduction. Both Catholicism and Protestantism came to Korea in times of great social and political upheaval. Historically, the introduction of Christianity went hand in hand with Koreans' early encounters with the Western world and their first experiences with modernization.

The most important factor in Christianity's relative success has been the similarities between Christian theology and the

Christian concept of God and the structures of Korea's traditional religions. Koreans' belief in a supreme being, together with the presence of shamans acting as spiritual mediators, helped overcome cultural differences inherent in Christian teachings. Their faith in an absolute and supreme being, once vague, was made specific. Christianity introduced a god that native religions had failed to define sufficiently. Christianity provided the theos missing from traditional religious thought.

The establishment of the concept of a divine being in such a specific manner provided Koreans an opportunity to reflect on how their traditional sense of salvation was realized morally in a sociological and historical context. Moreover, the emergence of a new community that encompassed men and women of all ages from all classes of society was a dramatic development because it pointed the way to the modern age.

Korea's religious tradition is not simply an amalgamation of native and foreign religions, however. The merging of religious cultures has also provided fertile soil for the emergence of new religions unique to Korea, religions which have appeared at critical junctures in Korea's history.

Nationalistic religions—most notably Ch'ŏndogyo, the "Religion of the Heavenly Way," Taejonggyo, a conservative sect with strong nationalistic overtones, Chŭngsan'gyo and Won Buddhism—are characterized by their fundamental assertion of Korea's primacy in the universe. These religions tended toward exclusive nationalism on occasion, but they have not been entirely self-centered in that they have tried to respond to threats to Korea's national identity through faith. They have also revealed a radical interpretation of modern history through concepts such as *kaebyŏk*, a thoroughly Korean theory of cosmic creation.

Indigenous religions have been handicapped to a certain extent because they do not share the universal vocabulary of the major world religions. They are, however, developing a new awareness and are beginning to play a more important role in modern society. All communities require a mythical foundation. Korea's indigenous religions contribute to the formation of historical identity in the language of traditional soteriology, the study of salvation as the effect of divine agency.

I have described, from the viewpoint of soteriology, how religions have developed in Korea, that is, the historical changes caused by the introduction of foreign religions.

Religion in modern Korean society is characterized by two factors. First, the religious atmosphere is richer than that of other cultures. This variety is not simply a quantitative matter. Throughout history, Koreans have interpreted imported religions in their own way, creating something meaningful within the context of their own culture. As a result, the Korean spiritual consciousness goes beyond the fundamental framework of native religions to embrace, in a mature and blended form, the mythos of Buddhism, the logos of Confucianism and the theos of Christianity. In addition, indigenous religions tell the ancient myths of old Korea. This richness—in a sense, a concentration of elements from all religions— is the most active and creative aspect of Korean religious life today.

This variety can serve as a model for the resolution of religious conflict. This does not mean, of course, that there are no religious conflicts in Korea. There have been persecutions and martyrs over time, but these were merely the results of specific circumstances, not a defining characteristic of Korea's religious history. Compared to Western cultures, Korea is relatively free of religious renunciation or conversion. It is not that Koreans do not understand the differences between religions; rather, they unconsciously know that differences can be overcome through harmony.

Secularization is gradually making inroads in Korea. Still, the tradition of tolerance plays a creative role. The power of religions has not diminished greatly; more than half the Korean people consider themselves religious, and the social pronouncements of religious leaders, of all faiths, are not taken lightly.

Korean religions are striving to offer a new soteriology which corresponds to the needs of modern society. They are focusing on current issues—democratization, economic justice, the environment, the quality of life, even unification—and are increasingly recognized for their role in contemporary affairs.

More important, however, is their role in the future. Certainly, the richness and harmony evident in Korean religion thus far will serve Korea well in the future. Variety and the ability to accommodate are essential to an open pluralist society. Creativity and effort, however, are also essential. Koreans must recognize the task ahead. Religious leaders must draw on a critical, analytic understanding of their own situation and address contemporary issues honestly. Fortunately, Korean religion is well-equipped for this task thanks to Korea's rich religious tradition. ◆

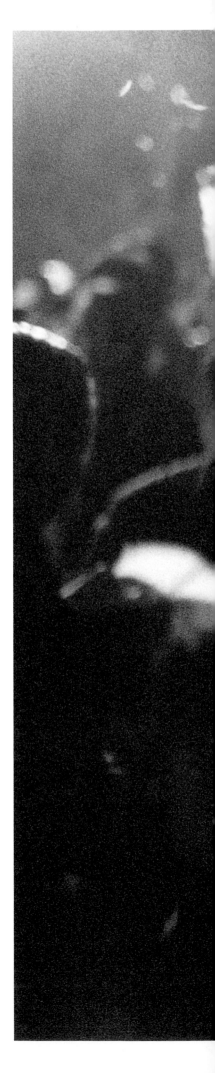

Indigenous Religions

Choi Joon-sik

Koreans have long adhered to a variety of religious beliefs, such as shamanism, indigenous to their culture, and others, including Confucianism, Buddhism and Taoism, imported from abroad. Toward the end of the Chosŏn Dynasty Korea saw the emergence of a new type of indigenous religion, beginning with the Tonghak ("Eastern Learning") Doctrine introduced by a young scholar Ch'oe Che-u (1824-1864). Indeed, the fifth day of the fourth lunar month in 1860, the day Ch'oe experienced his revelation, marked an unprecedented revolution in the history of Korean religion. Ch'oe was the first in a line of religious leaders, including Kang Il-sun (1871-1909), founder of the Chŭngsan belief, Pak Chung-bin (1891-1943), who founded Won Buddhism, and Na Ch'ŏl (1863-1916), founder of Tan'gun'gyo, the belief in Tan'gun, Korea's legendary founder. Never before had so many gifted religious leaders emerged in such a short period of Korean history.

The latter years of the Chosŏn Dynasty were a dark time during which the Korean people lost their sovereignty to the Japanese. Koreans attempted to revive their nation politically, militarily, economically and spiritually. The various indigenous religious movements were evidence of their efforts in the field of religion.

At present, there are somewhere between 300 and 400 new indigenous religious sects in Korea. Scholars divide these into approximately one dozen categories. First are the sects derived from the Tonghak Movement, best represented by the largest, Ch'ŏndogyo, the "Religion of the Heavenly Way." While no longer as influential as it was during the time of its founder, Ch'oe Che-u, and his disciple Ch'oe Si-hyŏng (1827-1898) or during the Japanese colonial period when it played a key role in the independence movement, Ch'ŏndogyo remains an important force in Korean society. More than 20 other sects, including Sich'ŏn'gyo, founded by Yi Yong-gu, a Tonghak apostate, in 1906, sprang from the Tonghak Movement. Only Ch'ŏndogyo remains active today.

Second to Ch'ŏndogyo in size is Tan'gun'gyo, the belief in Korea's legendary founder.

Taejonggyo, a conservative sect with strong nationalistic overtones, is the largest of the 20 or more sects affiliated with Tan'gun'gyo. However, the deteriorated condition of Taejonggyo headquarters on a hilltop in Seoul's Hongje-dong reflects the sect's pitiful status in modern Korean society, a stark contrast to the Japanese people's reverential treatment of Amaterasu Omikami, the Sun Goddess, the Japanese national progenitor, at the Ise imperial shrine in Nara. When visiting the Ise shrine several years ago I was struck by its size and carefully manicured grounds as well as the Japanese people's respectful attitude. During the Japanese colonial period, Taejong-gyo was the spiritual mainstay for Korean independence fighters in Manchuria, but it has lost much of its influence today.

Chŭngsan'gyo, founded by Kang Il-sun, comprised more than 60 sects in its heyday but is less popular in modern times. "The Great Peregrination" (*Taesun jŏn'gyŏng*), a written record of Kang's teachings, is an astonishing collection of religious elements borrowed from Confucianism, Buddhism, religious Taoism (Sŏndo), the cosmic principles of the *yin* and *yang*, geomancy and other beliefs. Kang is widely recognized as Korea's greatest religious syncretist. The largest remaining sect is found at Taesun Truth Church. Kang's teachings are also popular among university students, despite discordant relations between the Taesun Truth Church and student groups. Ironically, the core of Kang Il-sun's teach-

Traditional beliefs in the power of nature and tutelary deities have contributed to the development of modern indigenous religions such as Ch'ŏndogyo, housed in the Western-style building shown here.

Ch'oe Che-u

ing was the resolution of differences or deliverance from resentments, *haewon* in Korean. A number of smaller sects related to Chŭngsan'gyo are clustered around Kŭmsansa Temple in Chŏllabuk-do province where Kang Il-sun was most active.

Another denomination founded in the late Chosŏn period was Kim Il-bu's Namhak, which claimed to usher in a new era of creation though divination. Many indigenous religions have made similar assertions. Kim distinguished himself by providing a philosophical foundation for his claims through his theory of the "Right Divination" (*chŏng'yŏk*). Of the ten sects related to the Namhak lineage, the Gospel Singing and Dancing Church (Yŏnggamudohoe), which promotes an ecstatic atmosphere through dancing and the chanting of the five basic vowel sounds, is the best known.

Buddhist sects account for most of the new indigenous religions in modern times. With the revision of the Buddhist Property Management Act, the number of Buddhist sects has increased to about 80. The largest are the Ch'ŏnt'ae and Chin'gak sects. The Ch'ŏnt'ae sect accommodates many aspects of traditional Buddhism and prohibits marriage by monks or nuns. The Chin'gak

sect allows clergy to marry and has much in common with Esoteric Buddhism, including training in the recitation of mantras such as *Om mani padme hum*, literally, "Om, jewel of the lotus, hum." Monks and nuns of the Chin'gak sect are not required to shave their heads or give up their families. The Won Buddhism school, founded in the early twentieth century under the slogan "Let us reform our spirit as material changes reform our world" continues to grow and remains one of the most solid national religions of Korea.

Of the Christian sects active in Korea today, the Unification Church founded by the Reverend Sun Myung Moon (Mun Sŏn-myŏng) is by far the largest. In fact, the Unification Church is one of the largest churches in the Christian world and is worthy of note both for its positive and negative influences.

Of the new Christian churches in Korea, Pak T'ae-sŏn's "Village of Faith" is best known. At one time several thousand believers embraced Pak as their spiritual leader and shared in the village's communal lifestyle, but their numbers have decreased rapidly since his death.

Pak left a dark legacy. Cho Hŭi sŏng, a Pak disciple and founder of the Eternal Life Church (Yŏngsaenggyo), has been accused of involvement in the murder of more than 20 believers. Cho claimed the Pak era was over and took over as the "new savior," capable of offering perpetual youth through the Eternal Life Church, but he was arrested for operating a criminal organization that eliminated members who betrayed him or his church.

Let us turn now to religious groups derived from shamanistic, foreign or undetermined origins. Most religious groups founded by shamans consist of no more than a handful of believers. On the other hand, many of the religious groups founded overseas, such as the Mormon Church or the Jehovah's Witnesses, have many followers. Several Japanese religious groups, such as the Ch'angga Society, the Heavenly Principle Church (Ch'ŏlligyo), House of Growth (Saengjangŭi chip) and Ipchŏnggyosŏghoe, are also active in Korea. Of Chinese religious sects, Yiguandao (Ilgwando), a group which came to Korea to escape Mao's religious oppression in the 1950s, is most prominent. The Bahai faith of Iran and several Indian faiths have also attracted followers in Korea.

The philosophical origins of a number of sects are vague. The One Spirit Church (Han'ŏlgyo) was founded by Sin Chŏng-il, who received more than 40,000 votes when he ran for presi-

Wonbulgyo, a modern derivative of Buddhism, originated in Yŏnggwang, Chŏllanam-do province, where its early headquarters are still maintained (above).

dent several years ago. We should also note the existence of many "scientific" sects concerned with UFOs and other mysterious phenomena. Some people believe that extraterrestrial beings are the progenitors of the human race and perform regular rites to honor their "ancestors."

These sects have much in common for they emerged around the same period. Most are based on a belief that the end of the world is near, a notion perpetrated by their founders and justified by the sorry state of current affairs, the Bible's references to the end of the world, or Buddhism's concept of the Maitreya, or Future Buddha.

While this tendency toward eschatology is, in most cases, born of the founders' sincere belief in their ability to launch a new age, many sect leaders have taken advantage of it. The 1992 Tamisŏn Church incident, in which thousands of followers flocked to the church to await the end of the world, is one negative example of this phenomenon. However, we must remember that eschatology has been a factor in Christianity since Paul predicted the Second Coming of Christ.

End-of-the-world theories always refer to a savior. The leaders of Korea's new religions attempt to establish themselves as saviors, offering evidence to support their assertions of superiority. Many claim the injustices of the present world will be resolved on Judgment Day. Believers can escape the disaster and disease of that fateful day by gathering around the church, which will protect them until judgment is done. Korea will then become the center of the new world and the religious leader will rule the new world order.

Sun Myung Moon, founder of the Unification Church, claims Korea is the second Israel and Jesus Christ will be resurrected on Korean soil. Does that mean Moon, who has already proclaimed himself the second Adam, will become the resurrected Jesus? I leave that question to my readers. Pak Chung-bin, founder of Won Buddhism, was convinced Korean would become a universal language and Korea the world's moral leader. In one sense, it all seems quite absurd, and yet when one considers how Korea's image on the world stage has improved in recent years, one cannot help but wondering if he had the right idea. We will just have to wait and see.

The idea that a paradise on earth will greet us in the next life and that we will live in a utopia on earth, not in heaven—these concepts are quite explicit in indigenous religions such as Chŭngsan'gyo. The religion also predicts an end to all discrimination by class or sex.

Chŭngsan'gyo founder Kang Il-sun expressed these ideas most articulately. In his "Ritual of Cosmic Renewal" (Ch'ŏnji kongsa), Kang sought to launch a new age in which the resentment and dissatisfaction of all oppressed peoples, particularly women, farmers and laborers, would be alleviated. Equally important was Kang's insistence that his followers not only work to alleviate past resentments but also strive to avoid the creation of further resentment. With effort, a better world would come, bringing a more convenient life.

"In the coming age, people will farm without touching the earth." Was Kang predicting the development of mechanized agriculture? "They will cook their rice without fire." The invention of the electric rice cooker? "A large light will illuminate each village and the night will no longer be dark." Did Kang foresee the invention of electricity? It is remarkable how many modern conveniences he predicted.

One final point of interest: the tenets of these various indigenous religions are remarkably syncretistic. They all combine, complete and improve upon existing religious beliefs, from Confucianism, Buddhism and Shamanism to folk belief. However, these syncretistic tenets are not indiscriminately mixed. Each has developed within its own systematic logic. One belief may combine the morals of Confucianism, the ascetic practices of Taoism, the concept of karma and the three states of existence from Buddhism and the spiritual world of Shamanism, but it incorporates these elements according to its own systematic method.

Korea's newer religious traditions have positive and negative points. How should we judge them? Let me suggest a way. If, through the acceptance of any of these beliefs, a person is reunited with family or friends or learns to love, then we can say it is a good thing. On the other hand, if someone neglects their familial responsibilities, fights with their friends and family or invests all their money in the religion, it may be that the religion is at fault. Unfortunately, there are many bad religions in our society, and at times, our traditional religions have not served us much better. ◆

Chŭngsan'gyo is a highly syncretic belief, combining elements borrowed from Confucianism, Buddhism, Taoism and nationalism.

Catholicism

Choi Suck-woo

Although Catholicism was introduced to Korea years earlier, the religion drew its first converts in 1784. These early followers were scholars attracted to Catholicism for intellectual reasons rather than a strong belief in its religious tenets. Over time, Catholicism attracted many devout Korean converts, but its early adherents valued it as a challenge to the prevailing social and political order.

When Catholicism was introduced, Korea was dominated by Confucianism. It was by no means easy for Koreans, so long immersed in the Confucian tradition, to convert to an alien religion, but many braved numerous ordeals to create a proud history for Korean Catholicism.

The history of Catholicism in Korea was not always smooth. The church suffered from repeated persecutions, but ultimately survived, recovering from near extinction following the persecution of many followers. No sooner had the church won the freedom to worship than its existence was threatened by both Japanese colonial occupation of Korea in the earlier part of this century and the territorial division of the nation following World War II. Nevertheless, the Korean Catholic Church continues to develop today, despite its silent congregation in North Korea.

In 1984, its bicentennial year, the Korean Catholic Church consisted of three archdioceses, eleven dioceses and thousands of churches and chapels. More than 1,000 Korean priests serve in these institutions, and some 4,000 nuns and priests are affiliated with 65 religious orders.

The church also operates numerous hospitals, homes for the elderly and patients of Hansen's disease, kindergartens, Sunday schools, primary and secondary schools, special education facilities, vocational schools, colleges, universities and seminaries.

When the Korean Church was founded, Korea was a Confucian society closed to the outside world. The Chosŏn Dynasty, established in 1392, adopted Confucianism as its ruling ideology, but humanity is not content to live under any one ideology and always seeks new ideas. In the 18th century, many Koreans, especially the younger Confucian literati, began to reevaluate Confucianism. Their skepticism resulted in a quest for something new.

In the 17th century, Jesuit missionaries were active in China, translating and publishing books on Christianity and Western science with their Chinese converts. Korean tributary missions to the imperial court of China began to take an interest in the West, and books about European ideas soon found their way to Korea. These books were full of new ideas and were naturally of great interest to Korea's Confucian literati.

Korean intellectuals took a variety of approaches to Western learning. Some focused on technical knowledge, while others stressed philosophical knowledge, and still others considered both Western technology and philosophy valuable in their quest for new ideas. It was this third group of intellectuals that played the leading role in the establishment of the Korean Catholic Church.

Among the foreign texts influencing the development of Korean Catholicism were Matteo Ricci's *True Principles of Catholicism* (*Dian-zhu shin-i*) and *First Steps in Catholic Doctrine* (*Dian-xue zhu-han*), which were brought to Korea after they were published in China.

In the 1770s, Korean intellectuals began to study these Western texts in groups. Yi Pyŏk, Kwon Il-sin and Chŏng Yak-chŏn met in an isolated Buddhist temple to study Christian books. Finding what they were looking for in these texts, the intellectuals began to practice Christian doctrine. Yi Pyŏk asked Yi Sŭng-hun to go to Beijing to be baptized. Yi went in the winter of 1783 and was baptized and christened Peter. Returning home in 1784, he set up a house of worship with his friends. This was how the Korean Catholic Church was born, not by proselytizing missionaries but as a result

(Clockwise from above) The cathedral in Beijing where Yi Sŭng-hun, Korea's first Catholic, was baptized in 1784; Chŏltusan, a shrine to Catholic martyrs in Seoul; Haemi in Ch'ung-ch'ŏngnam-do province, the largest Christian holy ground in Korea; another site of Catholic persecution at Ch'ŏnjin'am in Kyŏnggi-do province

of the Korean literati's direct quest for new ideas. In other words, the initial attraction to Catholicism was intellectual rather than religious. Nowhere else in the Catholic world has a church been established in this manner. Korean Catholics take pride in the fact that their church was founded by laymen pursuing knowledge, instead of Western missionaries.

Upon his return to Korea, Yi Sŭng-hun baptized not only the friends with whom he studied but also several upper-class scholars interested in Christianity. In the church they founded in 1784, they preached that all men are equal before God and that all men must love one another. These teachings had great appeal to members of the upper class who were out of favor with the despotic Chosŏn court. New churches soon sprouted up in provincial areas, especially in the Ch'ungch'ŏng and Chŏlla provinces.

Catholicism also gave hope to people longing for a more equal society and thus posed a serious threat to the Confucian social system. As a result, the Chosŏn government banned Catholicism and persecuted

its followers. The persecution of the Korean Catholic Church began in 1785, just a year after it was founded. Kim Pŏm-u, an interpreter of Chinese and Catholic convert, was arrested while holding a religious gathering at his home in Seoul. The government first tortured him, then sent him to a remote place to force him to give up his religion. When that failed, he was put to death in 1786, becoming Korea's first Christian martyr.

This did not stop the spread of the religion. After Kim's death, Yi Sŭng-hun and others established a provisional ministry in an effort to launch an organized proselytizing movement. They soon learned, however, that the provisional ministry was in violation of Catholic doctrines and disbanded it. They also learned from the Chinese Church that ancestral memorial rites, so important to Confucianism, were considered pagan, and banned converts from conducting them. This ban resulted in even more severe persecution.

In 1791, Yun Chi-ch'ung and Kwon Sang-yŏn were executed for refusing to perform ancestral rites, and many other Catholic

Pope John Paul II visited Korea in June 1984 to canonize 103 martyrs in commemoration of the bicentennial of the Korean Catholic Church.

Kim Tae-gŏn, Korea's first Catholic priest

believers were arrested for the same reason. The persecutions spread across the country with increased intensity as the government realized that Father Zhou Wen-mu, a Chinese priest who had arrived in Korea toward the end of 1794, was involved in clandestine missionary work.

Despite this suppression and hardship, Catholicism continued to flourish. An increasing number of people converted to Catholicism, not only in the Ch'ungch'ŏng and Chŏlla regions but in other provinces as well. Converts lucky enough to escape persecution moved to remote mountain areas and there, in spite of many hardships, set up Catholic villages.

In the 50-year period from the founding of the church in 1784 until the establishment of the Korean Diocese in 1831, Father Zhou Wen-mu was the only foreign priest in Korea, and even he was martyred after only six years of missionary work. Thus it was chiefly Korean converts who carried on the faith during this early period. It was also these Korean laymen who asked the Beijing Diocese to send missionaries and wrote a letter to Rome requesting the establishment of a diocese in Korea.

Pope Gregory XVI ordered the establishment of a Korean Diocese in 1831 and consecrated a priest of the Foreign Mission Society of Paris as the first bishop of Korea. The Korean Diocese's independence from the Beijing Diocese was a reward for the Korean believers' aggressive and independent pursuit of Christian faith and marked a new chapter in the history of Korean culture.

The establishment of the Korean Diocese with French ties did not prevent further persecution. The government defended its Confucian traditions and continued to persecute Catholics from time to time. Priests of the Foreign Mission Society of Paris, on the other hand, continued to enter the country, launching missionary programs and educating Korean priests. In the first half of the 19th century French missionaries managed to send several young Korean converts abroad for education. As a result, Kim Tae-gŏn was ordained to the priesthood in 1845, and Ch'oe Yang-ŏp became the second Korean priest in 1849. In 1855, a seminary was set up to educate priests in Korea. The early French missionaries also translated many texts into Korean and collected data on Korean martyrs, which ultimately led to the canonization of 103 Korean martyrs in

1984. Thanks to these missionaries' efforts, the Korean congregation grew to 2,300 by 1865.

The Chosŏn government, dedicated to its closed-door policy, was not happy with the growth of Catholicism. It felt threatened by the advance of Western powers in Asia and was hostile to French missionaries. In 1866 a cruel persecution of Catholics was ordered by the Taewon'gun, King Kojong's father. Foreign priests, including bishops, and many laymen were killed in Seoul and other areas. The seminary, which opened in 1855, was also shut down. Catholicism survived, however, and the bloodshed did not prevent continued growth.

Beginning in 1876, the persecution of Catholics became less severe. Foreign missionaries were arrested but sent to China instead of being executed. On the other hand, many Korean followers were incarcerated and died in prison.

A treaty with France in 1886 brought religious freedom, though limited, for Korean Catholics. Foreign missionaries were allowed to carry out limited missionary activities. The treaty was a turning point in the history of Korean Catholicism.

In the latter half of the 19th century, Korea stood at a major crossroads. Treaties had been signed with Japan and the Western powers, including the 1886 pact with France which brought Korean Catholics freedom to worship.

In the 1880s, the government began to overlook the activities of foreign missionaries but did not guarantee full freedom of religion. Many laymen were still imprisoned for their faith. The reforms permitted the rapid growth of Korean Catholicism, but soon caused a new series of conflicts with the government, particularly on the provincial level. To resolve these conflicts, an agreement was concluded between the government and the Korean Diocese in 1899, providing more religious freedom for Catholics. This freedom was not simply the result of the agreement. It owed much to the suffering of early Catholic converts who were willing to die for their beliefs.

With the freedom to worship, the Korean Church abandoned its underground activities and began to train Korean priests in an newly established seminary. A cathedral was built in Seoul and churches were established in many cities. A printing house was also set up to publish Catholic books.

The Catholic Church also launched an

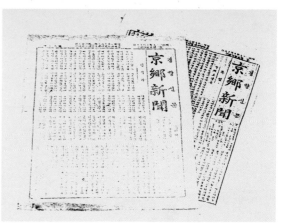

educational program for the lay community. The first Catholic school was established in 1882, and by 1910 when Korea was annexed by Japan, there were 124 Catholic schools. In 1906, the Church launched the *Kyŏnghyang Shinmun*, a weekly newspaper using only *han'gŭl* Korean script, to call for internal reforms of the nation through popular enlightenment about the outside world. The weekly carried many patriotic articles warning Koreans against Japanese aggression, and when Korea was annexed by Japan it was forced to close down.

Korean Catholics were active participants in anti-Japanese movements from the early years of this century. Many took part in armed struggles against the Japanese beginning around 1907. In 1909, An Chung-gŭn, a devout Catholic, assassinated Ito Hirobumi, the former Japanese Resident-General of Korea, in Manchuria for his role in the annexation of Korea.

Japan's annexation of Korea was a great test for the Korean people, and the Korean

The tomb of Kim Tae-gŏn, Korea's first Catholic priest, is found in Mirinae, Ansŏng County, Kyŏnggi-do province (above). The Kyŏnghyang Shinmun, a han'gŭl *newspaper, was inaugurated by the Catholic Church in 1906 (opposite).*

A modern painting of the Korean and French martyrs canonized by Pope John Paul II in 1984

Catholic Church shared in the national ordeal. Japanese colonial authorities attempted to use the church as a tool of colonial policy, alternating between threats and conciliation to achieve their goal. The church suffered greatly but stood firm and continued to grow and contribute to the development of Korean society through its educational and medical programs, although the Japanese authorities restricted religious freedom.

The Korean Catholic Church set up a new diocese in Taegu in 1911, and others in Wonsan, P'yŏngyang and Kwangju. In 1937, the Chŏnju Diocese was established with a Korean bishop for the first time. The educational, medical, voluntary service and cultural programs of the church also expanded. Many of these continue today.

Japan's occupation of Manchuria and World War II cast a dark shadow over the Korean Catholic Church. During the war, many laymen were forced to join the Japanese Imperial Army and work in Japanese munitions industries. Many

Catholic facilities were commandeered for war purposes, and foreign missionaries were either put under house arrest or deported. Students of Catholic schools were told to offer prayers at Japanese Shinto shrines, and in 1925, many university students were expelled for refusing to attend such shrines. In the 1930s, the Japanese authorities ruled that worship at Shinto shrines was a national rite, and on the basis of this rule, the Catholic Church was forced to recognize such worship. In addition, the Japanese forced the church to hold services and publish books in Japanese and to replace Western bishops with Japanese clerics. Despite this suppression, Father No Ki-nam was given the episcopate of the Seoul Diocese.

Liberation from Japanese rule in 1945 brought complete religious freedom for the Korean Catholic Church. There was no need to worry about the arrest of missionaries or the commandeering of church facilities. Services were held in Korean once again.

The situation in North Korea was quite different, however. Liberation did not bring full religious freedom. The Soviet occupying forces imposed many restrictions on religious activities and even persecuted some Catholics. As a result, churches in North Korea were silenced.

In the South, where full religious freedom was guaranteed, the Catholic Church initiated a variety of programs. Many Catholic organizations, including a youth association, were established, not only to propagate the gospel but also to serve the Korean people. Many new Catholic schools were built, the *Kyŏnghyang Shinmun* resumed publication as a daily, and the church began publishing many new periodicals to meet both the needs of the liberated and a divided country thirsting for democratic unification.

The Korean War in 1950 dealt a serious blow to Korean society and the church itself. Most church facilities, except a few parishes in the Taegu Diocese, were destroyed in the war, and many priests and laymen were killed or taken to North Korea by the communists. However, the church did not wallow in its losses. It launched relief efforts and voluntary programs for war victims, in many cases with the assistance of foreign churches and relief organizations.

Following the 1953 armistice, the church

contributed greatly to the reconstruction of the war-torn country. Proselytizing efforts intensified and many people, including intellectuals, converted to Catholicism. The church also set up credit unions at all dioceses to provide financial assistance to citizens and established the Catholic Youth Association and the Catholic Farmers Union to help workers and farmers increasingly alienated in the rapidly industrializing society.

In 1962, the Korean Catholic Church established its own hierarchic system. The Second Vatican Council, launched in the same year, had a great influence on the reform Korean Church, which stepped up reform programs and defined a new role for itself in Korean society. The Korean Church now had three archdioceses and eleven dioceses in southern Korea; Archbishop Kim Su-hwan was elected cardinal. With the Mass and other Catholic services performed in the Korean language, Catholicism found a solid position in Korean culture.

The Foreign Mission of Korea was established to dispatch Korean missionaries overseas, and the church was increasingly interested in local social problems resulting from Korea's rapid industrialization. This social commitment was the main thrust of various programs launched in 1981 when the church observed the 150th anniversary of the Korean Diocese. In 1984 Pope John Paul II visited Korea to canonize 103 martyrs in celebration of the bicentennial of the Korean Church.

The founding fathers of the Korean Catholic Church were Korean intellectuals who established the church without any help from foreign missionaries, then spread the gospel to all levels of Korean society, despite the rigid social stratification of the Chosŏn period. Their descendants have carried on this tradition, contributing to the development of Korean society through educational, medical, cultural and social programs, thus helping the Korean Catholic Church play an important role in Korea's modernization.

Today the Catholic Church is working to restore human dignity and enhance spiritual values in the face of Korea's rapid industrialization and the accompanying social and cultural changes. To achieve these ends, the church continues to reform itself while at the same time living up to the tradition established by its founding fathers. ◆

CHRISTIANITY AND KOREAN CULTURE

Suh Kwoeng-il

It was only after the Korean-American Treaty in 1882 that Protestantism was introduced to Korea, nearly 100 years after Catholicism. Horace N. Allen of the Northern Presbyterian Church came to Korea in 1884, followed by Horace G. Underwood and Henry G. Appenzeller the following year. Even as these American missionaries were preparing for evangelization in Seoul, Korean Christians, such as Sŏ Sang-ryun and Paek Hong-chun, were actively promoting Christian belief in the northwestern part of the peninsula, and preparations were underway for the establishment of a church in Songch'ŏn, Hwanghae-do province.

Protestantism spread relatively rapidly through Chosŏn society because its advent coincided with the opening of Korean ports after centuries of relative isolation. Once the country was opened to international trade, Korea became the arena for a power struggle between Japan, China and Russia, and after the Sino-Japanese and Russo-Japanese wars, it was annexed by Japan. Koreans accepted Protestantism more readily than the Chinese or Japanese because they associated it with deliverance from Japanese aggression.

The transmission and development of early Protestantism were directly linked to the national tragedies in the closing days of the Chosŏn Dynasty. Many Koreans, humiliated and frustrated by Japanese aggression, sought a solution to their nation's dilemma in the Protestant churches, known for their energy and organizational capacity. Protestant churches grew rapidly, naturally associating themselves with patriotism and loyalty.

Having witnessed traditional Qing China's defeat by a modernized Japan, Koreans were determined to shed tradition and conventional thought in favor of modernization. They turned to Christianity for the means of modernization. The Christian

(Above) Missionaries and lay persons involved in the translation of the Bible into han'gŭl: *(from left, back row) Mun Kyŏng-ho, Kim Pyŏng-jun and Chŏng Tong-pyŏng; (from left, front row) William D. Reynolds, H.G. Underwood, J.S. Gale and G.H. Jones. (Right) Yŏngnak Church in the heart of Seoul*

leadership was expected to lead the modernization movement. As Korea opened to Western culture, reformers promoted Christianity in their drive for enlightenment. Missionaries worked to establish schools, hospitals and publishing companies as means of disseminating the religion; *han'gŭl*, the Korean alphabet, was rediscovered in the Korean translation of the Bible; alcohol, tobacco and opium were banned; and wedding and funeral ceremonies were simplified. With the expansion of educational opportunities for women, sexual equality and women's rights received considerable support. The introduction of Christianity and the development of the church also contributed to the prevention of bureaucratic corruption. Christians organized against government officials who violated human rights and ignored legal procedures, and resisted unlawful taxation and bureaucratic extortion. From its onset, Christianity roused a strong sense of social reform and a spirit of independence in the face of foreign aggression.

Christianity, in the form of Catholicism and Protestantism, provided momentum for the reformation and development of the Korean people. As traditional society crumbled, values changed. The importance of the individual was recognized as were citizens' rights vis-à-vis the monarchy and bureaucracy. There was also a new nationalist consciousness.

Today, 100 years since the introduction of Protestantism and 200 years since that of Catholicism, Christians account for over one-quarter of the entire population. But

Koreans were quick to embrace Christianity and many of the institutions related to it. Among these were Western-style schools, hospitals and churches. Ewha Haktang, the predecessor to today's Ewha Womans University (above), was founded in 1886 by American Methodist missionaries. Soongjun (Sungjŏn) University was founded in P'yŏngyang but has operated in Seoul since the Korean War. At right, its students receive Bible training at the P'yŏngyang campus around 1900.

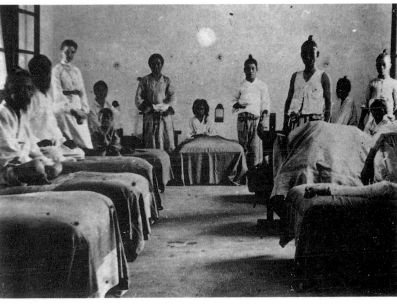

Protestantism in Korea circa 1900: (from top) Solae Church in Changyŏn, Hwanghae-do province, built in 1883, the first Protestant church on Korean soil; the original Ewha Haktang in Seoul; the Changdohoe Theological Seminary in P'yŏngyang; and the theological seminary affiliated with Seoul's Methodist Church. In 1900, St. Luke Hospital in Seoul was one of the few places a Western-style bed could be found (left).

The Christ's Church around 1900 (above); Korean bibles: a 1900 translation of the New Testament (near right below) and the Ross Version of the New Testament translated in 1887 (far right below); Ch'unghyŏn Church, the largest church in Seoul's upscale Kangnam district (bottom)

how has Christianity affected our society? Have Christian values, such as freedom, equality, justice and peace, really taken root in Korean culture? Have modern concepts of human rights, civil rights and national rights matured? How has Korean culture has grown ethically?

Protestantism was a powerful driving force in the enlightenment of modern Korea. The British missionary R. J. Thomas highlighted the differences between Catholicism and Protestantism in his evangelical work. Rather than contradict Korean governmental policies or values, he sought to discover similarities between Korean culture and Christianity. According to Thomas, "Protestantism is based on Heavenly Ways meant to guide the people and correct evils. Therefore, it is already endowed with the Confucian precepts of charity, justice, loyalty and filial piety. Protestants differ from Catholics in that we try to make all people good."

The Protestant church attempted to harmonize with Confucian philosophies and ethics, asserting that Protestant ethical teachings were no different from Confucian precepts aimed at advancing humanity through the promotion of charity and virtues.

The void left by the decline of traditional religions such as Confucianism, Buddhism and Taoism at the end of the Chosŏn period caused a great religious yearning in the Korean populace and contributed to the ready acceptance of Protestantism. It also encouraged the spread of Tonghak ("Eastern Learning"), a mixture of Confucianism, Buddhism and Taoism so named to distinguish it from Catholicism which was known as *Sohak*, or "Western Learning." The first Protestant missionaries represented American denominations. They were friendly and understanding of the Korean situation, and Koreans responded positively to their honesty, humanitarianism and sense of justice.

The religious point of view of God-centered Christianity and the ethical point of view of man-centered Confucianism precluded any harmonious dialogue but Protestantism allowed for some dialogue because its God-centered ideology was based on the principle of God's humanization or incarnation. The Protestant church sought to participate in the development of Korean culture and modernization on the grounds that God had intervened in human history by taking the form of human flesh.

It did not attempt to confront or transcend Korean traditions; rather it actively sought to convert them. Thus, toward the end of the Chosŏn period, Korean Christians came to realize that the promotion of the Christian spirit meant the promotion of enlightenment and national welfare.

They further believed that education was vital to the enlightenment and that the promotion of God's ways was vital to education. Early Protestants saw enlightenment, education and religion as one and the same and believed Christianity provided momentum for cultural reform. A report to the International Missionary Conference held in Edinburgh in 1910 concedes "Christianity in Korea is hailed not so much as a religion as an educator." Replacing Buddhism and Confucianism which had traditionally provided the impetus for cultural development and reform, the Protestant church took on the role of reformer and creator of a new culture. Its influence was best represented by changes in the values of Koreans who embraced the Christian faith.

Christianity went by many different names in Korea. It was called *Sohak* ("Western Learning"), *Ch'ŏnjuhak* ("Heavenly Father Learning"), *Sahak* ("Evil Learning"), and *Mugunmubu chihak* ("Kingless, Fatherless Learning"), and its believers were often called *yesujaeng'i* ("Jesus freaks") or *yesugun* ("Jesus gangsters"). Catholicism was generally referred to as a kind of "learning" while the more pejorative yesujaeng'i and yesugun were reserved for Protestants. These terms reflect the paths taken by Catholic and Protestant clerics and missionaries. Protestantism was first propagated among the lower classes and spread upward to the middle class, whereas Catholicism was first embraced by upper class intellectuals and later appealed to the common people. In both cases, Christian values of equality and love spread, doing away with differences between nobility and slaves, men and women, young and old. J. E. Fisher suggests the Christian contri-

bution to Korean culture was the promotion of equality and human rights which transcended the class system. Christianity overcame the existing Confucian system and created a new ethical ideal.

Sexual equality was one of the most innovative ideas advocated by the Christian church during the enlightenment period. At that time, women were not treated equally, in the home or in society. Chosŏn was a monogamous society, but concubines were publicly acknowledged. Women were helpless in the face of their husbands' indiscretions because remarriage by women was socially forbidden. The Christian movement sought to restore women's rights. Christians stressed the need for women's education, arguing educated mothers were better equipped to raise children and that the development of human resources would contribute to the general development of the country. They also sought to realize sexual equality by encouraging women's activities. Although traditional society's rigid class system was abolished by government reforms in 1894 (*Kabo kyongjang*), true class leveling began within the Christian church. The church proclaimed all humans were equal as each was God's precious creation. This concept was associated with the idea that all humans are equal under the law.

The traditional Korean world view was decidedly fatalistic. This fatalism explains the popularity of fortunetelling in Korea. Christianity promoted realistic reasoning, suggesting that the individual controlled his or her personal fate. The church introduced Western ideas, revealed the absurdity of superstition and idolatry, led the fight against superstition, and disseminated the new Christian morality. The church's ban on drinking, smoking and ancestral memorial ceremonies originated not in the teachings of the Bible but in the practical belief that they undermined enlightenment efforts. Ancestral rites were based on the Confucian concept of filial piety. At the time, the Christian church criticized ances-

Christianity has had a substantial influence on modern Korean culture. As the number of churches grows, church design has become an important architectural genre. Seoul's Kyŏngdong Methodist Church was designed by one of Korea's foremost modern architects, the late Kim Su-gŭn, in 1981.

tral rites for lacking the true spirit of filial piety. It argued that traditional rites were steeped in pretense and formality and ran contrary to the spirit of enlightenment. In the eyes of the enlightenment movement, the church's stand against ancestral rites did not contradict the Confucian filial piety philosophy; rather it offered a new interpretation in Christian terms. Christians honored their ancestors by worshiping God and revering their living parents. As the closed, traditional society collapsed and a new democratic society emerged, the Christian church established new values to promote enlightened humanity.

Protestantism called for humanity to rise above nature and take its place as developer and master of natural forces. It reminded man that he was God's supreme creation. The church also preached the dignity of labor and asserted that all occupations were equally honorable. Every person should acquire skills and contribute to the development of the community by devoting themselves to their occupation. The church declared that an enlightened man was an independent, self-reliant person, responsible, cooperative and compassionate.

On the basis of the Bible's teachings, the Christian church taught Koreans to resist their ruler should he violate common justice and human rights. The traditional concept of a ruler "caring for" or "looking after" the people did not satisfy the Christian vision of a democratic society.

Korea's modern history has been the history of popular nation- building. Based on a belief in the undeniable human right to freedom and equality, Christian humanism worked to surmount the autocratic monarchism of the Chosŏn and developed into a nationalistic movement aimed at recovering Korea's sovereignty from Japanese colonial rule.

In fact, Japan's annexation of Korea was the first national crisis to confront Protestantism in Korea. In 1907, a massive revival movement unfolded in the Protestant churches in 1907 as Christians actively waged an anti-Japan movement. The "Movement for One Million Souls for Christ" spread throughout the country around 1909. American and English missionaries had adopted a policy of separating religion from politics, so Christianity failed to channel national outrage in an active response to Japan's aggression. Rather they converted it to religious fervor, thus impos-

ing a certain limit on their anti-Japanese movement. Christians energetically pursued patriotic enlightenment, education and social activities but were far less devoted to the organization of a volunteer army to rescue the country. Consequently, the Korean church was relatively quiet on Japan's annexation of Korea. In fact, the religion should be criticized for its internalization and political indifference. While the church may have identified with national problems internally, it should have expressed its concern outwardly and actively.

After Christians actively took part in the March First Movement, Koreans reconsidered Christianity and the number of church-goers grew rapidly. The church became increasingly autocratic and class-oriented, however. Young people deserted the church, which was increasingly populated by women. The church failed to keep pace with contemporary nationalist movements. It became ideologically conservative, ignoring issues such as socialism and tenant and labor rights. This new conservatism, together with the clergy's intellectual poverty, meant Christianity could not respond to the nationalist needs of the Korean people.

While the Christian church suffered under Japanese colonial rule, it responded passively, simply trying to escape reality, concentrating on internalization and piety. The Japanese ordered Koreans to attend rites honoring the Japanese emperor at Shinto shrines, and many Christians complied. They not only kept silent or actively collaborated with Japanese, some even offered theological justification for the Shinto rites. By the end of colonial rule, Korean Christian leaders had deserted their principles and the church was little more than a colonial government pawn.

Following liberation from Japanese rule, Korean Christians should have campaigned for the eradication of all vestiges of colonial rule, but they did not. On the contrary, with the rise of the Syngman Rhee government, the clergy powerful at the end of the colonial period returned to power, banishing anyone demanding penitence from the church. Lacking experienced professionals, the government employed bureaucrats, police and military with collaborationist backgrounds, effectively excluding from the government anyone dedicated to the nationalist cause. Opportunism, slander and flattery were rampant, and social values were shaken to their roots. Korean

Protestantism was marked by extreme dissension and fragmentation, especially after the Korean War.

Christianity saw impressive growth in the 1970s as Korea pushed for industrialization. Millions of Koreans embraced the religion following the church's call for the evangelization of the entire nation. Nevertheless, the general attitude of Korean Christianity has not matched the progress made by the Korean people in other fields. Neon crosses punctuate the skyline across the country, but that does not mean the Christian church is contributing to the development of Korean culture. While the early church made truly great contributions to the reform of values in Korea, the modern church has yet to recover the reputation for morality and honesty it earned in the 1910s.

Korea's Christian community has made important contributions to the anticommunist movement following liberation from Japan, to the civil rights and human rights movements since the 1970s, and to a spiritual revitalization movement in recent years. The National Conference of Christian Women launched this revitalization movement in an effort to promote cooperation within the community, to take a more forward-looking view and to overcome the materialism and greed of modern society.

The development of Korean Protestantism reflects our national history. Christianity has played a leading role in many of the nation's events over the last century, and by rediscovering itself through introspection and self-criticism, it will prepare itself to confront the tasks facing Korea. ◆

Every Sunday more than 20,000 people flock to services at the Full Gospel Church's main chapel on Seoul's Yŏŭido. Thousands more watch live broadcasts of the services carried at 13 local affiliates around the country. The Full Gospel Church has the most members of any Protestant church in Korea.

APPENDICES

GLOSSARY

Amitabha—Buddha of Infinite Light who presides over the Western Paradise.

Ananda (Ananda)—the historical Buddha's cousin and trusted disciple, known for his remarkable memory and ability to recite the Buddha's teachings which he had heard directly.

Avalokitesvara (Kwanseŭm posal)—the bodhisattva of compassion, said to have been born from a ray of light emanating from the head of the Amitabha Buddha. This bodhisattva is generally considered the receiver of the world's pain. In fact, the Sanskrit Avalokitesvara means the "Hearer of Cries."

Avatamsaka-sutra—*Flower Garland Sutra* which perfected the teachings of Mahayana Buddhism.

Avatamsaka School (*Hwaŏmjong*)—An important school of Chinese Buddhism, the Avatamsaka School teaches the equality of all things and the interdependence of all life. This school's teachings were introduced to Korea in the seventh century by Master Ŭisang of the Silla Kingdom.

Bhaisajyaguru (Yaksayŏrye bul)-the Medicine Buddha.

Bodhidharma—the twenty-eighth patriarch after the historical Buddha and the first Chinese patriarch of Zen Buddhism.

bodhisattva (*posal*)—in Mahayana Buddhism, someone who seeks buddhahood through the systematic practice of the perfect virtues but renounces complete entry into nirvana until all beings are saved.

Book of Changes (I Qing)—a Chinese book of wisdom and oracles, essentially based on Confucianism but including Taoist ideas. Dates from the transition period between the Yin and Zhou dynasties.

Buddhism—A religious and philosophical system founded in India in the sixth century B.C., Buddhism teaches that right living, right thinking and self-denial will enable a person to achieve enlightenment, a state of release from earthly and bodily pain, anguish and desire. Buddhism is generally believed to have been introduced to Korea from China during the fourth century A.D.

changsŭng—spirit posts stationed in pairs at the entrances to villages to protect residents and ensure community peace and prosperity. Traditionally villages held periodic rites to honor the spirits embodied in the posts.

Ch'ŏndogyo—"The Religion of the Heavenly Way," an offshoot of the Tonghak (Eastern Learning) Movement, teaches that man and God are one. In the late 19th and early 20th centuries, the sect became the focal point for Korean opposition to foreign aggression.

Chongmyo—the royal ancestral shrine of the Chosŏn Dynasty.

Chŭngsan'gyo—A modern indigenous religion founded by Kang Il-sun in the late 19th century, Chŭngsan'gyo is a nationalist belief system incorporating elements of Buddhism, Confucianism and Taoism, as well as Tonghak and some Western religions. The religion predicts an end to all discrimination, by class or sex.

Confucianism—A state doctrine combining philosophical, religious, ethical and sociopolitical aspects of the teachings of Confucius (551-479 B.C.), Confucianism is based on the belief that humanity is inherently good. It also stresses the proper relationship between the individual and the surrounding society and cosmos.

Dharani-sutra (Pure Light Sutra)—the sutra devoted to Amitabha Buddha. A Korean scroll printing of this sutra, possibly dating from between 704 to 751, is believed to be the oldest extant wood block printing in the world.

dharma (*pŏp*)—the teachings of the Buddha, truth.

Doctrinal School of Buddhism (Kyojong)—the lineage focusing on the study of the Tripitaka, the Buddhist textual canon.

Esoteric Buddhism—A doctrine strongly influenced by the Tantric sects of Hinduism, Esoteric Buddhism assumes that the ultimate reality cannot be expressed by words and is best suggested by magical signs and symbols.

"five elements" (obang) —metal, wood, water, fire and earth. The Chinese naturalists of the late Zhou period believed that all nature is made of varying combinations of these "five elements." The concept developed into an extensive philosophy-science which includes geomancy.

geomancy—the method of divination used to determine sites for settlements, buildings and burial grounds. Based on naturalist theories about the "five elements" governing all natural phenomena, geomancy is still practiced in modern Korea.

Great Learning (Da Xue)—one of the main Confucian texts, establishing eight ways to practice Confucius' teachings. These methods are explained in terms of the relationship between sequence, cause and effect, and the importance of matter.

Hinayana Buddhism (Sosŭng)—literally the "Lesser Vehicle," a derogatory term used by believers in Mahayana Buddhism. Hinayana is actually a form of early Buddhism generally referred to by its own followers as Theravada, the "Teaching of the Elders."

History of Koryŏ (Koryŏsa)—a history of the Koryŏ Kingdom compiled by Chosŏn scholars in 1451.

History of the Three Kingdoms (Samguk Sagi)—a history compiled by the Confucian scholar Kim Pu-sik upon the order of Koryŏ King Injong in 1146.

hwarang—elite units of young men trained to assist the Silla army. The hwarang (literally "flower of youth") were known for their military skills, valor and strong moral values.

hyangga—Silla's "native songs," varying in length from four to eight or ten lines. The hyangga were recorded in *idu*, which employed Chinese characters as phonetic symbols and to express synonymous Korean nouns.

hyanggyo—public schools, specializing in Confucian studies, which were operated in each county from Koryŏ times.

kangsinmu—shamans who receive their calling through possession by a deity.

Kashyapa (Kasŏp)—the Buddha's loyal disciple who actively promoted the religion following the Buddha's passage to the Western Paradise.

kibok—praying for the fulfillment of worldly desires.

kisaeng—Korean female entertainers, trained in poetry, music and dance.

Ksitigarbha (Chijang posal)—the bodhisattva that helps those in torment.

Kukchagam—the National University established in the Koryŏ capital in 992. It was the kingdom's highest educational institute, teaching the Confucian classics and practical subjects such as law, calligraphy, accounting and, in later years, military tactics.

kunja—a virtuous man as defined by Confucian principles.

kut—shamanistic rites.

kwagŏ—the system of state civil service examinations first instituted in the early years of Koryŏ as a means of recruiting government officials. During the Chosŏn period, the system took on even greater importance.

Mahayana Buddhism—One of the two major schools of Buddhism, Mahayana is called the "Great Vehicle" (*Taesŭng*) because it opens the way of liberation to many people and expresses the intention to liberate all beings. In Mahayana, the individual seeks enlightenment for the sake of all beings.

Maitreya Buddha (Mirŭk)—the Future Buddha.

Manjusri (Munsu posal)—the bodhisattva of wisdom, who, in Korea, resides on Mt. Odae.

Meditation School of Buddhism (Sŏnjong)—the Buddhist lineage which attempts to achieve enlightenment through meditation, transcending words.

Memorabilia of the Three Kingdoms (Samguk Yusa)—a record of important history, traditions and legends compiled by the Buddhist monk Iryŏn in the late 13th century.

mokt'ak—a hand-held bell-shaped wooden percussion instrument used by Buddhist monks to announce and accompany chanting sessions.

mudang—the common, but pejorative, term for a shaman.

mudra (suin)—the hand gestures signifying the identity and powers of Buddhist images.

Munmyo—the National Shrine to Confucius, modeled after that of the Chinese dynasties.

naerim-gut—initiation ceremony in which a deity is enshrined in the body of a shaman.

Neo-Confucianism—the philosophical synthesis of Confucian thought and other philosophical schools (mainly Taoism and Buddhism) arising from the intellectual ferment that occurred in Chinese society from the third to eighth centuries. Neo-Confucian thinkers hoped to recreate the ideal Confucian society while incorporating metaphysical elements gleaned from Buddhism and Taoism.

Oriental zodiac—The 12 "earthly branches" (*sibijisinsang*) combine in a sequence of paired Chinese ideographs to form the traditional cycle of sixty. Each "earthly branch" is represented by a different animal, symbols found throughout Korean art and folk crafts.

pagoda—A Buddhist architectonic form indigenous to China, Japan and Korea, which developed out of Indian stupa, pagodas serve as containers for relics of the Buddha (sarira).

p'ansori—oral narrative sung by a professional singer accompanied by a single drummer.

pŏmp'ae—ceremonial Buddhist chants without rhythmic cycle, pattern or harmony, performed by specialized monks at certain rites.

pyŏlsin-gut—a shamanistic rite and a village-wide festival dating from ancient times and still practiced in some rural communities.

sadaebu—a class of Neo-Confucian literati which began to appear as aristocratic government declined during the period of Koryŏ military control. Many of these scholar-officials continued to administer government affairs during the Chosŏn period.

Saddharmapundarika-sutra (Lotus Sutra)—Perhaps the most famous Sanskrit sutra, the *Lotus Sutra* considers the nature of the manifestations of the Buddha and has been especially important in Mahayana and Zen Buddhism.

Sajiktan—Chosŏn national altar honoring the gods of land and grain.

Sakradevanam Indra (Chesŏk)—a famed god from ancient Indian myths, who was later embraced as a guardian god in Buddhism.

Sakyamuni Buddha (Sŏkkamoni)—the historical Buddha, born to a princely family in northeast India in the late sixth century B.C.

Samantadhadra (Pohyŏn)—the bodhisattva venerated as the protector of all those who teach the dharma.

sarira—relics of the Sakyamuni Buddha, generally ashes or bone fragments, which confer a quality of sacredness on a stupa or pagoda.

sesŭpmu—hereditary shamans who inherit their calling from their ancestors.

Shamanism—Originating among prehistoric Russo-Tungus tribes, Shamanism is based in the belief that the visible world is pervaded by invisible spirits that affect the lives of the living.

Sirhak—"Practical Learning," a reformist school of thought directed against the preoccupation among Chosŏn bureaucrats with Chinese literature and the speculative side of Neo-Confucianism. Sirhak thinkers called for a practical, empirical approach to government and learning.

sottae—spirit poles erected in or around villages in an area believed to be ruled by spirits that influence village fortune. Sottae may be traced to the worship of trees, a form of animism widely practiced among the primitive peoples of East Asia.

Sŏkchŏnje—memorial rites honoring Confucius and his disciples in the second and eighth lunar months at Seoul's Munmyo, the National Shrine to Confucius.

sŏnbi—a gentleman-scholar who embodies the precepts of Confucianism and is known for his knowledge and upstanding character.

Sŏnggyun'gwan—the National Confucian Academy, a successor to Koryŏ's Kukchagam, which was established in Koryŏ capital in 992. It was renamed Sŏnggyun'gwan in 1308 and remained the highest educational institute throughout the Chosŏn period.

sŏwon—private academies which also

257

and respected scholars. The sŏwon, together with *hyanggyo* county schools, provided the basic Confucian education during the Chosŏn period.

stupa (*pudo*)—Originally memorial monuments over the mortal remains of the historical Buddha and other respected figures, stupas also served as symbolic reminders of various decisive events in the life of the historical Buddha.

t'aegŭk—A symbol originating in Chinese culture, the t'aegŭk consists of two comma-shaped figures representing the cosmic principles of *yin* and *yang* and indicating the interaction of opposites, as well as symbolizing the creation of the cosmos and the reciprocal action of these principles in all daily phenomena. The juxtaposition of the red and blue comma-shapes found in the Korean version of this symbol signifies continual change, or the world in flux.

Taejonggyo—An indigenous Korean religion with strong nationalistic overtones affiliated with Tan'gun'gyo, Taejonggyo centers around a belief in Tan'gun as the divine progenitor.

Tan'gun—the mythical founder of Korea, believed to have been born of a heavenly father and a woman from a bear-totem tribe.

Tan'gun'gyo—the belief in Tan'gun, Korea's mythical founder.

Tano—The fifth day of the fifth lunar month, Tano is the largest religious festival held in the Kangwon region and dates from ancient times. During the festival, tutelary deities are honored and various folk practices aimed at promoting good health through the summer months are performed.

Taoism—a Chinese philosophy based on the teachings of Lao-zi and Zhuang-zi (sixth century B.C.) and advocating simplicity and selflessness. The term also refers to religious Taoism which was concerned with the attainment of immortality.

Theravada Buddhism—One of several sects of Hinayana Buddhism and the more conservative of the main branches of Buddhism today, the "Way of the Elders" is dominant in Sri Lanka, Burma, and Thailand.

Tripitaka—a collection of Buddhist scriptures, rules and treatises. The Tripitaka Koreana was compiled in the early 11th century. Wood blocks dating from the 13th century, containing the entire Tripitaka Koreana, are housed at Haein Temple.

Tonghak (Eastern Learning)—a religious and social movement launched by Ch'oe Che-u in the late 19th century. The Tonghak doctrine combined elements of Confucianism, Buddhism, Shamanism and Catholicism in an effort to rescue peasants from the widespread poverty and unrest of late Chosŏn society.

Vairocana (Pirojana-bul)—the first of the five transcendent Buddhas, often called the Brilliant One.

yangban—literally the "two corps," the yangban were a class of scholar-officials during the Koryŏ and Chosŏn periods.

Yogacara Sect (*yusik hakp'a*)—a school of Mahayana Buddhism that relied on introspective meditation for salvation. Literally, the "consciousness-only" school.

Zen Buddhism (Korean Sŏn, Chinese Chan)—The meditative sect of Buddhism, which developed in China during the sixth and seventh centuries, Zen differs from other sects in seeking enlightenment through introspection and intuition rather than in the study of texts.

A Note on Pronunciation & Proper Names

The romanization of all Korean words and names in this volume follows the McCune-Reischauer system, except for some idiosyncratic spellings, such as Seoul, the capital city, and the preferred spellings of authors or public figures already familiar to those in the West.

The only diacritical mark not found in the English alphabet is the breve (˘), which sometimes appears above *o* or *u*. Romanized Korean vowels are pronounced as follows:

> *ŏ: u* in r*u*n
> *ŭ: oo* in b*oo*k
> *o: aw* in l*aw*
> *u: oo* in m*oo*n
> *a: a* in f*a*ther
> *i: ea* in l*ea*p
> *e: e* in s*e*t
> *ae: a* in s*a*t
> *oe: way* in s*way*

An apostrophe indicates an aspirated consonant or the division between two syllables that might otherwise be ambiguous as in the case of Tan'gun, the mythical founder of Korea.

Chinese has in most cases been rendered in the Pinyin system of romanization.

All surnames precede the given names, as is the traditional Korean practice. Kings are referred to by their posthumous titles. Buddhist monks are referred to by their Buddhist names.

ABOUT THE AUTHORS

An Byung-ju is a graduate of Sung Kyun Kwan University's Department of Oriental Philosophy where he is now Professor of Philosophy and Director of the Taedong Cultural Research Center. His publications include *Twelve Korean Philosophers* and *Chosŏn Neo-Confucianism and Japanese Neo-Confucianism*.

Chang Chong-ryong is Professor of Korean Literature at Kangnŭng National University where he received his undergraduate degree. He received his doctorate from Choong-ang University. His publications focus on folklore of the Kangwon region and include *Research on the Folk Practices and Folk Songs of Korea and China*, *Village Beliefs of the Samch'ŏk Region* and *Tutelary Deities of Kangwon-do Province*.

Choe Chul is presently Professor of Korean Literature at Yonsei University. He received his B.A. and M.A. from Yonsei University and attended the graduate course in Korean literature at Dongguk University. He has published several works on literature from the Silla period, focusing on *hyangga*.

Choi Hyun-gak is Professor of Sŏn (Zen) Studies at Dongguk University and Director of Dongguk University's Sŏn Research Center. He has translated a number of works on the Meditation School of Buddhism and has written extensively on the subject.

Choi Joon-sik received his Ph.D. in religion from Temple University in the United States and is presently Professor of Korean Studies at Ewha Womans University. He has published and edited several volumes on Korean religion and thought, including *Korean Religion, Korean Religious Masters* and *The Development of Korean Religion*.

Choi Rai-ok is Professor of Korean Language Education at the College of Education at Hanyang University and

Dean of Bethesda Normal College. He received his Ph.D. from the Department of Korean Literature at Seoul National University's Graduate School of Education. His publications include *A Study of Korean Legends*, *Oral Literature* and *Proverbs from Chŏllabuk-do Province*.

Choi Suck-woo is a Catholic priest presently working at the Institute for the Study of Korean Church History. He graduated from the Department of Theology at Sungshin College and received graduate degrees in theology from Belgium's Leuven University and Bonn University. His publications are *Faith and Life*, *Religion in North Korea*, *The History of the Korean Catholic Church* and *Studies of the History of the Korean Church*.

Chung Chin-hong is a graduate of the Department of Religion at Seoul National University where he is now a professor. Among his publications are *An Introduction to Religion*, *Understanding Religious Culture* and *The Development of Korea's Religious Culture*.

Chung Byong-jo is Professor of Korean Ethics at Dongguk University and Dean of the Wonhyo Study Center at the Korean Buddhism Research Institute. He received his Ph.D. from Dongguk University. He has written numerous publications on Korean Buddhism and religion, including *A Study on the Cultural History of Buddhism* and *Korean Religion in Transition*.

Hahn Man-young graduated from Seoul National University's Graduate School of Korean Music and received his Ph.D. from Japan's Ochanomizu University. He was a professor in the Department of Korean Music at Seoul National University from 1969 to 1991 and is now active as a minister. His publications on Korean music include *A Study of Korea's Buddhist Music*, *Research on Traditional Korean Music* and a volume of English essays enti-

tled *Studies in Korean Traditional Music*.

Hwang Rushi graduated from the Department of Journalism at Ewha Womans University and is now Professor in the Department of Korean Literature at Kwandong University. Her research has focused on Korean Shamanism and her publications include *Rites and the Shaman in Korea*, *The Theatrical Elements in Shamanistic Rites* and *A Survey of Shamanistic Rites*.

Hwang Sun-myung is Professor of Religion at Myŏngji Technical College. He received his undergraduate and graduated degrees in religion from Seoul National University and has numerous works on the religion and ethics of Korea, including *A History of Popular Religious Movements*, *Occupational Ethics* and *A Social History of Religions Under the Chosŏn Dynasty*.

Im Dong-kwon graduated from the Department of Korean Literature at Kukhak University (now Korea University) and did his graduate studies at Kyunghee University. He is now Professor Emeritus at the Department of Folklore at Choong-ang University and Chairman of the Folklore Subcommittee of the Cultural Property Committee. His numerous publications include *A History of Humanity*, *The History of Korean Folklore*, *Understanding Korean Folk Literature* and *Women and Folk Songs*.

Keum Jang-tae is Professor of Religion at Seoul National University. He received his undergraduate degree in Religion from Seoul National University and did his graduate work at Sung Kyun Kwan University. His writings have focused on Korean Confucianism and include *Confucianism and Korean Thought*, *A Study of Korea's Practical Learning* and *Confucianism and Korean Society*.

Kim Kwang-on graduated from the Department of Archeology and Anthropology at Seoul National University and did his graduate work at Tokyo University. He is presently Professor of Folklore at Inha University and Director of Inha University Museum and is known for his many writings on Korea's traditional culture. Among his publications are *Korea's Traditional Houses, Folk Practices in Korea, Geomancy* and *Ah! Koguryŏ*.

Kim Tae-gon studied Korean Literature at Kukhak University (now Korea university) and Kyunghee University and received his doctorate in literature from Tokyo University. He is presently Professor of Korean literature at Kyunghee University and is actively involved in the folklore studies community. Among his publications are *Korean Folklore Studies, Studies in Korean Shamanism, Principles of Korean Folklore Studies* and *Korean Myths*.

Ko Chang-soo is a graduate of Sung Kyun Kwan University and presently serves as Korea's Ambassador to Pakistan. Throughout his diplomatic career, he has written and translated poetry in both Korean and English. He has also won the Korean Translation Award for his translation of Korean poetry into English.

Lee Eun-yun is a graduate of the Department of the History of English Literature at Kongju Normal College. He is presently Deputy Managing Editor of the *Joong-ang Economic Daily* and writes extensively on Korean journalism and culture.

Lee Jong-chan is Professor of Korean Literature at Dongguk University. He graduated from the Department of Korean Literature at Dongguk University and received his Ph.D. from Hanyang University. Among his publications are *Korea's Zen Poetry* and *A History of Korea's Chinese Script Literature*.

Lee Ki-dong is Professor of Confucian Studies at Sung Kyun Kwan University. He did his graduate work in literature at Japan's Tsukuba University and has written broadly on Asian culture and philosophy. Among his publications are *Understanding the Korean and Japanese Economies Through Philosophy* and *The Book of Changes Made Easy*.

Lee Sang-il is a graduate of Seoul National University Department of German Literature. He did postgraduate work at Zurich University's Folk Museum and received his doctorate in literature at Sung Kyun Kwan University where he is now Professor of German Literature. Many of his publications focus on Korean culture. They include *Korea's Spirit Posts, Shamanistic Rites and Practices in Korea* and *Festivals and Folk Dramas*.

Park Sung-bong is a graduate of Hanguk University of Foreign Studies' Department of Swedish and the Department of Aesthetics at Sweden's Uppsala University. He presently teaches at Hanguk University of Foreign Studies and Myongji University. His publications include *The Aesthetics of Popular Art* and an anthology of translated essays entitled *Theories on the Aesthetics of Popular Art*.

Park Sun-young graduated from the Department of Buddhism, Dongguk University and the Graduate School of Education, Korea University. He has been a professor at the Department of Education, Dongguk University since 1977 and is presently Dean of the College of Education. Among his publications are *The Educational Philosophy of Buddhism* and *The Philosophy of Education*.

The Ven. Popchong is a poet and presently chief monk at Purim Hermitage, attached to the Chogye Order. His many publications include *The Buddhist Canon, The Sakyamuni Buddha* and *Sutra-pitaka*.

Rhi Bou-yong is Professor of Psychiatry at Seoul National University's College of Medicine. He graduated from Seoul National University's College of Medicine and studied at the Jung Institute in Zurich where he received his accreditation as a Jungian analyst. Among his publications are *Analytical Psychology, Lost Shadows* and *Why Do We Despair?*.

Suh Kwoeng-il is Professor of Religion Hanshin University.

Suh Kyoung-yo is Dean of the College of Confucian Studies and Professor of Confucian Studies at Sung Kyun Kwan University where he did his graduate studies in philosophy. His writings focus on Korean Confucianism and include a volume on Kim Chŏng-hŭi and a study of unique elements of Korea's Confucianism.

Yoon Yee-heum is Professor of Religious Studies at Seoul National University. He graduated from Seoul National University, received his M.A. at Vanderbilt University and his Ph.D. at Northwestern University in the United States. He is well known for his writings which include *Religion and Modern Life* and *A History of World Religion*.

Yun Sa-soon graduated from Korea University's Department of Philosophy where he now teaches. His research focuses on the work of Chosŏn philosopher Yi Hwang. Among his publications are *Korean Confucianism* and *Neo-Confucianism and Practical Learning in Korea*.

INDEX

WORLD CHRONOLOGICAL TABLE

	KOREA	CHINA	JAPAN	THE WEST
B.C. 5,000	Paleolithic Age Neolithic Age			
2,000		Bronze Age	Jomon Period	Early Mesopotamia Egyptian Kingdoms
1,000		Shang Dynasty (1766-1122) Zhou (1122-256)		Greek Civilization
500	Bronze Age Ancient Chosŏn	Spring and Autumn Era (770-476) Iron Age		Founding of Rome (735)
	Iron Age Puyŏ	Warring States Era (475-221) Qin Dynasty (221-206) Western Han Dynasty (206 B.C.-A.D. 9)	Bronze Age Yayoi Period	Socrates (469-399) Alexander the Great (356-323) First Punic War (264-241) Second Punic War (219-201)
200 100	Confederated Kingdoms of Samhan (Three Han States)			
A.D.	Three Kingdoms: Silla (57 B.C.-A.D. 935) Koguryŏ (37 B.C.-A.D. 668) Paekche (18 B.C.-A.D. 660) Kaya (42-562)			Birth of Christ
200		Shin Dynasty (8-25)		
300		Eastern Han Dynasty (26-221) Three Kingdoms (220-280) Qin Dynasty (265-420)	Iron Age Tumulus Period	Christianity adopted as the state religion of Roman Empire (392) Roman Empire divided (395)
400 500		Northern & Southern Dynasties (420-581)		Anglo-Saxons established in Britain (449)
600			Asuka Period (552-645)	Mohammed (570-632)
700	Parhae Kingdom (669-928) Unified Silla Kingdom (618-935)	Sui Dynasty (581-618) Tang Dynasty (618-906)	Nara Period (645-794)	Hegira (622) and beginning of Islamic era
800			Heian Period (794-1185)	
900	Koryŏ Kingdom (918-1392)			Charles the Great crowned first Holy Roman Emperor (800)
1000		Five Dynasties (906-960)		
1100		Song Dynasty (960-1279)		First Crusade (1096-1099)
1200			Kamakura Period (1185-1392)	
1300		Yüan Dynasty (1279-1368)		Magna Carta (1215) Marco Polo (1254-1324)
1400	Chosŏn Kingdom (1392-1910)	Ming Dynasty (1368-1644)	Muromachi (Ashikaga) Period (1392-1568)	The Hundred Years' War (1618-1648)
1500				Gutenberg's Press (1438) Columbus discovered America (1492)
1600			Momoyama Period (1568-1615)	Martin Luther launches reform of the church (1517)
1700		Qing Dynasty (1644-1911)	Tokugawa Period (1615-1867)	The Thirty Years' War (1618-1648)
1800				American Independence (1776) French Revolution (1789-1793)
1900	Taehan Empire Proclaimed (1897)		Meiji Period (1868-1912)	American Civil War (1861-1865)
	Annexation by Japan (1910) Establishment of the ROK (1948) Korean War 1950-1953	Establishment of the ROC (1912) Establishment of the PRC (1949)	Taisho Period (1912-1926) Showa Period (1926-1988) Heisei Period (1989-)	World War I (1914-1918) World War II (1939-1945)

Koguryŏ (37 B.C.-668)

Ruler	Reign
Tongmyŏng	37 B.C.- 19 B.C.
Yuri	19 B.C.- A.D. 18
Taemusin	18-44
Minjung	44-48
Mobon	48-53
T'aejo	53-146
Ch'adae	146-165
Sindae	165-179
Kogukch'ŏn	179-197
Sansang	197-227
Tongch'ŏn	227-248
Chungch'ŏn	248-270
Sŏch'ŏn	270-292
Pongsang	292-300
Mich'ŏn	300-331
Kogugwon	331-371
Sosurim	371-384
Kogugyang	384-391
Kwanggaet'o	391-413
Changsu	413-491
Munja	491-519
Anjang	519-531
Anwon	531-545
Yangwon	545-559
P'yŏngwon	559-590
Yŏngyang	590-618
Yŏngnyu	618-642
Pojang	642-668

Parhae (698-926)

Ruler	Reign	Ruler	Reign
Ko	698-719	Kan	817-818
Mu	719-737	Sŏn	818-830
Mun	737-794	Yijin	830-857
Wonŭi	794	Kŏnhwang	857-871
Sŏng	794	Kyŏng	871-893
Kang	794-809	Wigye	893-906
Chŏng	809-812	Ae	906-926
Hŭi	812-817		

Paekche (18 B.C.-660)

Ruler	Reign
Onjo	18 B.C.- A.D. 28
Taru	28-77
Kiru	77-128
Kaeru	128-166
Ch'ogo	166-214
Kusu	214-234
Saban	234
Koi	234-286
Ch'aekkye	286-298
Punsŏ	298-304
Piryu	304-344
Kye	344-346
Kŭnch'ogo	346-375
Kŭngusu	375-384
Ch'imnyu	384-385
Chinsa	385-392
Asin	392-405
Chŏnji	405-420
Kuisin	420-427
Piyu	427-455
Kaero	455-475
Munju	475-477
Samgŭn	477-479
Tongsŏng	479-501
Muryong	501-523
Sŏng	523-554
Ŭidŏk	554-598
Hye	598
Pŏp	599-600
Mu	600-641
Ŭija	641-660

Silla (57 B.C.-618)

Ruler	Reign
Pak Clan	
Hyŏkkŏse	57 B.C.-A.D. 4
Namhae	4-24
Yuri	24-57
Sŏk Clan	
T'arhae	57-80
Pak Clan	
P'asa	80-112
Chima	112-134
Ilsŏng	134-154
Adalla	154-184
Sŏk Clan	
Pŏrhyu	184-196
Naehae	196-230
Chobun	230-247
Ch'ŏmhae	247-261
Kim Clan	
Mich'u	262-284
Sŏk Clan	
Yurye	284-297
Kirim	298-309
Hŭrhae	310-355
Kim Clan	
Naemul	356-402
Silsŏng	402-417
Nulchi	417-458
Chabi	458-479
Soji	479-500
Chijŭng	500-514
Pŏphŭng	514-540
Chinhŭng	540-576
Chinji	576-579
Chinp'yŏng	579-632
Sŏndŏk (Queen)	632-646
Chindŏk (Queen)	647-654
Muyŏl	654-661

Unified Silla (619-935)

Ruler	Reign
Kim Clan	
Munmu	661-681
Sinmun	681-692
Hyoso	692-702
Sŏngdŏk	702-737
Hyosŏng	737-742
Kyŏngdŏk	742-765
Hyegong	765-780
Sŏndŏk	780-785
Wonsŏng	785-798
Sosŏng	798-800
Aejang	800-809
Hŏndŏk	809-826
Hŭngdŏk	826-836
Hŭigang	836-837
Minae	838-839
Sinmu	839
Munsŏng	839-857
Hŏn-an	857-861
Kyŏngmun	861-875
Hŏn-gang	875-886
Chŏnggang	886-887
Chinsŏng (Queen)	887-898
Hyogong	898-912
Pak Clan	
Sindŏk	913-917
Kyŏngmyŏng	917-924
Kyŏngae	924-927
Kim Clan	
Kyŏngsun	927-935

Koryŏ (918-1392)

Ruler	Reign
T'aejo	918-943
Hyejong	943-945
Chŏngjong	945-949
Kwangjong	949-975
Kyŏngjong	975-981
Sŏngjong	981-997
Mokchong	997-1009
Hyŏnjong	1009-1031
Tŏkchong	1031-1034
Chŏngjong	1034-1046
Munjong	1046-1083
Sunjong	1083
Sŏnjong	1083-1094
Hŏnjong	1094-1095
Sukchong	1095-1105
Yejong	1105-1122
Injong	1122-1146
Ŭijong	1146-1170
Myŏngjong	1170-1197
Sinjong	1197-1204
Hŭijong	1204-1211
Kangjong	1211-1213
Kojong	1213-1259
Wonjong	1259-1274
Ch'ungyol	1274-1308
Ch'ungsŏn	1308-1313
Ch'ungsuk	1313-1330
Ch'unghye	1330-1332
Ch'ungsuk	1332-1339
Ch'unghye	1339-1344
Ch'ungmok	1344-1348
Ch'ungjong	1348-1351
Kongmin	1351-1374
U	1374-1388
Ch'ang	1388-1389
Kongyang	1389-1392

Chosŏn (1392-1910)

Ruler	Reign
T'aejo	1392-1398
Chŏngjong	1398-1400
T'aejong	1400-1418
Sejong	1418-1450
Munjong	1450-1452
Tanjong	1452-1455
Sejo	1455-1468
Yejong	1468-1469
Sŏngjong	1469-1494
Yŏnsan	1494-1506
Chungjong	1506-1544
Injong	1544-1545
Myŏngjong	1545-1567
Sŏnjo	1567-1608
Kwanghae	1608-1623
Injo	1623-1649
Hyojong	1649-1659
Hyŏnjong	1659-1674
Sukchong	1674-1720
Kyŏngjong	1720-1724
Yŏngjo	1724-1776
Chŏngjo	1776-1800
Sunjo	1800-1834
Hŏnjong	1834-1849
Ch'ŏlchong	1849-1864
Kojong	1864-1907
Sunjong	1907-1910

KOREA IN THE THREE KINGDOMS PERIOD

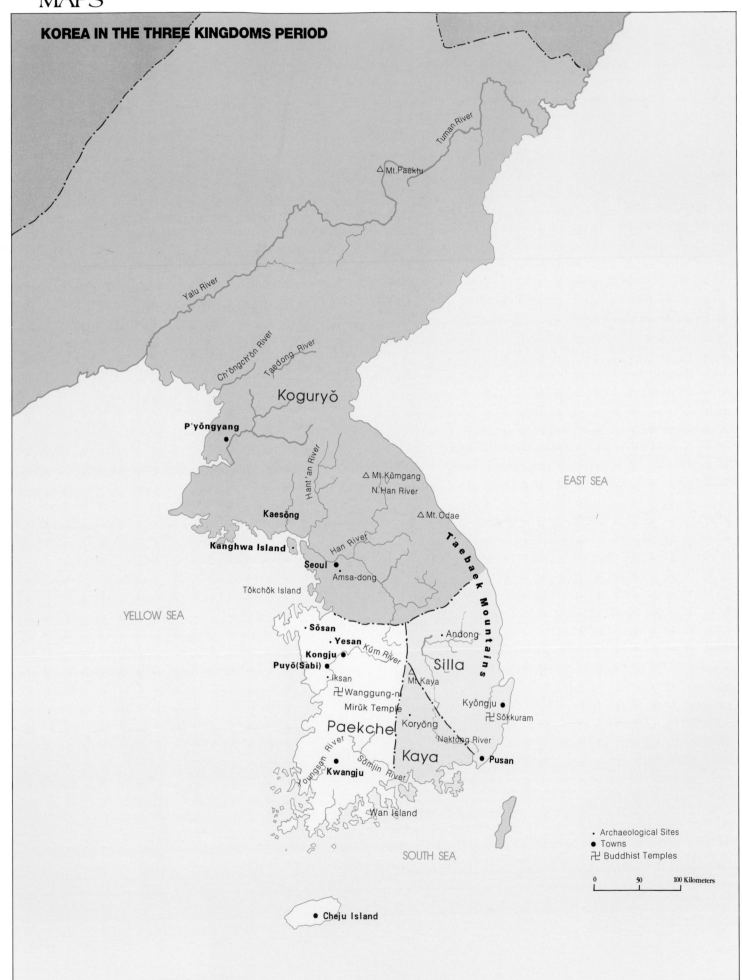

Yalu River

Ch'ŏngch'ŏn River

Taedong River

Tuman River

△ Mt.Paektu

Koguryŏ

● P'yŏngyang

Hant'an River

△ Mt.Kŭmgang

N.Han River

EAST SEA

Kaesŏng

△ Mt.Odae

Kanghwa Island ●

Han River

Seoul ●

T'aebaek Mountains

Amsa-dong

Tŏkchŏk Island

YELLOW SEA

● Sŏsan

● Yesan

Andong

Kŭm River

Silla

● Kongju

Puyŏ(Sabi) ●

● Iksan

Mt.Kaya

卍 Wanggung-ni

Kyŏngju ●

Mirŭk Temple

Koryŏng

卍 Sŏkkuram

Paekche

Naktong River

Kaya

● Pusan

Youngsan River

Sŏmjin River

● Kwangju

Wan Island

● Archaeological Sites
● Towns
卍 Buddhist Temples

SOUTH SEA

0   50   100 Kilometers

● Cheju Island

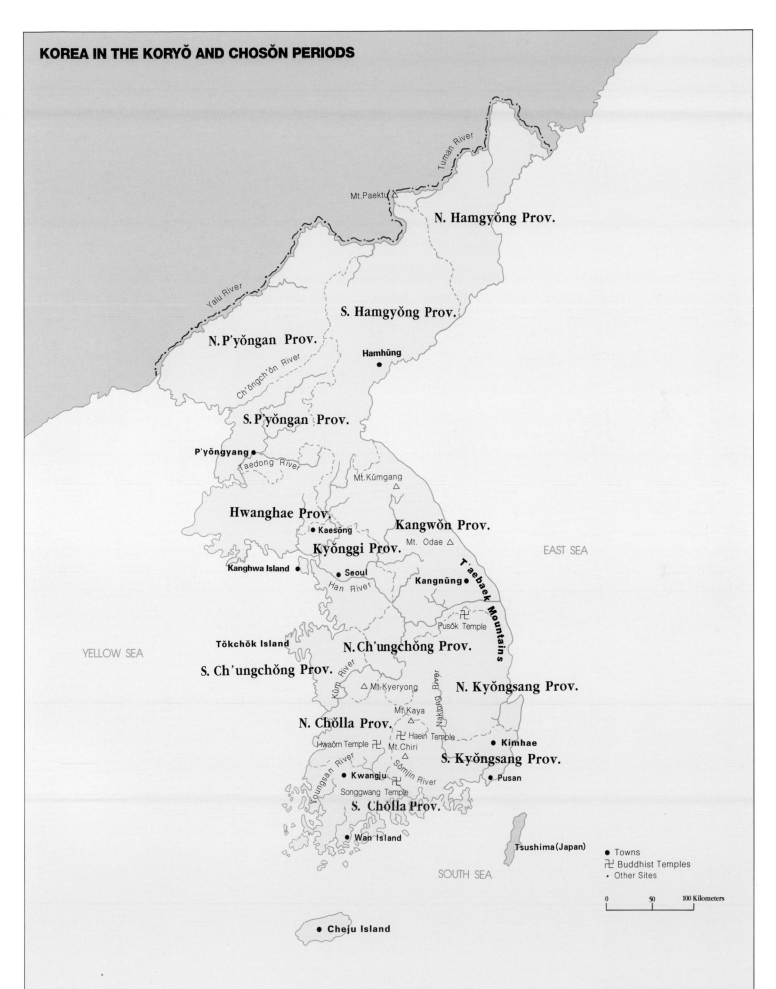

KOREA IN THE KORYŎ AND CHOSŎN PERIODS

N. Hamgyŏng Prov.

Mt.Paektu △

Tuman River

Yalu River

S. Hamgyŏng Prov.

N. P'yŏngan Prov.

Ch'ŏngch'ŏn River

Hamhŭng •

S. P'yŏngan Prov.

P'yŏngyang •

Taedong River

Mt.Kŭmgang △

Hwanghae Prov.

Kangwŏn Prov.

• Kaesŏng

Kyŏnggi Prov.

Mt. Odae △

EAST SEA

Kanghwa Island •

• Seoul

Kangnŭng •

Han River

T'aebaek Mountains

卍 Pusŏk Temple

YELLOW SEA

Tŏkchŏk Island

N.Ch'ungchŏng Prov.

S. Ch'ungchŏng Prov.

Kŭm River

Naktong River

△ Mt.Kyeryong

N. Kyŏngsang Prov.

Mt.Kaya △

N. Chŏlla Prov.

卍 Haein Temple

Hwaŏm Temple 卍 Mt.Chiri

S. Kyŏngsang Prov.

• Kimhae

Yŏngsan River

Sŏmjin River

• Kwangju 卍

• Pusan

Songgwang Temple

S. Chŏlla Prov.

• Wan Island

Tsushima (Japan)

• Towns

卍 Buddhist Temples

• Other Sites

SOUTH SEA

0   50   100 Kilometers

• Cheju Island

269